T0215224

Hyper-V for VMware Administrators: Migration, Coexistence, and Management

ISBN-13 (pbk): 978-1-4842-0380-4

ISBN-13 (electronic): 978-1-4842-0379-8

Managing Director: Welmoed Spahr
Lead Editor: Gwenan Spearing
Technical Reviewer: David Cobb and Ken Mauldin
Editorial Board: Steve Anglin, Mark Beckner, Gary Cornell, Louise Corrigan, Jim DeWolf, Jonathan Gennick, Robert Hutchinson, Michelle Lowman, James Markham, Matthew Moodie, Susan McDermott, Jeffrey Pepper, Douglas Pundick, Ben Renow-Clarke, Gwenan Spearing, Matt Wade, Steve Weiss
Coordinating Editor: Melissa Maldonado
Copy Editor: April Rondeau
Compositor: SPi Global
Indexer: SPi Global
Artist: SPi Global

Distributed to the book trade worldwide by Springer Science+Business Media New York, 233 Spring Street, 6th Floor, New York, NY 10013. Phone 1-800-SPRINGER, fax (201) 348-4505, e-mail orders-ny@springer-sbm.com, or visit www.springeronline.com. Apress Media, LLC is a California LLC and the sole member (owner) is Springer Science + Business Media Finance Inc (SSBM Finance Inc). SSBM Finance Inc. is a Delaware corporation.

For information on translations, please e-mail rights@apress.com, or visit www.apress.com.

Apress and friends of ED books may be purchased in bulk for academic, corporate, or promotional use. eBook versions and licenses are also available for most titles. For more information, reference our Special Bulk Sales–eBook Licensing web page at www.apress.com/bulk-sales.

Any source code or other supplementary material referenced by the author in this text is available to readers at www.apress.com. For detailed information about how to locate your book's source code, go to www.apress.com/source-code/.

Hyper-V for VMware Administrators

Migration, Coexistence, and Management

Brien Posey

Apress®

I would like to dedicate this book to my wife, Taz. Writing a book is a time-consuming process that inevitably results in family and chores being neglected. Taz has always been remarkably understanding of my writing schedule and my hectic travel schedule, and I want to thank her for her continued love and support.

Contents at a Glance

Contents

About the Author

Brien Posey is a freelance technology writer and 13-time Microsoft MVP with over two decades of IT experience. Prior to going freelance, Brien was CIO for a national chain of hospitals and healthcare facilities and served as a network engineer for the United States Department of Defense at Fort Knox. Brien has also worked as a network administrator for some of the largest insurance companies in America.

When Brien isn't busy writing or speaking at technology events, he enjoys adventure travel with his wife, shredding waves in his cigarette boat, scuba diving, and flying RC aircraft. In addition, Brien is currently working toward his most ambitious goal yet—becoming a civilian astronaut.

About the Technical Reviewers

David Cobb is a system engineer for CheckAlt Payment Solutions, a provider of automated and electronic check transaction processing since 2005. He is a Microsoft Certified Trainer, training people on SQL Server since 2002. David is also the principal consultant for Cobb Information Technologies, Inc., founded in 1996, which provides technology consulting with a focus on SQL Server.

Ken Mauldin has been in the Information Technology field for more than 35 years, starting out as a burn-in and test tech with mini-mainframe computers. Along the way, Ken has worked as an instructor, a technical trainer and Microsoft Certified Trainer (MCT), a systems administrator, an IT manager, a systems engineer, and a consultant. For the past several years, Ken has worked extensively in the virtualization world with Hyper-V and VMware. In his spare time, Ken is also an author and a blogger. Currently, he is a technical trainer for Fortinet, a company that specializes in next-generation firewall and unified threat-management solutions.

Acknowledgments

I would like to say thank you to all of the wonderful people that I have gotten to work with at Apress. I especially want to thank Gwenan, Chris, and Melissa for being so accommodating with the production schedule. I know it wasn't easy. I also want to thank David and Ken for the technical review of the book. Again, I know it wasn't easy. My most sincere apologies if I have accidentally overlooked anyone.

Introduction

Greetings! I'm Brien Posey. For those of you who don't know me (or my work), I am a freelance technology writer and a 13-time Microsoft MVP. Given my background, it should come as no surprise that I spend a lot of time working with Microsoft's Hyper-V. Even so, it wasn't just my Hyper-V background that made me decide to write this book. There were actually a few different things.

One of the main reasons why I wanted to write this book was because I have had a lot of people asking me about Hyper-V migrations recently. Apparently, there are quite a few VMware shops that are either making the move to Hyper-V or are looking at the possibility of running multiple hypervisors. I thought that writing a book would be a way in which I could help with those sorts of projects.

Before I move on, let me just say up front that I am not going to tell you that Hyper-V is superior to VMware. Conversely, I don't believe that VMware is better than Hyper-V. Hyper-V got off to a bit of a rocky start in the Windows Server 2008 and 2008 R2 days, but today it is a very capable enterprise-class hypervisor. There are some things that Hyper-V does better than VMware, but there are other things that VMware does better than Hyper-V. VMware and Hyper-V are both excellent hypervisors, and I am not writing this book as a way of bashing VMware.

The reason that I say that is to underscore the idea that I am not encouraging a migration from VMware to Hyper-V because I think that VMware is inadequate. Every organization has their own reasons for migrating, but oftentimes the real driving factor behind a migration is economics. In certain situations, Hyper-V can be much more cost effective than VMware. I am going to spend some time talking about licensing costs later on.

I also wanted to write this book because even though migrating from Hyper-V to VMware isn't overly difficult, it can be a jarring experience. Hyper-V and VMware actually have a lot of similarities, but the management interfaces could not be more different. Back in the 2008–2010 time frame, I was working exclusively with Hyper-V. One day I was asked to work on a project that required me to use VMware. Even though I was familiar with the basic concepts that VMware uses, I have to confess that I felt like a fish out of water. Performing even the simplest of tasks took a lot of effort because I didn't know my way around the VMware interface. Going from VMware to Hyper-V can be just as abrupt of a transition, so I wanted to write this book as a way of showing you what you need to know about Hyper-V, and how the various Hyper-V features compare to what you are currently using in a VMware environment.

With that said, let me give you an idea of what you can expect from this book. First, I am going to make this book as hands on as I possibly can. I am actually going to walk you through the migration process in a step-by-step manner.

Of course, blindly following a set of instructions would probably be a bad idea, so I am going to explain some things along the way. For the purposes of this book, I am going to assume that you have a basic working knowledge of VMware, but that you have never worked with Hyper-V before. Of course, if there is something that you already know about Hyper-V, you can always skip ahead rather than reading my explanation.

One last thing that I want to mention is that I am going to try to keep things simple. I don't do this as a way of insulting anyone's intelligence. It's just that there are a couple of benefits to simplicity. The most obvious benefit is that simple explanations are easier to understand. I am going to do my best to explain things in plain English and keep the tech jargon to a minimum.

The other benefit to simplicity is that I think simple examples are a little bit more relevant to the real world. Let me explain.

A while back, someone asked me to do a technical review of an Exchange Server 2013 book. The book was excellent, and the author really knew his stuff. The problem was that the examples used in the book were a little too complicated. The author had been super ambitious and constructed a lab environment that mimicked a global enterprise. Even though it was just a lab environment, there were dozens of servers being used. While I applaud the author's ambition and work ethic, my opinion was that the complexity of the lab architecture got in the way of some of the concepts that the author was trying to teach.

That being the case, my plan is to do things a little bit differently. During the lab portions of this book, I am not going to build an enterprise-scale environment. Instead, I am going to keep things relatively small. Even so, everything that I am going to show you can be scaled to fit the enterprise. In other words, I am going to start with the basics and then build on those concepts throughout the book. In doing so, I am going to make every effort to keep the material relevant to the real world as well as easy to understand.

■ ■ ■

CHAPTER 1

Hyper-V Basics

Welcome to the world of Hyper-V. In this first chapter, I am going to provide you with an overview of everything that you need to know in order to get started. In doing so, I am going to leverage your knowledge of VMware in order to make the content a little bit easier to understand. My intent for this chapter is not to provide a comprehensive discussion of Hyper-V, but rather to give you enough to get started and to familiarize you with the basics.

The first thing that I plan to talk about is how to get Hyper-V installed. From there, I will devote the rest of the chapter to key concepts, relating them to their VMware counterparts. By the end of the chapter, you will have a solid foundation in the basics of Hyper-V and we can then move on to more advanced topics in subsequent chapters.

Initial Deployment Considerations

The first thing that you need to know about Hyper-V is that you have a few different options when it comes to deployment. Microsoft offers a standalone Hyper-V server that you can download for free. Hyper-V is also included with Windows Server. In fact, Hyper-V has been a part of Windows Server since Windows Server 2008 was released. For the purposes of this book, I am going to be using Windows Server 2012 R2, with Hyper-V installed in a server role.

It is worth noting that Microsoft gives you a choice of performing a server core installation or a full-blown GUI-based installation. A server core installation is a Windows Server installation that lacks most of the GUI components. This type of deployment essentially forces you to manage Hyper-V either remotely or entirely from the command line.

The concept of whether it is better to deploy Hyper-V using a server core or a GUI-based deployment has been hotly debated. Some people claim that server core deployments are ideal because the resources that would otherwise be used by the GUI can instead be used for running virtual workloads. Others claim that it is better to use the GUI because doing so makes the configuration and management process a lot easier.

In the introduction to this book, I promised you that I was going to do my best to keep this book easy to understand. That being the case, I am going to use a GUI-based deployment. If you prefer to use a server core deployment, you can still do everything that I am going to show you in this book. Windows Server 2012 and 2012 R2 give you the option of uninstalling the GUI after you are done using it. I will show you how to do that at the end of this chapter.

There is one more server question that I want to answer before I move on. This question has to do with why I am going to be using Windows Server 2012 R2 rather than going with the free version of Hyper-V. It all has to do with licensing. When you use the free version of Hyper-V, you have to purchase the appropriate virtual machine licenses. On the other hand, Windows Server 2012 R2 includes some virtual machine licenses. The actual number of licenses that are included vary depending on how you chose to license your server.

Another thing that I want to point out before I move on is that you are going to need to make some decisions about how your Hyper-V servers will connect to the network and how they will participate in the Active Directory. My advice is to include at least three physical NICs in each of your Hyper-V servers (if your servers can accommodate more NICs, it is a good idea to do so). One NIC in each server should be reserved for management traffic.

While I am on the subject of management traffic, I need to point out that there is no rule that says that your Hyper-V servers have to be members of an Active Directory domain. However, you lose some functionality related to management and failover clustering if you choose not to join your Hyper-V servers to such a domain.

My recommendation is to create a dedicated Active Directory forest for your Hyper-V servers. Each of your Hyper-V servers should participate in the forest as a member server. The lab environment that I will be using throughout this book consists of two domain controllers that are running on physical hardware. These domain controllers exist solely for the purpose of providing Active Directory (and DNS) functionality to the Hyper-V servers. You should never configure a Hyper-V server to act as a domain controller.

Hyper-V Licensing

Before you build a Hyper-V infrastructure, it is important to understand Microsoft's licensing requirements. The way that Microsoft licenses Hyper-V is a little bit different from what you might be used to in a VMware environment.

As previously mentioned, Microsoft does offer a free version of Hyper-V. If you choose to use the free version then you are only required to license the virtual machine contents (the guest operating system, the applications, etc.)

For the purposes of this book, I am going to assume that Hyper-V is being deployed as a role within Windows Server 2012 R2. Microsoft does not make Windows Server 2012 R2 freely available for production use, but if you need a copy for lab purposes then you can download Microsoft's 180-day free evaluation, or you can get a free copy through an MSDN subscription (MSDN software is not licensed for production use). It is worth noting that Microsoft offers four different editions of Windows Server 2012 R2, but only the Standard Edition and Datacenter Edition are suitable for virtualization.

A Windows Server 2012 R2 Standard Edition license includes two virtual Operating System Environment (OSE) licenses running on a server with up to two physical processors. Multiple Standard Edition licenses can be aligned to support a higher number of OSEs.

It is important to note that the parent operating system should only be configured to run the Hyper-V role and any required infrastructure components (such as antivirus software or backup agents). Not only is doing so considered to be a best practice, but also this configuration is actually addressed within Microsoft's licensing policies.

A Windows Server 2012 R2 Datacenter Edition license includes an unlimited number of Operating System Environment (OSE) licenses.

The main thing that you need to understand about licensing Hyper-V is that Windows Server 2012 R2 licenses cannot be applied to virtual machines. A Windows Server license can only be applied to a physical server. Of course, this raises the question of what happens when a virtual machine is live migrated to another host server. Because the virtual machine itself is not licensed, the destination host must be licensed for a sufficient number of virtual machines to be able to accommodate the inbound VM. Because of the way that Windows Server licensing works, it is usually going to be more cost effective in the long run to purchase Datacenter Edition licenses.

Regardless of whether you use Windows Server 2012 R2 Standard Edition or Datacenter Edition, you will need an appropriate number of client access licenses (CALs). A CAL is required for every user or device that connects to the server.

Important Points to Remember:

- You will usually spend less on licensing in the long run if you run Hyper-V as a Windows Server role.

- Windows virtual machines running on Hyper-V are not licensed. The Hyper-V host is licensed, and the OS license extends to the VMs.

- Windows Server Standard Edition and Datacenter Edition are both suitable for virtualization, but Datacenter Edition is almost always the better choice.

- Regardless of how your Hyper-V environment is licensed, a CAL is required for every user or device that connects to a Windows Server.

The Lab Installation Process

Now that I have spent some time talking about the basic configuration that we are going to be using and have given you some information about the way that Microsoft licenses Hyper-V, it's time to get our hands dirty and actually install Hyper-V.

Requirements

I have designed this book as a lab manual of sorts. The idea is that everything that I am covering can be completed in small scale or scaled up to an enterprise environment. I used a lot of physical hardware when I wrote this book, but there are some ways to scale things back if you need to use fewer physical machines. Here is what I used:

- One server running VMware ESX 5.5

- Three servers running Hyper-V

- One server acting as a domain controller, certificate server, DNS, and DHCP server

- A server running vCenter

- A server running System Center 2012 R2 Virtual Machine Manager

- An NAS server that supports iSCSI connectivity

If you need to trim down the required hardware then you can run your domain controller, vCenter, Virtual Machine Manager, and an NAS-based file server on virtual machines. The reason why I used three Hyper-V servers is because doing so made it easy to create a clustered Hyper-V deployment, but if you only want to experiment with VMware–to–Hyper-V migrations, then you can do so without building a failover cluster.

Before you get started it's also a good idea to plan your IP address usage as well as the naming conventions that you will use for domains, servers, virtual machines, etc.

Earlier in this book, I explained that I am going to assume that you have a basic understanding of VMware, but no experience with Hyper-V. That being the case, I am going to start at the very beginning. First, I am going to walk you through installing Windows Server 2012 R2. From there, I will show you how to configure a server to act as a domain controller. Once we have done that, I will show you how to join a server to your domain and install Hyper-V. If you already know how to perform any of these tasks, then feel free to skip ahead.

I seriously considered saving myself some time by not writing a walkthrough of the Windows installation and domain controller configuration processes. The reason why I decided to go ahead and include them is because every procedure that I am going to show you in this book is based around having a Hyper-V deployment connected to a management forest. As such, I wanted to maximize your chances of success by providing step-by-step procedures for the benefit of those who might not have much experience with Windows Server 2012 R2. For those of you who do have a good working knowledge of Windows Server, please bear with me for a little while, or just skip ahead a couple of chapters.

Installing Windows Server 2012 R2

There are actually a number of different ways to install Windows Server 2012 R2. For the purposes of this book, we will be installing the operating system from an installation DVD. You can complete the installation process by performing these steps:

1. Insert the installation DVD and boot the server from the DVD.

2. When prompted, specify your language, time and currency format, and keyboard or input method, as shown in Figure 1-1.

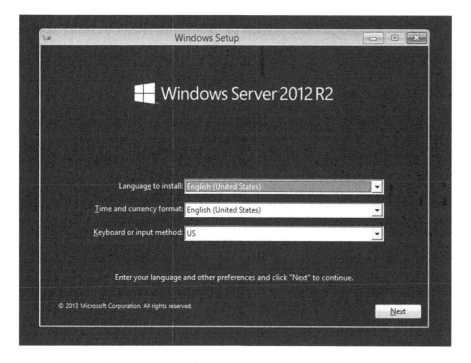

Figure 1-1. *Specify your language, time and currency format, and keyboard or input method*

3. Click Next.

4. Click Install Now.

5. When prompted, enter your product key.

6. Click Next.

7. Select the operating system that you want to install. As you can see in Figure 1-2, Windows Setup defaults to performing a Server Core installation. All of the procedures within this book are going to be based on the assumption that your servers have a GUI interface. As such, make sure that you choose the Server with a GUI option.

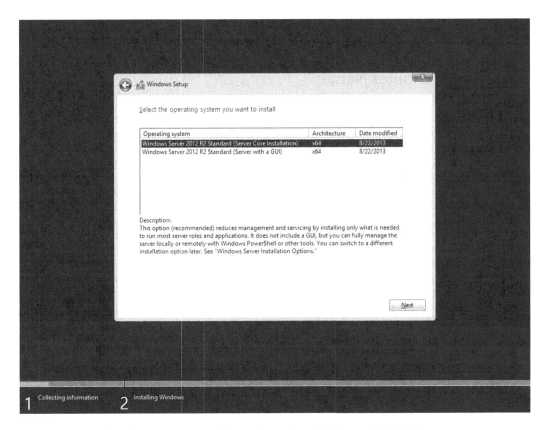

Figure 1-2. Windows Setup wants to perform a Server Core deployment by default

8. Click Next.

9. Select the I Accept the License Terms check box and click Next.

10. When prompted as to what type of installation you want to perform, choose the Custom Install Windows Only (Advanced) option.

11. Select the volume to which you want to install Windows.

12. Click Next. Upon doing so, the file copy process will begin.

13. When the copy process completes, you will be prompted to enter and confirm your administrator password. In a Windows environment the Administrator account is the equivalent to VMware's Root account.

The initial Windows Server installation is now complete. In the next section I will walk you through some post-installation tasks.

Post-Installation Tasks

Once Windows Server 2012 R2 has been installed, there are a number of post-installation tasks that you may want to perform. For instance, it is common to configure various group policy settings to meet your organization's security requirements. I really want to get to the discussion of VMware coexistence and migration as quickly as I can, so I'm not going to spend time talking about any post-deployment tasks except for the ones that are necessary for achieving our objectives. The main post-deployment tasks that I will be focusing on are changing the computer name and configuring the server's IP address.

Changing the Computer Name

After the Windows Server installation process completes, one of the first things that you will probably want to do is to change the computer name. This makes it easier to identify the computer on the network.

Before I show you how to change the computer name, I want to quickly point out a detail that will come into play later on when we start creating Hyper-V virtual machines. Hyper-V uses virtual machine names to identify virtual machines. These virtual machine names do not however, automatically match the computer names. As you pick out a naming convention, it is important to remember that the names that you assign will need to be assigned to the server and to the virtual machine (if the server is being virtualized).

For the purposes of this book, we will be setting up a domain controller that will also act as a DNS server. This machine will run on physical hardware, so you won't have to worry about assigning it a virtual machine name. As a best practice, your management network should contain two domain controllers, both running on physical hardware.

As we work through the labs in this book, we are also going to be setting up some Hyper-V servers. These servers will also run on physical hardware, so you won't have to worry about assigning them virtual machine names either. All of the other machines that we will be creating as we go along will be virtual.

So now that I have talked a little bit about the plan for our labs, let's take a look at how you can change a server's name. To change the computer name, follow these steps:

1. Log in to the server using an account that has administrative access.

2. Right click on the Start button and choose the System command from the resulting shortcut menu, as shown in Figure 1-3.

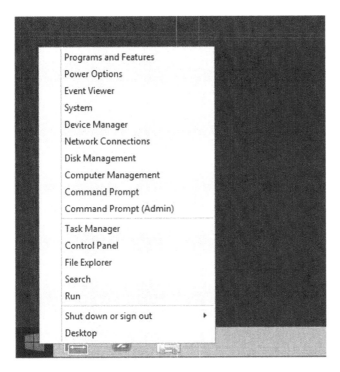

Figure 1-3. Right click on the Start button and choose the System command from the resulting shortcut menu

3. When the System dialog box appears, click on the Change Settings link found in the Computer Name, Domain, and Workgroup Settings section.

4. Windows will now open the System Properties dialog box. Make sure that the Computer Name tab is selected, and click on the Change button.

5. Enter a new computer name, as shown in Figure 1-4.

Figure 1-4. Enter a new computer name and click OK

6. Click OK.

7. Click OK again to acknowledge the reboot requirement.

8. Click Close.

9. Click Restart Now.

Assigning an IP Address

The next thing that you will probably want to do after assigning a computer name is to provision the server with an IP address. Technically, Windows servers are able to acquire an address from a DHCP server. However, you are going to need to provision your domain controller with a static IP address since the domain controller will also be acting as a DNS server. In a production environment, it is a good idea to configure both of your physical domain controllers to act as DNS servers so that you still have name-resolution capabilities, even if a domain controller fails.

As a best practice, you should also consider provisioning your Hyper-V servers with static IP addresses. You don't necessarily have to do so, but it will make things a little bit easier for you later on as we work through the configuration process.

You can assign a static IP address to a Windows 2012 R2 server by completing these steps:

1. Log in to the server using administrative credentials.

2. Right click on the Start button and choose the Control Panel option from the shortcut menu.

3. When the Control Panel opens, click on the Network and Internet link, shown in Figure 1-5.

Figure 1-5. *Click on the Network and Internet link*

4. Click on the Network and Sharing Center link.

5. Click on the Change Adapter Settings link.

6. Right click on the listing for your server's network adapter and choose the Properties command from the shortcut menu. If no network adapter is listed on this screen, it may mean that you need to install a driver for your network adapter.

7. When the adapter's properties dialog box appears, click on Internet Protocol Version 4 (TCP/IPv4) and click Properties.

8. Click on Use the Following IP Address, as shown in Figure 1-6.

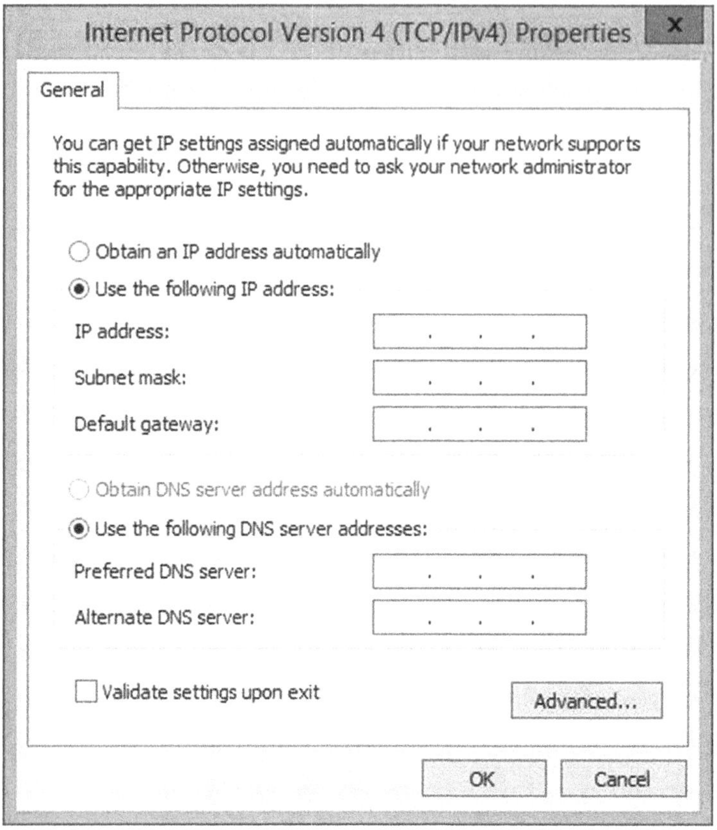

Figure 1-6. *Click on Use the Following IP Address*

9. Enter your IP address, subnet mask, and default gateway.

10. Click on Use the Following DNS Server Addresses.

11. Enter the IP addresses of your DNS servers. The labs in this book will assume that your domain controller is acting as a DNS server, so this will be your domain controller's IP address.

12. Click OK.

Configuring a Domain Controller and DNS Server

Now that we have a Windows Server up and running, it's time to configure that server to act as both a domain controller and a DNS server. Remember, we are creating a dedicated management forest that exists for the sole purpose of allowing us to manage our Hyper-V environment. So with that said, you can turn your server into a domain controller and DNS server by completing the following steps:

1. Log in to your server using administrative credentials.

2. Open the Server Manager.

3. Choose the Add Roles and Features command from the Server Manager's Manage menu.

4. Windows will now launch the Add Roles and Features Wizard. Click Next to bypass the wizard's Before You Begin page.

5. Choose the Role-Based or Feature-Based Installation option and click Next.

6. Make sure that the Select a Server from the Server Pool option is selected and verify that the correct server is selected.

7. Click Next.

8. When the Server Roles page appears, select the Active Directory Domain Services role, as shown in Figure 1-7.

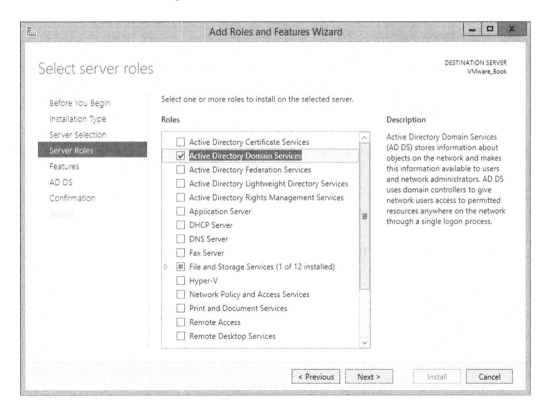

Figure 1-7. *Select the Active Directory Domain Services role*

9. Windows will prompt you to install some additional features. To do so, click on the Add Features button.

10. Click Next.

11. When you arrive at the wizard's Features page, click Next.

12. The next page that you will see is the AD DS page. Click Next.

13. When you reach the Confirmation page, click Install.

14. When the installation process completes, click Close.

So far we have installed the necessary roles and features, but we haven't actually configured our server to act as a domain controller. If you look at Figure 1-8, you will notice that there is a yellow triangle with an exclamation point in it next to the Manage menu within Server Manager. This icon indicates that there are additional tasks that need to be performed.

Figure 1-8. *The yellow triangle indicates that there is more work to be done*

To complete the process of setting up a domain controller, perform the following steps:

1. Click on the previously mentioned yellow triangle.

2. Click on the Promote this Server to a Domain Controller link. This will cause Windows to launch the Active Directory Domain Services Configuration Wizard.

3. On the wizard's Deployment Configuration page, choose the Add a New Forest option.

4. Enter a root domain name. Since this is going to be a management forest, I will be calling it MGMT.com.

5. Click Next.

6. On the Domain Controller Options page, enter and confirm an Active Directory Restore Mode (DSRM) password. You can accept the default values for all of the other settings. It is very important to leave the Domain Name System (DNS) Server check box selected.

7. Click Next.

8. The DNS page will display a warning message indicating that a delegation for the DNS server cannot be created because the authoritative parent zone cannot be found. Click Next to acknowledge the warning.

9. When prompted, enter a NetBIOS name for the domain. The NetBIOS name should match the root domain name (minus the .com portion of the name).

10. Click Next and you will be prompted to supply a series of database paths. Click Next to accept the defaults.

11. You should now see a summary of the installation options that you have selected. Take a moment and review the summary information. If everything appears to be correct, click Next.

12. Windows will now take a moment and perform a prerequisite check. It is normal to receive a couple of warning messages on this page, but you shouldn't receive any errors. Assuming that no errors are present, click the Install button.

Setting Up Hyper-V

Now that we have a domain controller and DNS server up and running, the next step is to install Hyper-V. For the purposes of this book, I recommend setting up at least three Hyper-V servers. The reason for this is that we are eventually going to be building a Hyper-V cluster, and the process is a little bit easier if you have three Hyper-V servers to work with.

The Hyper-V servers will need to run on physical hardware. You can install Windows, configure the computer name, and provision an IP address using the same procedures that I just provided.

Joining a Domain

Once Windows is up and running, you will need to join your Hyper-V servers to the management domain that you created earlier. Doing so is very similar to the technique that you used when assigning a name to a server. In fact, you can assign a computer name and join a domain at the same time.

The instructions listed below assume that you have already assigned an IP address to your server and that the server is configured to use your domain controller as a DNS server. If the server is configured to use a DNS server that is not aware of your Active Directory domain then the domain join will fail.

To join your Hyper-V server to a domain, complete these steps:

1. Right click on the Start button and choose the System command from the resulting menu.

2. When the System dialog box opens, click on the Change Settings link.

3. When the System Properties dialog box appears, make sure that the Computer Name tab is selected and then click the Change button.

4. Select the Domain radio button.

5. Enter the name of the domain that you want to join, as shown in Figure 1-9.

6. Click OK.

7. When prompted, enter a set of domain administrator credentials.

Figure 1-9. *Enter the name of the domain that you want to join and click OK*

Installing Hyper-V

Now that your Hyper-V server has been joined to your management domain, it is time to install the Hyper-V role. As a best practice, you shouldn't install any other roles onto the server (the File and Storage Services role is installed by default, however, and should not be removed). You can install the Hyper-V role by completing these steps:

1. Log in to your server using an account that has administrative credentials.

2. Open Server Manager.

3. Choose the Add Roles and Features command from the Server Manager's Manage menu. When you do, Windows will launch the Add Roles and Features wizard.

4. Click Next to bypass the wizard's Before You Begin page.

5. Choose the Role-Based or Feature-Based Installation option.

6. Click Next.

7. Make sure that the Select a Server from the Server Pool option is selected and ensure that your Hyper-V server is selected within the server pool, as shown in Figure 1-10.

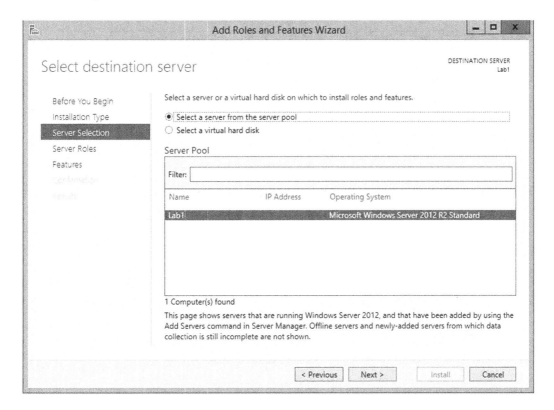

Figure 1-10. *Make sure that your server is selected*

8. Click Next.

9. Select the Hyper-V role.

10. When Windows prompts you to install the required features, click the Add Features button, as shown in Figure 1-11.

Figure 1-11. *Click the Add Features button*

11. Click Next.

12. When the wizard displays the list of available features, click Next.

13. Click Next on the Hyper-V introductory page.

14. Select the network adapters that you want to make available to your virtual machines, as shown in Figure 1-12. This network adapter will be the adapter through which your virtual machines communicate with the physical network. Be sure to reserve at least one network adapter for host management traffic. In a lab environment you can get away with using a single NIC in your servers, but in a production environment it is a good idea to provision your servers with as many NICs as possible.

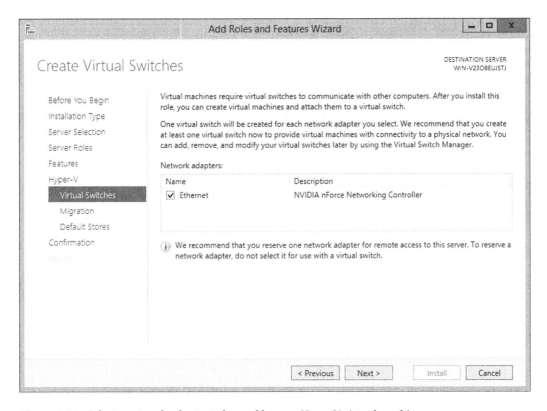

Figure 1-12. *Select a network adapter to be used by your Hyper-V virtual machines*

15. Click Next.

16. You will now see a page asking if you want to allow the server to send and receive live migrations of virtual machines. Live migrations are the Microsoft version of vMotions. Go ahead and enable live migrations and click Next.

17. When prompted, click Next to accept the default stores.

18. The wizard will now display a confirmation. Take a moment to review the information on the page and then click the Install button.

19. When the role-installation process completes, click the Close button.

20. Although Windows may not display a prompt, it is necessary to reboot the server to complete the deployment of the Hyper-V role.

Important Concepts to Understand

By now you should have Hyper-V up and running, but before I move on to the next chapter I want to help you to become more familiar with some basic Hyper-V concepts. As I previously mentioned, there are a lot of similarities between Hyper-V and VMware, but common tasks are performed in very different ways. That being the case, I want to spend the rest of this chapter drawing some parallels between the two hypervisors.

The vSphere Client

As you are no doubt aware, the vSphere server console provides a very minimal interface. You can use it to perform some very basic tasks, such as setting the root password or setting the server's IP address, but you can't perform virtual machine management through the server console. Instead, VMware management is performed through a Web interface or through the vSphere Client.

Hyper-V does things differently. There is no direct Hyper-V equivalent to the Web interface or to the vSphere Client. The primary tool for managing Hyper-V is the Hyper-V Manager. You can access the Hyper-V Manager by opening the Server Manager and choosing the Hyper-V Manager option from the Tools menu, as shown in Figure 1-13.

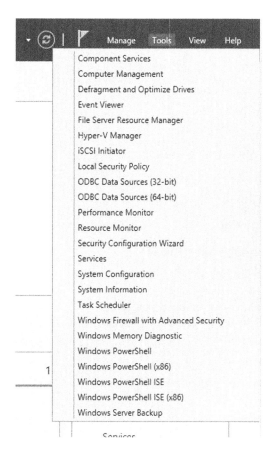

Figure 1-13. *You can launch the Hyper-V Manager by selecting the Hyper-V Manager command from the Server Manager's Tools menu*

You can see what the Hyper-V Manager looks like in Figure 1-14. As you can see in the figure, the Hyper-V Manager console is arranged into a few different sections. The section on the left lists your Hyper-V host servers. By default, the Hyper-V Manager only connects to a single Hyper-V host, but it can be configured to connect to multiple hosts.

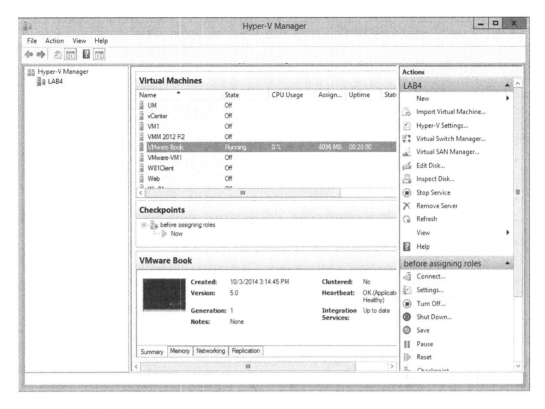

Figure 1-14. *This is the Hyper-V Manager*

The top, middle section lists all of the virtual machines that exist on the selected server. This section allows you to see some basic virtual machine information, including the virtual machine's state, CPU usage, memory usage, uptime, and more.

The section in the very middle of the console lists any existing checkpoints for the currently selected virtual machine. *Checkpoints* is Microsoft speak for a feature that is more commonly referred to as *snapshots*.

The lower middle section displays some summary information for the currently selected virtual machine, including a preview of the virtual machine console. Incidentally, if you want to access the virtual machine's console, all you have to do is to double click on the virtual machine (within the virtual machine list).

The upper right section lists some actions that apply to Hyper-V as a whole. For instance, you can use this section to create a new virtual machine or to access the virtual switch manager.

The section in the lower right portion of the console lists actions that can be performed against the currently selected virtual machine. For instance, you can use this section to connect to a virtual machine (access its console), power the virtual machine on or off, or adjust the virtual machine's settings.

Although the Hyper-V Manager is the primary tool for managing Hyper-V, it is not the only interface for doing so. You can also use Windows PowerShell. Although we will have to occasionally use PowerShell for various tasks within this book, comprehensive PowerShell-based management of Hyper-V is beyond the scope of this book. If you want to know more about using PowerShell to manage Hyper-V, check out my free eBook: *The Hands-on Guide: Understanding Hyper-V in Windows Server 2012* (`www.veeam.com/wp-backup-posey-henley-zerger-understanding-hyper-v-in-windows-server-2012.html`). I have written a 2012 R2 version of this book, but as of the time of writing, my 2012 R2 book has not yet been made available. Incidentally, I also recommend downloading that book if you want to know more about Hyper-V. This book will discuss the basics of using Hyper-V, but my ultimate goal in this book is to help you to migrate VMware workloads to a Hyper-V environment. The book mentioned above is more about working with Hyper-V on a day-to-day basis.

The third option for managing Hyper-V is a tool called System Center Virtual Machine Manager. System Center Virtual Machine Manager is an add-on product from Microsoft that allows Hyper-V deployments to be centrally managed (it also offers many other capabilities). You can think of System Center Virtual Machine Manager as being similar to VMware's vCenter Server. We will be spending a lot of time working with System Center Virtual Machine Manager later in this book.

Important Things to Remember:

- Hyper-V does not have a direct equivalent to the vSphere Client or to VMware's Web interface.

- Windows Server includes a Hyper-V management tool called the Hyper-V Manager.

- Hyper-V can also be managed through PowerShell.

- Larger Hyper-V deployments are commonly managed through System Center Virtual Machine Manager.

- System Center Virtual Machine Manager is a separate product and is not included with Hyper-V.

The Datastore

As I'm sure you know, VMware virtual machines are created within a datastore. Hyper-V, however, has no equivalent to a VMware datastore. It is technically possible to create a Hyper-V virtual machine on any path that is accessible to the host operating system. This can be a local disk, SAN storage, and so on.

Of course, just because you can do something doesn't necessarily mean that you should. Virtual machines should be kept on high-speed storage arrays that have some built-in redundancy. My personal preference is to use a RAID 1+0 array. RAID 5 and 6 work well too, but they don't deliver as good of write performance as RAID 1+0.

Microsoft supports installing Hyper-V virtual machines onto Direct Attached Storage (DAS), an iSCSI target, a Fibre Channel SAN, or an SMB file share (SMB 3.0 or above only). It is possible to create virtual machines on other storage types, but it is important to use only supported storage.

While I am on the subject of storage, I also want to mention that like VMware, Hyper-V allows you to create virtual hard disks of a fixed size or thinly provisioned virtual hard disks (which Microsoft refers to as a dynamically expanding virtual hard disk). I will be talking more about Hyper-V storage in the next chapter.

Important Things to Remember:

- Hyper-V does not use datastores.

- Hyper-V VMs can be installed on Direct Attached Storage (DAS), an iSCSI target, an SMB 3.0 file share, or on a Fibre Channel SAN.

- Hyper-V virtual machines should be stored on highly available, high-speed arrays.

The Virtual Machine Console

One of the first things that you will need to know about the Hyper-V Manager is how to go about accessing a virtual machine's console. The process is actually very simple. All you have to do is to double click on the listing for a virtual machine. However, if the virtual machine is running Windows Server 2012 R2 or Windows 8.1, you may see a prompt asking you to choose your preferred screen resolution (see Figure 1-15). If you receive this prompt then it means that you have connected using enhanced session mode, which is a new mode that gives you a few extra capabilities. You must simply choose your preferred resolution and click Connect. As an alternative, you can close the dialog box, and Windows will use the default resolution and a non-enhanced session instead.

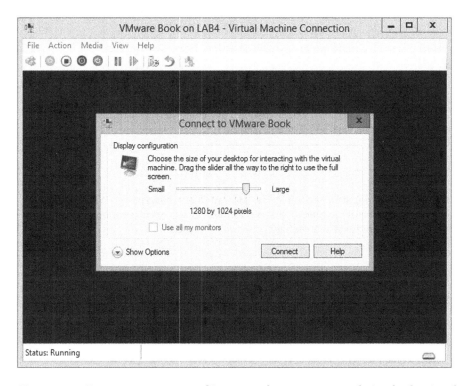

Figure 1-15. *You may see a prompt asking you to choose a screen resolution for the virtual machine console*

When the virtual machine console opens (see Figure 1-15), you will notice a row of icons along the top of the console screen. Table 1-1 provides a list of the icons and what they do.

Table 1-1. *Virtual Machine Console Toolbar Buttons*

Button	Function
	Ctrl, Alt, Delete
	Start
	Turn Off
	Shut Down
	Pause
	Reset
	Checkpoint (which is similar to creating a VMware snapshot)
	Revert (which is like rolling back a VMware snapshot)
	Enhanced Session

In case you aren't familiar with Enhanced Session Mode, it is something that is new to Windows Server 2012 R2. Enhanced Session Mode makes it possible to redirect resources from a local computer to the virtual machine. The resources that you can redirect in an enhanced session include:

- USB devices
- Some plug-and-play devices
- The Windows clipboard
- Printers
- Smart cards
- Audio
- Display configuration

Capturing a DVD Drive

While I am on the subject of resource redirection, I want to show you how to redirect a DVD drive within the Hyper-V console. However, I need to point out that Hyper-V supports two different generations of virtual machines. What I am about to show you only works for first-generation virtual machines (which Microsoft refers to as Generation 1 virtual machines). I will talk about virtual machine generations a little bit later on in this chapter.

So with that said, if your server is equipped with a physical DVD drive, that drive can be redirected to a virtual machine. The catch is that only one virtual machine can access the DVD drive at a time. If you attempt to capture a DVD drive that is in use, the process will fail. The exact nature of the failure depends on whether or not the virtual machine is running.

If you are working from the console of a running virtual machine and you try capturing a DVD drive that is already in use, you will receive an error message stating that capturing the drive failed.

If you attempt to capture an in-use DVD drive from a virtual machine that is powered off, then the capture process will succeed. However, when you attempt to power the virtual machine on, you will receive an error message if the DVD drive is still in use by another virtual machine.

You can capture a physical DVD drive by completing these steps:

1. Open the Hyper-V Manager.

2. Double click on the virtual machine to open its console.

3. ' Click on the console's Media menu.

4. Select the DVD Drive ➤ Capture commands (see Figure 1-16).

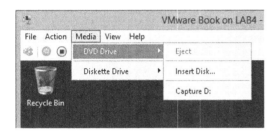

Figure 1-16. *To capture a physical DVD drive, select the DVD Drive ➤ Capture commands from the console's Media menu*

The process for releasing a DVD drive is very similar. To release a DVD drive, complete these steps:

1. Open the Hyper-V Manager.

2. Double click on the virtual machine to open its console.

3. Click on the console's Media menu.

4. Select the DVD Drive ➤ Eject commands from the menu.

It is worth noting that you are not limited solely to using a physical DVD drive. In fact, Generation 2 virtual machines cannot use a physical DVD drive at all (more on that later). As an alternative to using a physical DVD drive, you can capture an ISO file and treat it as a DVD drive.

If you want to capture an ISO file, you can do so by completing these steps:

1. Open the Hyper-V Manager.

2. Right click on the virtual machine that needs access to the ISO file, then select the Settings command from the shortcut menu (see Figure 1-17).

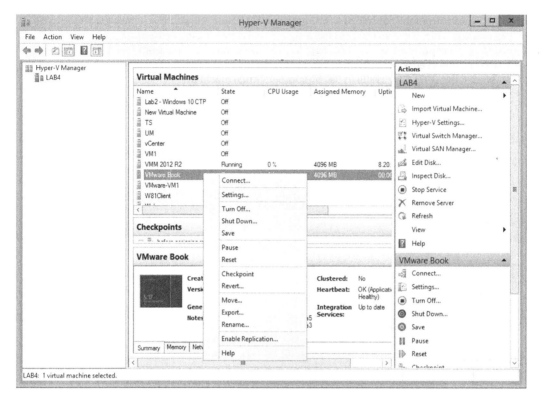

Figure 1-17. *Right click on the VM and choose the Settings command from the shortcut menu*

3. When the virtual machine's Settings screen appears, look to see if any IDE controllers are present. If IDE controllers do exist (which will usually be the case for Generation 1 virtual machines) then expand IDE Controller 1 to reveal the DVD drive (see Figure 1-18).

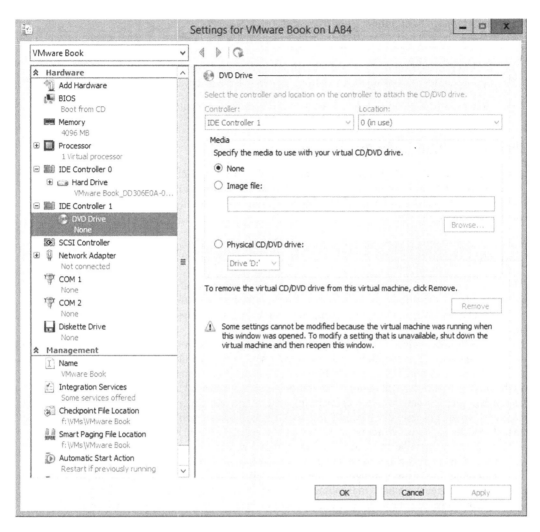

Figure 1-18. *Select the DVD drive if it exists*

4. If no IDE controllers exist, click on the SCSI controller, select the DVD Drive option, and click Add.

5. Regardless of which virtual machine generation is being used, select the Image File option.

6. Click the Browse button and then browse to the image file that you want to use.

7. Click OK.

8. Click OK to complete the process.

Important Things to Remember:

- Only one VM at a time can capture a physical DVD drive.

- If a VM cannot capture a physical DVD drive, it is usually because the drive is in use by another VM. Releasing the drive from the VM will make it available for capture.

- Generation 2 VMs cannot use physical DVD drives, but *can* capture ISO files.

The Virtual Machine Settings

During my discussion of the DVD drive, you got a preview of the virtual machine Settings screen. You can use the Settings screen to add, remove, or reconfigure hardware for any virtual machine. Some hardware can be added or modified while the virtual machine is running. Other virtual hardware changes can only be performed while the virtual machine is shut down.

VMware Tools

In a VMware environment, VMware Tools improve a virtual machine's performance and functionality. VMware Tools offer capabilities such as better graphics performance, better mouse performance, clock synchronization, and copying and pasting between virtual machines and the client desktop (among other things).

Hyper-V has its own equivalent to VMware Tools. Microsoft calls this component Integration Services. A virtual machine that has Integration Services installed is said to be enlightened. As is the case with VMware virtual machines and VMware Tools, Hyper-V virtual machines can function without Integration Services, but they will perform a lot better if Integration Services is installed.

It is worth noting that newer Microsoft operating systems include Integration Services by default. However, only Windows Server 2012 R2 and Windows 8.1 have the latest version of Integration Services. If you install an older version of Windows within a virtual machine, you will need to update Integration Services. Even if you are installing a current-generation Windows operating system, it is a good idea to check and see if Integration Services needs to be updated, because Microsoft routinely releases updates to its software. Incidentally, the Hyper-V Integration Services are also available for several common Linux builds. Microsoft has gone to great lengths to make Windows Server 2012 R2 Hyper-V Linux friendly.

In the case of Linux VMs, the technique that you would use to install Integration Services varies depending on the flavor of Linux that you are running. For Windows VMs, you can install Integration Services by completing the following steps:

1. Open the Hyper-V Manager.

2. Double click on the virtual machine on which you want to install Integration Services. This will cause the virtual machine's console to open. The virtual machine must be running, and you must be logged in to the guest operating system, before you will be able to install Integration Services.

3. Select the Insert Integration Services Setup Disk command from the virtual machine console's Actions menu (see Figure 1-19).

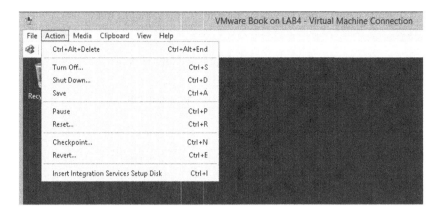

Figure 1-19. Select the Insert Integration Services Setup Disk command from the Actions menu

4. When the AutoPlay screen appears, click on the Install Hyper-V Integration Services option. There is a chance that you might instead see a message telling you that a previous version of Hyper-V Integration Services has been detected (see Figure 1-20) or that the VM already has the latest version of Integration Services installed. In either case, click OK.

Figure 1-20. You may see a message indicating the presence of an earlier version of Hyper-V Integration Services

The same basic procedure can be used to upgrade a virtual machine that is running an earlier version of Integration Services. The only real difference between the procedures is that if an outdated version of Integration Services is detected then Hyper-V will display a message indicating that an earlier version of Integration Services was detected. You can click OK to upgrade to the latest version.

One of the most important things that you need to know about Integration Services is that it is composed of multiple components. When you install Integration Services, all of these components are installed by default, but not every service is automatically enabled. Hyper-V allows you to choose which of the Integration Services you want to enable or disable on a per-virtual-machine basis.

Of all of the components that make up Integration Services, only the Guest Services component is not enabled by default. Guest Services was first introduced with Windows Server 2012 R2. This service makes it possible to use PowerShell to copy a file from the host operating system to a running virtual machine without having to establish a network path. The reason why Guest Services is disabled by default is because having the ability to inject a file into a running VM by using PowerShell could pose a security risk. As such, you should only enable Guest Services if needed.

You can enable or disable individual Integration Services components by completing these steps:

1. Open the Hyper-V Manager.

2. Right click on the virtual machine that you want to configure and then choose the Settings command from the shortcut menu.

3. When the virtual machine's Settings screen appears, go to the Management section.

4. Click on Integration Services.

5. Use the check boxes to enable or disable individual Integration Services (see Figure 1-21).

6. Click OK to complete the process.

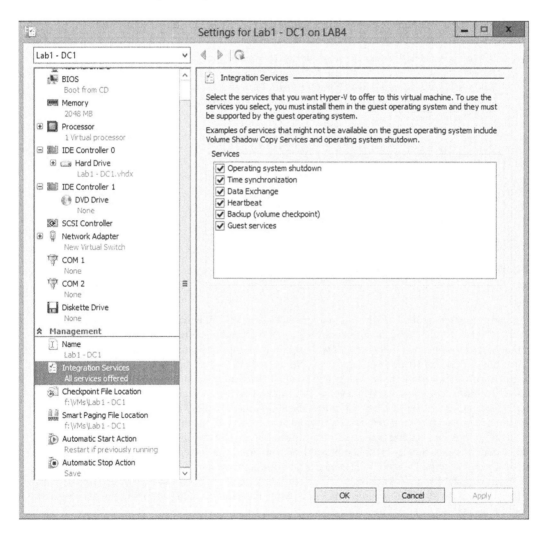

Figure 1-21. You can enable and disable the integration services on an individual basis

Important Things to Remember:

- Integration Services is the Hyper-V equivalent to VMware Tools.

- Integration Services can be enabled or disabled individually.

- Future versions of Hyper-V will make Integration Services available through Windows Update.

Virtual Machine Generations

One of the really important concepts that must be understood prior to creating a Hyper-V virtual machine is that of virtual machine generations. Windows Server 2012 R2 allows for the creation of Generation 1 or Generation 2 virtual machines.

Generation 1 virtual machines are the first-generation virtual machine format, which has been in use since Hyper-V was first introduced as a part of Windows Server 2008. These first-generation virtual machines offer tremendous flexibility, but might not always perform as well as Generation 2 virtual machines.

Although Generation 2 virtual machines do offer some distinct advantages over their first-generation counterparts, there are also a number of limitations associated with second-generation virtual machines. It is extremely important to choose the most appropriate virtual machine generation based on your needs, because once a virtual machine has been created you cannot change its generation. I should also point out that virtual machine generations are a virtual machine–level attribute. There is no limitation that prevents you from mixing first-generation and second-generation virtual machines on a single server. So with that said, let's take a look at the criteria that must be considered when deciding between Generation 1 and Generation 2 virtual machines.

Performance aside, the main benefit to creating Generation 2 virtual machines is that they provide better support for SCSI virtual hard disks. Generation 1 virtual machines allowed for the use of SCSI virtual hard disks, but there were some limitations. Specifically, you couldn't boot from a SCSI virtual hard disk and you couldn't place the paging file onto a SCSI virtual hard disk. These limitations go away with Generation 2 virtual machines.

Generation 2 virtual machines also provide improved support for PXE boot. First-generation virtual machines allowed for PXE boot, but you had to install the Legacy Network Adapter. This requirement does not exist for Generation 2 virtual machines.

I previously hinted that Generation 2 virtual machines tend to perform better than their first-generation counterparts. A big part of this performance improvement comes from the fact that Generation 2 virtual machines do not support IDE emulation. Rather than relying on IDE emulation drivers, Generation 2 VMs use synthetic SCSI drivers. The emulation layer is eliminated and the virtual machine is able to use the VMBUS to communicate with the parent partition.

Just as emulated IDE drivers have been removed, so too have the legacy network adapter drivers. These drivers have also been replaced with VMBUS drivers.

The actual performance gain that is realized by using Generation 2 VMs varies depending on the virtual machine's workload. According to some estimates however, operating systems can be installed on Generation 2 VMs twice as quickly as they can be installed on Generation 1 VMs, and the boot process has been estimated to be 20% faster.

In spite of the many benefits provided by Generation 2 VMs, there are at least two disadvantages to using them. The first disadvantage is that, as previously mentioned, there is no DVD support. The best you can do is to link the VM to an ISO file that will act as a virtual DVD drive.

The other disadvantage is that, because Generation 2 VMs do not support various types of legacy hardware emulation, they can only be used with a supported OS. Initially, Microsoft only supported the following operating systems on Generation 2 VMs:

- Windows Server 2012

- Windows Server 2012 R2

- 64-bit versions of Windows 8

- 64-bit versions of Windows 8.1

Microsoft now supports running various Linux builds on Generation 2 VMs.

To get a better feel for the differences between Generation 1 and Generation 2 virtual machines, take a look at the figures below. Figure 1-22 shows the Settings window for a Generation 1 virtual machine, while Figure 1-23 shows the settings for a Generation 2 virtual machine.

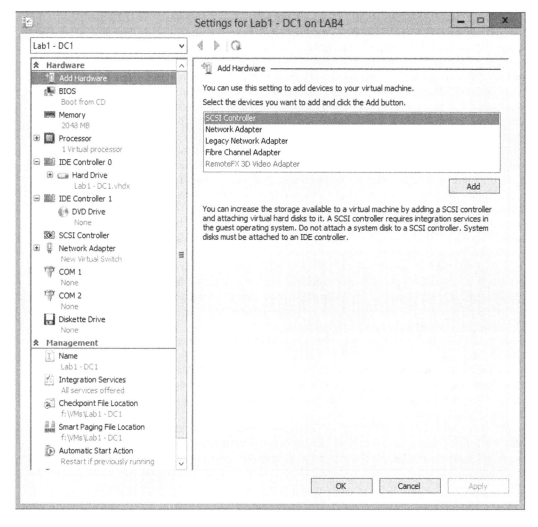

Figure 1-22. *This is the Settings window for a Generation 1 virtual machine*

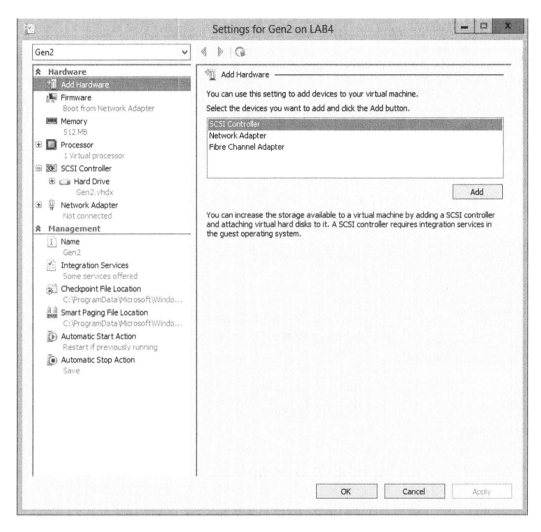

Figure 1-23. *This is the Settings window for a Generation 2 virtual machine*

Important Things to Remember:

- Hyper-V supports both Generation 1 and Generation 2 VMs.

- Generation 1 VMs offer better overall compatibility for guest operating systems.

- Generation 2 VMs generally offer better performance, but only support specific operating systems and do not support physical DVD drives.

Dynamic Memory

Although we haven't actually created a virtual machine yet, I wanted to take the opportunity to point out that, as with VMware, Hyper-V provides the ability to provision virtual machines with dynamic memory. I will walk you through setting up a virtual machine in the next chapter, but since I am covering VMware equivalent features, I wanted to go ahead and talk a bit about dynamic memory for Hyper-V virtual machines.

You can access a virtual machine's Dynamic Memory settings by completing the following steps:

1. Open the Hyper-V Manager.

2. Select the virtual machine whose memory you want to adjust.

3. Click Settings.

4. When the virtual machine's Settings screen is displayed, select the Memory tab (see Figure 1-24).

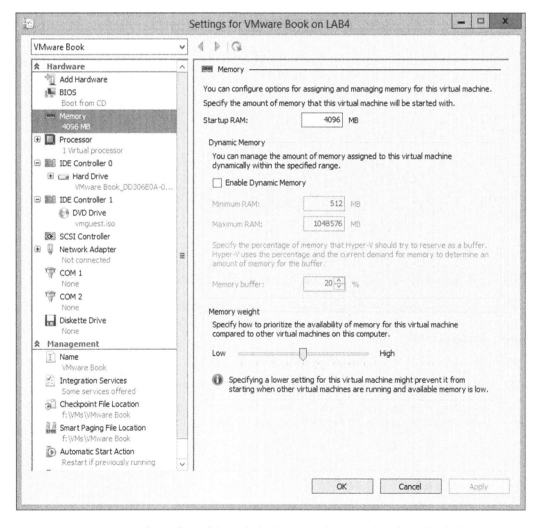

Figure 1-24. *Memory can be configured through the Memory tab on the virtual machine's Settings window*

There are a number of different settings that are used for controlling dynamic memory usage. Here are the settings that you need to know about:

- Enable Dynamic Memory – The Enable Dynamic Memory check box allows you to toggle between dynamic memory and static memory for the VM.

- Startup RAM – This is the amount of memory that the virtual machine is assigned at boot time. If dynamic memory is not being used then the Startup RAM is the total amount of memory assigned to the VM.

- Minimum RAM – This value represents the least amount of memory that will ever be available to a VM. It is common for the Minimum RAM value to be lower than the Startup RAM value because it is common for a VM to consume more memory during the boot process than while it is idle.

- Maximum RAM – The maximum RAM is the most memory that the virtual machine can consume.

- Memory Buffer – The memory buffer is a percentage of the current demand for memory that Hyper-V should try to reserve as a buffer.

- Memory Weight – This setting is a memory prioritization setting. During times when the server is low on physical memory, VMs with a high memory weight will be assigned memory before memory is assigned to lower priority VMs. In extreme situations, a low memory weight can prevent a VM from booting if VMs with higher memory weights need the memory.

Although it does not appear on the Memory tab, you should also be aware of the Smart Paging File location. As mentioned in the section above, it is possible (and common) for the Minimum RAM to be assigned a value that is less than the Startup RAM. However, configuring a virtual machine's memory in this way can lead to complications if the virtual machine is rebooted.

Imagine for a moment that a VM is assigned 2 GB of Startup RAM, but has a minimum RAM value of 512 MB (these are Hyper-V's default values). Now let's suppose that this VM is idle and is only using 512 MB of memory at the moment. Let's also assume that the other VMs are consuming the remaining memory.

If the VM is rebooted, it will not be able to claim a sufficient amount of memory to allow the boot process to complete. The VM needs more memory than the 512 MB that was released during the reboot process. The solution to this problem is to use the Smart Paging File.

The Smart Paging File is a dedicated paging file that allows the VM to use physical storage to make up for shortages in RAM during a reboot. This is the only time that the Smart Paging File is used. You can control the location of a virtual machine's Smart Paging File by going to the Smart Paging File tab, found within the virtual machine's Settings page (see Figure 1-25).

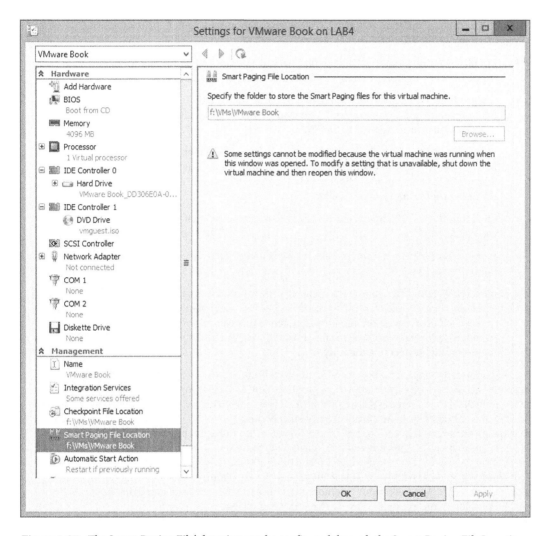

Figure 1-25. *The Smart Paging File's location can be configured through the Smart Paging File Location tab on the virtual machine's Settings window*

Removing the GUI

Earlier in this chapter, I promised you that I would show you how to remove the GUI from a Windows Server 2012 R2 server. I strongly recommend keeping the GUI until you have finished working through this book, but it is of course ultimately up to you as to if or when to abandon the GUI.

There are two main things that you need to know about removing the GUI. First, doing so requires the host server to be rebooted. Second, you can complete the process by using PowerShell.

Although it's easy to think of a GUI as either being turned on or turned off, Windows Server actually has three GUI modes. These modes are:

- Server Core (Figure 1-26) – There is no real GUI to speak of.

- Minimal Server (Figure 1-27) – Server Manager, the Microsoft Management Console, and some parts of the Control Panel are accessible.

- Full Server (Figure 1-28) – All GUI features are accessible.

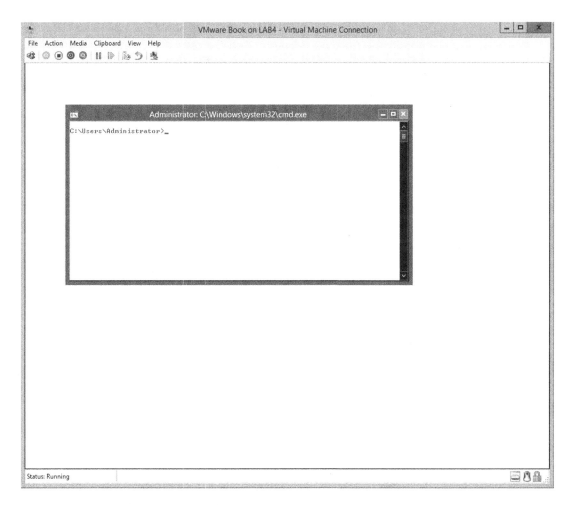

Figure 1-26. *This is the Server Core configuration*

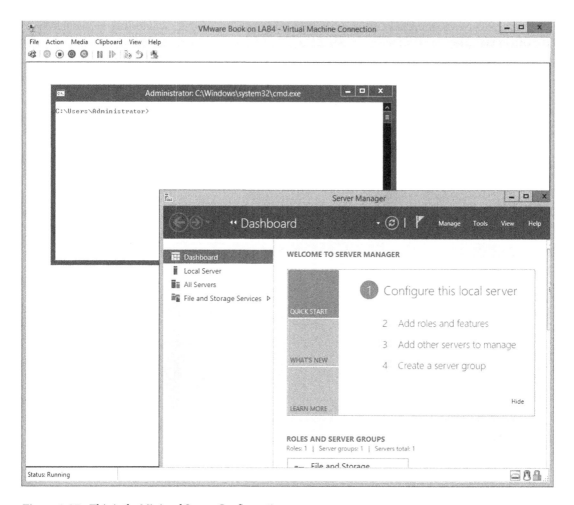

Figure 1-27. *This is the Minimal Server Configuration*

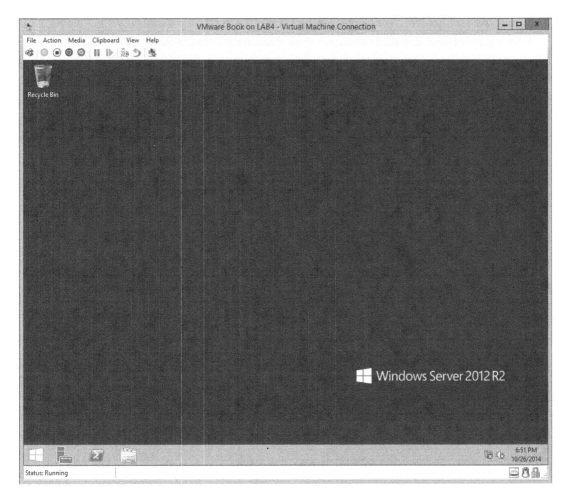

Figure 1-28. *This is the Full Server configuration*

So, with that said, here are some commands that you can use to switch between the various modes:

- To switch from Full installation to Server Core use this command (see Figure 1-29):

```
Uninstall-WindowsFeature Server-Gui-Mgmt-Infra
```

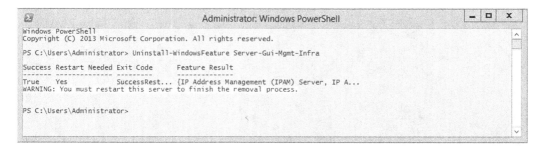

Figure 1-29. *You can use this command to switch to a Server Core configuration*

- To switch from Server Core to Minimal Server GUI mode use this command:

```
Install-WindowsFeature Server-Gui-Mgmt-Infra
```

It is worth noting that Server Core opens a Command Prompt window, not a PowerShell window. You must enter the PowerShell command to switch to PowerShell mode prior to using a PowerShell cmdlet.

- To switch from Server Core to full GUI mode use this command (see Figure 1-30):

```
Install-WindowsFeature Server-Gui-Shell
```

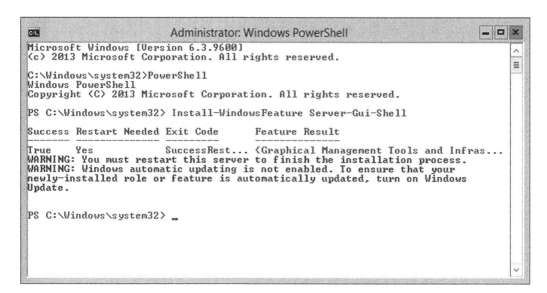

Figure 1-30. *You can use this command to switch back to the full GUI mode*

I also want to show you a variation of this last command. If you want to switch from Server Core to a full GUI mode, but you also want to install the Desktop Experience, you can do so by using this command:

```
Install-WindowsFeature Server-Gui-Mgmt-Infra Server-Gui-Shell Desktop-Experience
```

Moving On

This chapter has been something of a crash course in installing and working with Hyper-V. Obviously, Hyper-V has a huge number of features and capabilities that I did not cover in this chapter. My goal here was to cover some of the basics and familiarize you with the way that some of the most common tasks are performed in a Hyper-V environment. I will be discussing some other common tasks as we go along, especially in the last chapter of the book.

In the next chapter, my plan is to show you how to expand your Hyper-V deployment by building a failover cluster. By doing so, you will be able to make your virtual machines fault tolerant.

CHAPTER 2

■ ■ ■

Building a Failover Cluster

In the previous chapter, I showed you how to get Hyper-V up and running. Although you can run virtualized workloads on a standalone Hyper-V server, doing so is a bad idea because the host server can become a single point of failure. If the Hyper-V server were to fail, then all of the virtualized workloads that are running on the server would also fail, resulting in a major outage. The best way to prevent this from occurring is to create a Windows failover cluster. That way, your virtual machines can be made fault tolerant.

Cluster Planning

Before you cluster your Hyper-V deployment, you are going to need to do some planning with regard to the cluster architecture. The first thing that you need to understand is that there is no such thing as a "Hyper-V Cluster," even though I may casually use the term once in a while. Instead, "Hyper-V Clusters" are based on the Windows Failover Clustering Service. As such, the cluster exists at the Windows Server level, not at the Hyper-V level. Hyper-V is merely a server role that is installed onto a server that is acting as a cluster node.

I want to take just a moment and clarify some terminology before I move on. In Microsoft speak, there is a big difference between a server role and a clustered role. When it comes to a clustered Hyper-V deployment, Hyper-V is a server role that is installed on the cluster nodes, but Hyper-V is not treated as a part of the cluster. Instead, virtual machines are "clustered" on an individual basis. The virtual machines are treated as clustered roles. A clustered role is a specific task or service (in this case a virtual machine) that is made fault tolerant. Other examples of clustered roles might include the DNS or DHCP services.

Windows failover clusters are based on the Majority Node Set (MNS) model. The simple way to explain a Majority Node Set cluster is that the majority of the cluster nodes must be running in order for the cluster to remain functional. However, Microsoft has made some changes in Windows Server 2012 R2 that bend these rules a bit.

In order to remain a viable resource, a cluster must maintain *quorum*. Prior to Microsoft's newly redesigned cluster architecture, quorum could only be maintained if a majority of the cluster nodes remained functional. Microsoft defined a majority as half plus one. Suppose, for example, that a cluster consisted of ten nodes. Since half plus one of the nodes must remain functional, a total of six nodes would be required to remain online in order for the cluster to retain quorum.

Microsoft chose to modernize the quorum model in order to overcome shortcomings in the old model. Consider my previous example, in which a cluster with ten nodes required six nodes to remain functional in order for the cluster to retain quorum. If five nodes were to drop offline, the cluster would lose quorum, even though the remaining five nodes were completely functional. While the odds of having five nodes fail all at once might seem remote, this type of failure is common for clusters that span multiple datacenters. Imagine for a moment that the previously referenced ten-node cluster spans two datacenters, with five nodes in each location. If the WAN link between the two datacenters were to fail, then Windows would interpret the link failure as a multi-node failure. Neither site would be able to communicate with the nodes at the other site; therefore, both locations would lose quorum.

The solution to preventing this sort of problem has long been to place a witness server in a third location. The witness server gets counted as a cluster node even though it does not have the ability to host clustered virtual machines. As such, whichever site is still able to communicate with the witness server would retain quorum.

When Windows is checking to see if a cluster has quorum, it tests its ability to communicate with each node. A node's response to this test is referred to as a vote. Each node in the cluster gets a vote, as does the witness server (if one is used). The challenges and costs involved in designing a cluster so as to avoid losing quorum as a result of WAN link failures led Microsoft to modernize the Majority Node Set model. Most of the changes are based around the way that the voting process works.

One such change is that the witness server's quorum vote is now dynamic. The witness server only casts a vote if there are an even number of cluster nodes and a vote is needed to act as a tie breaker. Conversely, if a witness server fails then its vote is not considered in making quorum calculations. By the way, when we build a cluster later in this chapter, we won't be making use of a witness server.

So, if a witness server's job is now to act as a tie breaker, you might wonder what happens if a cluster contains an even number of nodes and no witness server. In that type of situation, Windows automatically removes the voting rights from a random cluster node. This allows the cluster to act as though it has an odd number of nodes, thereby preventing the dreaded 50–50 split.

Windows Server 2012 R2 makes it possible to manually configure the quorum model. The primary tool for managing Windows Failover Clusters is the Failover Cluster Manager console, which you will see later in this and other chapters. If at a later time you decide that you want to adjust the quorum votes for the cluster, you can open the Failover Cluster Manager, select your cluster, and click on More Actions ➤ Configure Cluster Quorum Settings. Doing so launches a wizard that you can use to adjust the quorum settings for the cluster.

Cluster Scalability

One of the most important considerations when building a failover cluster is scalability. You will need to take into account the capabilities of both Hyper-V and the Windows Server Failover Clustering Service. Essentially, this means making sure that the cluster can scale to meet your requirements. Here are the primary limits that you will need to keep in mind as you create a failover cluster:

- Hyper-V supports a maximum of 1,024 virtual machines per host server (including cluster nodes). It is actually possible to create more than 1,024 virtual machines per host, but only 1024 virtual machines can be powered on at any given time.

- For clustered Hyper-V deployments, you can only include about 8,000 virtual machines in the entire cluster. Large clusters could theoretically accommodate more virtual machines if the host VM limitation were the only thing being taken into account. For example, a ten-node cluster with a per-node limit of 1,024 VMs should theoretically be able to accommodate over 10,000 VMs. However, Microsoft sets the maximum number of virtual machines per cluster to 8,000.

- A failover cluster based on Windows Server 2012 R2 can include up to 64 nodes.

- Each Hyper-V server within the cluster can include up to 4 TB of RAM.

Although the limits mentioned above are important, there are often practical limits that come into play long before the cluster grows large enough to reach any of the hard limits. This book isn't intended to serve as a comprehensive discussion of failover clustering, but the following sections identify a few things to think about.

How Many Clusters Should You Build?

There is no rule that says that you can only have one failover cluster. It is sometimes better to build several small clusters than to build one big one. That way, you aren't putting all of your eggs in one basket. If a cluster-level failure were to occur, the VMs in external clusters would continue to function.

Using multiple clusters can also result in better virtual machine performance in some situations. Clustered Hyper-V deployments do not absolutely require the use of shared storage, but it is usually recommended to use shared storage whenever possible. In a large cluster you could have dozens of servers that are all accessing the same storage device at the same time (assuming that VMs are running on each node). Unless the storage device can accommodate the demand, the storage could become a major bottleneck. Very often organizations see better performance by deploying a series of smaller clusters, each with their own dedicated storage. That way, there isn't one single storage device that is forced to carry the full burden of the cluster's I/O demands.

Another advantage to using multiple clusters is that doing so makes it possible to define service tiers. Tiered service architectures are beyond the scope of this book, but the basic idea is that you could use relatively low-end server and storage hardware for minimally important or non-performance or latency-intensive workloads, and use a cluster with higher-end hardware for mission-critical or high-performance workloads. In case you are wondering, Hyper-V allows a running virtual machine to be live migrated between clusters if necessary.

Important Things to Remember:

- It is sometimes beneficial to build multiple clusters.

- Building multiple clusters can make it easier to define service tiers.

- Having multiple clusters can help you to reduce the load on your storage infrastructure.

Failover Cluster Architecture Considerations

It might at first seem that the per-host VM limit is completely at odds with the cluster VM limit. If each host can run 1,024 VMs, and a cluster can include up to 64 nodes, then how come you can only run 8,000 virtual machines instead of the theoretical limit of 65,536?

There are a few different reasons for this. First, not every cluster node is capable of running 1,024 virtual machines. This is especially true for resource-intensive virtual machines. It is entirely possible that a cluster node might only be able to handle running a few VMs, depending on its physical hardware and the scale of the workload. In my own organization, I have a host server that only runs a single VM. The VM needs nearly all of the resources of a physical server, but I chose to virtualize it anyway so that I could take advantage of the flexibility that is offered by virtualization. So one of the reasons why a cluster can have so many nodes is because not every node will be capable of running a huge number of virtual machines. In fact, having a high node limit may even allow you to use commodity hardware in your cluster rather than relying on high-end (and expensive) servers.

Another reason why there is a big mismatch between the per-node limit and the per-cluster limit on the maximum number of VMs is because completely maxing out every cluster node would be a bad thing. The entire purpose of a failover cluster is to allow virtual machines to keep running in the event of a node failure. In that type of situation, there must be adequate resources elsewhere within the cluster to accommodate the virtual machines from the failed node.

On the surface, the concept of leaving room for VMs from a failed node to fail over would not seem to account for much of the difference between node maximums and cluster maximums. Keep in mind however, that a Windows failover cluster can span multiple datacenters. With that in mind, imagine what would happen if an entire datacenter were to fail. The remaining nodes in a remote datacenter would need to be able to absorb the virtual machines from the failed nodes. In that type of situation, the remote datacenter would need to have a substantial amount of host resources free in order to accommodate the workloads that have failed over.

Setting Up Cluster Storage

One of the major considerations that you will have to take into account prior to building a Windows Failover Cluster is the cluster's storage type. Hyper-V is actually very flexible with regard to the types of storage that can be used, and there are a number of different supported options for cluster storage. All of these options fall into two main categories—shared storage or non-shared storage. Both are supported, but as a best practice you should use shared storage whenever possible.

For the purposes of this book, I am going to show you how to build a cluster that is based on shared storage, but with one caveat—I am going to be taking a mostly hardware-agnostic approach. My reason for doing this is that I want this book to be relevant to as many people as possible. If I got into a deep discussion of storage arrays and proprietary hardware I risk losing focus and also alienating some of my readers.

Most real-world shared storage implementations for clustered Hyper-V deployments tend to be SAN-based and are connected via either iSCSI or Fibre Channel. For the purposes of this book, I am going to build a simple iSCSI target that resides on an SMB 3.0 file server. I will then show you how to establish iSCSI connectivity from your cluster nodes.

Regardless of the storage solution that you choose to use, there are a few important things to keep in mind:

- The storage architecture must be supported by Microsoft. There are plenty of unsupported storage architectures that work, but using them is a bad idea. You should never run an unsupported configuration in a production environment.

- The storage array needs to deliver a sufficient level of IOPS to accommodate the cumulative demand of the virtual machines that will eventually reside on the cluster storage.

- The storage array should provide protection against physical disk failures.

- You must make sure that your storage connectivity provides sufficient bandwidth to prevent it from becoming a bottleneck. The fastest storage array in the world won't do you much good if your storage connectivity can't handle all of the storage traffic. I am going to be talking more about bandwidth a little bit later on.

Now that I have talked about my general approach to storage, let's go ahead and establish iSCSI connectivity to what will eventually become our cluster-shared volume.

Preparing Your Cluster Nodes

For the sake of demonstration, I am going to show you how to build a Windows Failover Cluster consisting of three cluster nodes (a node is a server that acts as a member of the cluster). I will show you how to configure your servers as failover cluster nodes a little bit later in this chapter. My main goal right now is to show you how to set up an iSCSI target. Even so, you can save yourself some work later on by taking care of a bit of prep work right now.

The first thing that you need to do is to install Windows Server 2012 R2 onto each of the physical servers that will act as a cluster node. You can use the instructions from Chapter 1 to complete the Windows Server installation. After Windows Server has been installed, be sure to join each server to the management domain. It's also OK to go ahead and install the Hyper-V role onto each of the servers.

I also recommend assigning each server a name that reflects its purpose within the cluster or the organization as a whole. For the purposes of this book, I am going to use the computer names Lab1, Lab2, and Lab3. The 1, 2, and 3 designate the server's positions within my rack. As you will recall from the previous chapter, I named my management domain MGMT.com. As such, the fully qualified domain name of server Lab1 would be Lab1.MGMT.com.

Starting the iSCSI Initiator and Documenting the IQN

Once the servers are up and running, the next thing that you will need to do is to start the iSCSI Initiator. The reason why we are doing this now is because each cluster node will have a unique iSCSI Qualified Name (IQN). You will need to know the IQN for each of your cluster nodes when you eventually set up the iSCSI target. Incidentally, the IQN is based on the server's name. Therefore, make sure to name the servers and join them to your management domain before starting the iSCSI Initiator.

Starting the iSCSI Initiator and documenting each server's IQN is a simple process. To do so, complete these steps:

1. Open the Server Manager.

2. Click on the Tools menu and then click on the iSCSI Initiator option.

3. You should now see a message telling you that the iSCSI Initiator is not running. If prompted, click Yes to start the iSCSI Initiator. If you do not see this message or this prompt, it simply means that the iSCSI Initiator is already running.

4. When the iSCSI Initiator's dialog box opens, go to the Configuration tab and then write down the Initiator Name (see Figure 2-1).

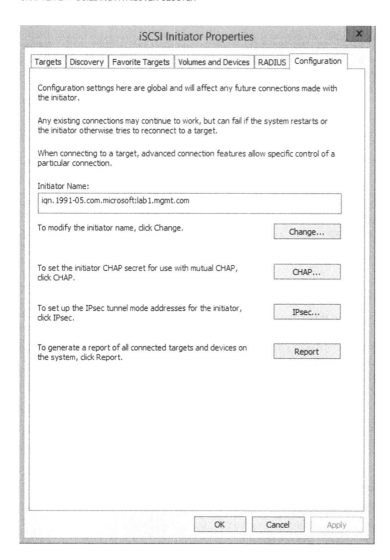

Figure 2-1. Write down the IQN for each cluster node

5. Repeat this process for each node in the cluster.

Creating an iSCSI Target

Now we are ready to build an iSCSI target that can be used for storing clustered Hyper-V virtual machines. There are two main steps involved in building the target. First, we have to install the iSCSI Target Server component. This component is included with Windows Server as a part of the File and Storage Services role, but must be manually deployed. The second step in the process is the actual configuration.

Deploying the iSCSI Target Component

The process of deploying the iSCSI target component is very similar to deploying any other server role. The iSCSI target is part of the File and Storage Services role. The role is installed by default, but the iSCSI target is not. To deploy the iSCSI target, complete these steps:

1. Log on to the Windows Server that will host the iSCSI target. This server should not be one of the cluster nodes. If an external storage array is being used then you can either establish an iSCSI connection directly to the array (if supported) without following the steps in this section, or you can use Windows Server as a bridge between the cluster nodes and the storage array. As previously mentioned, I am taking a hardware agnostic approach to storage and will be using a Windows Server with an internal storage array. I provisioned the array using Windows Storage Spaces, but that is beyond the scope of this book.

2. Open Server Manager (on the server that will host the iSCSI target).

3. When Server Manager opens, select the Add Roles and Features command from the Manage menu. This will cause Windows to launch the Add Roles and Features Wizard.

4. Click Next to bypass the wizard's Welcome page.

5. You should now see the wizard's Select Installation Type page. Select the Role-Based or Feature-Based Installation option and click Next.

6. Verify that the server that will host the iSCSI target is selected and click Next.

7. You will now be taken to the Select Server Roles page. Verify that the File and Storage Services Role is installed. This role should be installed by default.

8. Expand the File and Storage Services container.

9. Expand the File and iSCSI Services container.

10. Select the iSCSI Target Server option (see Figure 2-2). If at any point during this step or the next step you are prompted to install additional features, click the Add Feature button.

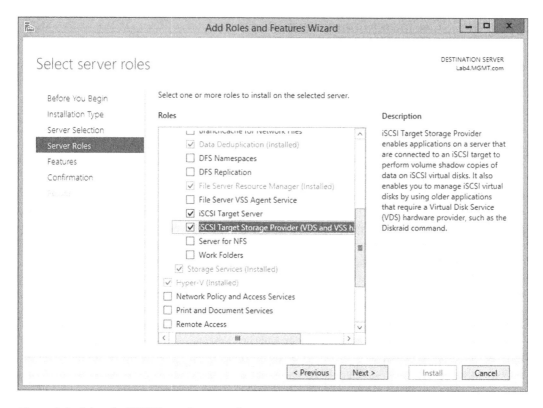

Figure 2-2. *Select the iSCSI Target Server option*

11. Select the iSCSI Target Storage Provider Option.

12. Click Next.

13. You should now see the Select Features page. You don't have to worry about installing any extra features, so just click Next.

14. You should now see a page showing the roles and features that you have selected for installation. Take a moment to verify that both the iSCSI Target Server and the iSCSI Target Storage Provider are listed (see Figure 2-3).

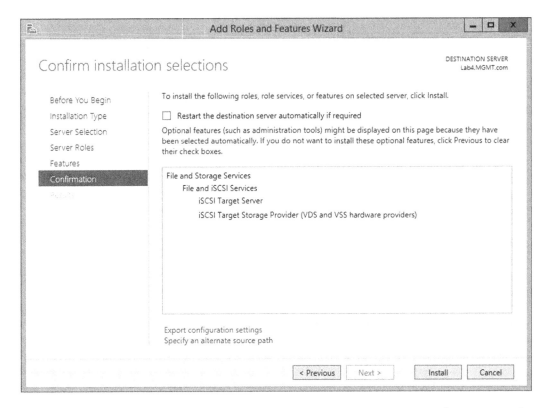

Figure 2-3. *Verify that both the iSCSI Target Server and the iSCSI Target Storage Provider are going to be installed*

15. Click Install.

16. When the installation process completes, click Close.

Configuring the iSCSI Target

Now that the iSCSI target components have been installed, we need to configure the iSCSI target. Remember, unlike VMware, Hyper-V has no concept of a datastore. You can store virtual machines on any disk that is accessible to the operating system. For the purpose of this book, we will be creating a virtual disk on top of our physical storage. It is this virtual disk that will become our iSCSI target.

While we are at it, we will also need to choose an authentication method that our iSCSI Initiators can use to connect to the iSCSI target. We will also need to provide the iSCSI target with the names of the iSCSI Initiators. After all, we don't want just any random initiator to be able to connect to our cluster storage.

So the process of configuring the iSCSI target requires us to complete several different tasks. The following procedure performs all of the required tasks:

1. Open the Server Manager on the server that will host your iSCSI target.

2. Click on the File and Storage Services container, located within the console tree.

3. Click on the iSCSI container (see Figure 2-4).

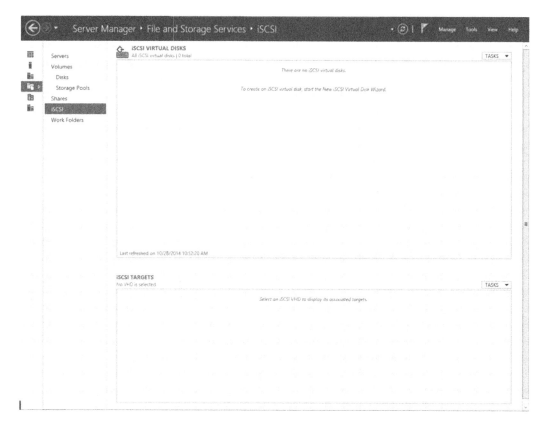

Figure 2-4. *Select the iSCSI container*

■ **Note** If you are working through this procedure in a lab environment, then you do not need dedicated hardware in order to create an iSCSI target. You can instead create the iSCSI target on your domain controller if sufficient storage space is available. In a production environment, however, dedicated storage is always recommended.

---

4. Click on the link labeled To Create an iSCSI Virtual Disk, Start the New iSCSI Virtual Disk Wizard. As the name of the link implies, this will cause the iSCSI Virtual Disk Wizard to be launched (see Figure 2-5).

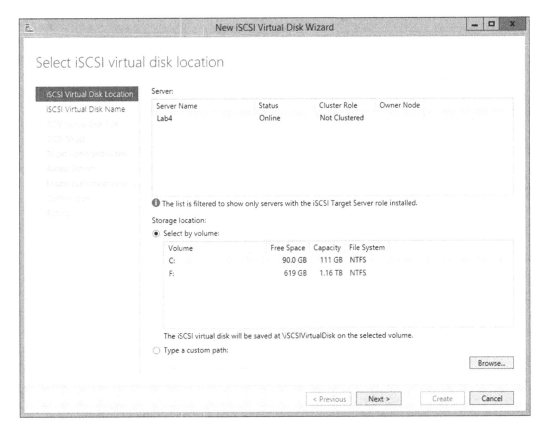

Figure 2-5. *Click on the link labeled To Create an iSCSI Virtual Disk, Start the New iSCSI Virtual Disk Wizard*

5. Select the volume on which you want to create the virtual disk.

6. Click Next.

7. Enter a name for the virtual disk that you are creating.

8. Enter a description for the virtual hard disk. Although entering a description is optional, it is a good idea to do so. Real-world deployments often involve multiple virtual hard disks, and it is important to be able to tell them apart.

9. Note the path where the virtual disk will be stored. By default, the virtual disk will be stored on the selected volume in the iSCSIVirtualDisks folder (see Figure 2-6).

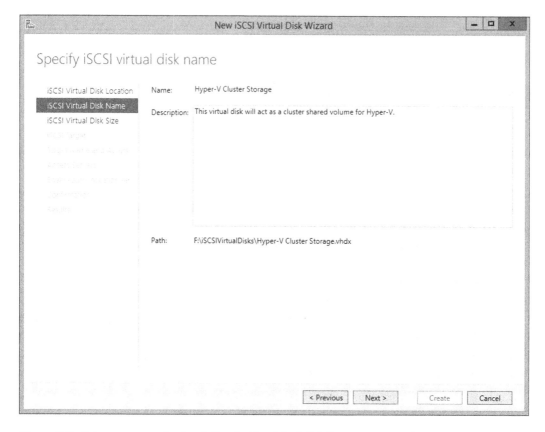

Figure 2-6. *Enter a name and a description for the virtual disk that you are creating*

10. Click Next.

11. Specify the desired size for the iSCSI virtual disk (see Figure 2-7).

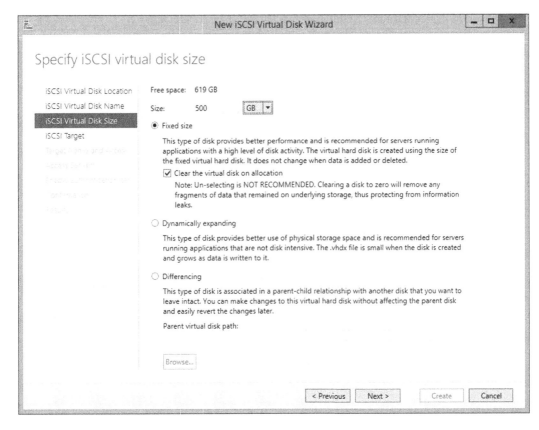

Figure 2-7. Specify the desired size for the virtual hard disk

12. Choose the virtual disk type. Like VMware, Hyper-V supports creating virtual disks of a fixed size or thinly provisioned (dynamically expanding) virtual disks. When it comes to creating a virtual disk that will act as an iSCSI target, it is best to create a fixed-size virtual disk, because doing so will provide better write performance than will a dynamically expanding virtual disk.

13. Click Next.

14. Choose the New iSCSI Target option.

15. Click Next.

16. Enter a name for the new iSCSI target.

17. Enter a description for the new iSCSI target. Once again, the description is optional, but as a best practice you should enter a meaningful description.

18. Click Next.

19. You will now need to enter the names of your iSCSI Initiators. To do so, click on the Add button.

20. If the iSCSI Initiators show up in the initiator cache, you can select those initiators. Otherwise, Set the Type option to IQN.

21. Enter the names of your iSCSI Initiators (see Figure 2-8) and click OK.

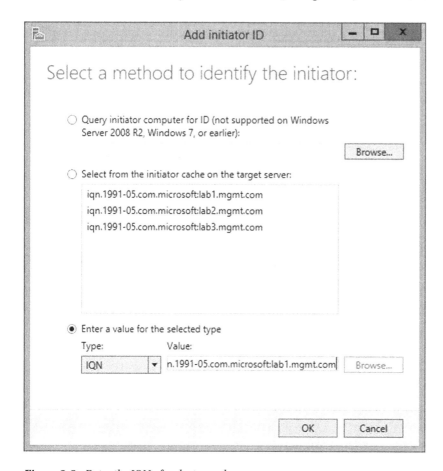

Figure 2-8. *Enter the IQN of a cluster node*

22. Click the Add button (see Figure 2-9) and repeat the process to add any additional required IQNs.

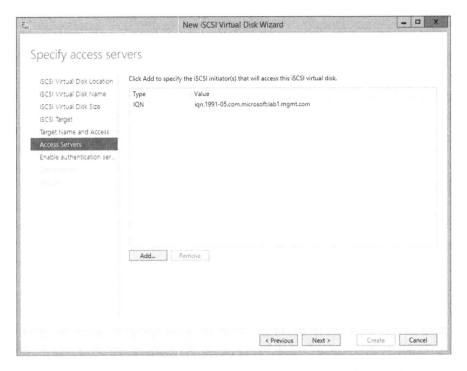

Figure 2-9. *Click the Add button and then enter the IQN of another cluster node*

23. Once all of the IQNs have been added, take a moment to verify that you typed the names correctly with no spelling or punctuation errors.

24. Click Next.

25. Choose the option to use CHAP Authentication. Authentication is optional, but you need to use authentication to prevent unauthorized use of your cluster storage.

26. Enter a CHAP username. The username can be anything that you want.

27. Enter and confirm a CHAP password. The password must be at least 12 characters in length (see Figure 2-10).

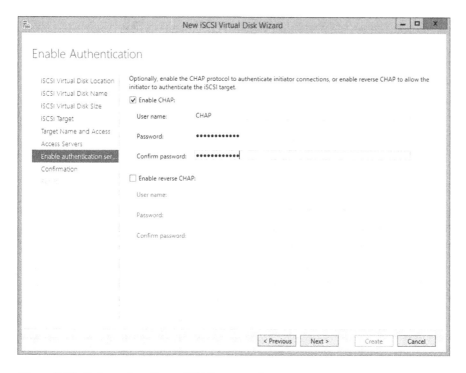

Figure 2-10. *Enter and confirm a CHAP password*

28. Click Next.

29. You should now see a confirmation page detailing your selected configuration. Take a moment to verify that the information is correct. This is extremely important, because any mistakes could cause storage connectivity to fail.

30. Click Create.

31. When the configuration process completes, click Close.

Attaching to the iSCSI Target

Now it is time to attach the cluster nodes to the iSCSI target that you created. The process for doing so is relatively easy, but you must follow this procedure very carefully because it is easy to accidentally attach the target in a way that effectively prevents it from being used by the cluster. With that said, you can attach your cluster nodes to the iSCSI target by completing the following steps on each of your cluster nodes:

1. Open the Server Manager on a cluster node.

2. Choose the iSCSI Initiator command from the Tools menu.

3. Select the iSCSI Initiator's Targets tab.

4. Enter the IP address of the server that is hosting the iSCSI target. You should enter this information into the Targets field.

5. Click the Quick Connect button. Upon doing so, the iSCSI target should be listed as inactive (see Figure 2-11). There are two different targets listed in the figure because the server that is hosting my iSCSI target is being used for other purposes beyond writing this book. If you are setting up iSCSI for the first time, you should only see one target.

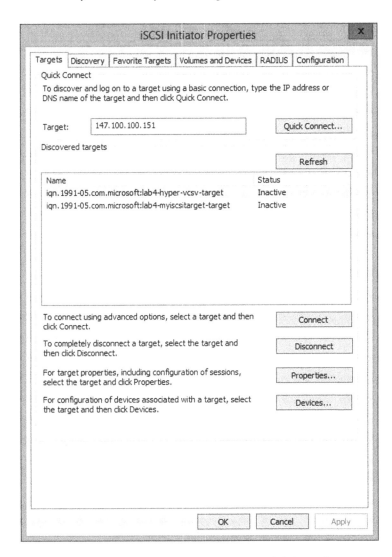

Figure 2-11. *Enter the iSCSI target's IP address and click Quick Connect*

6. Select the iSCSI target and click the Connect button.

7. Select the Add this Connection to the List of Favorites option.

8. Select the Enable Multi-Path check box (Figure 2-12). This is the most critical step in the entire process. Without multi-path enabled, the other cluster nodes will be unable to connect to the target.

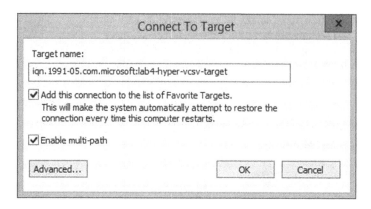

Figure 2-12. *It is CRITICALLY IMPORTANT to select the Enable Multi-Path check box*

9. Click the Advanced button.

10. Select the Enable CHAP Log On check box.

11. Enter your CHAP username into the Name field.

12. Enter your CHAP password into the Target Secret field (see Figure 2-13).

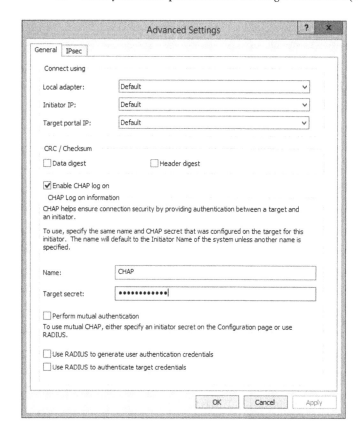

Figure 2-13. *Enter your CHAP username and password*

13. Click OK.

14. Click OK again.

15. Verify that the iSCSI target is listed as Connected (see Figure 2-14).

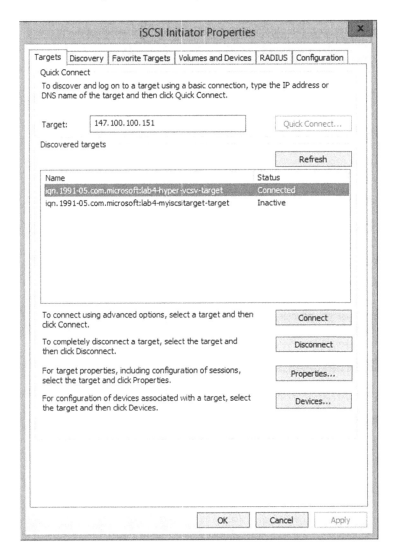

Figure 2-14. Make sure that the iSCSI target is connected

16. Repeat this procedure on all of your cluster nodes.

Preparing the iSCSI Target for Use

By now, all of your failover cluster nodes should be connected to the iSCSI target. Even so, the iSCSI target isn't quite ready to use. As you will recall, the iSCSI target makes use of a virtual hard disk. Like a physical hard disk, a Microsoft virtual hard disk needs to be provisioned by creating partitions and volumes. The easiest way to complete this task is to use the legacy Disk Management console. You can prepare the iSCSI target by completing the following steps on one of your cluster nodes (you do not need to repeat the process for each node):

1. Enter the DISKMGMT.MSC command at the server's Run prompt.

2. Locate the iSCSI target through the Disk Management console.

3. Right click on the disk that is associated with the iSCSI target and choose the Online command from the shortcut menu (see Figure 2-15). Upon doing so, the disk's status should change to Not Initialized.

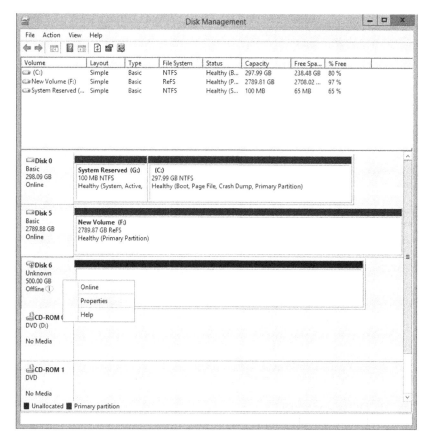

Figure 2-15. *Right click on the iSCSI target disk and select the Online command from the shortcut menu*

▪ **Note**   In some cases you may find that the iSCSI target is not listed and that when you attempt to attach the VHD for the iSCSI target, Windows reports that the disk is being used by another process. If you encounter this issue, you may be able to work around it by right clicking the virtual disk and choosing the Disable option. Next, right click on the virtual disk again and choose the Remove option, but do not delete the disk. You should then be able to attach to the target and access it through the Disk Management console.

4.   Right click on the disk that is associated with the iSCSI target once again, and choose the Initialize Disk command from the shortcut menu (see Figure 2-16).

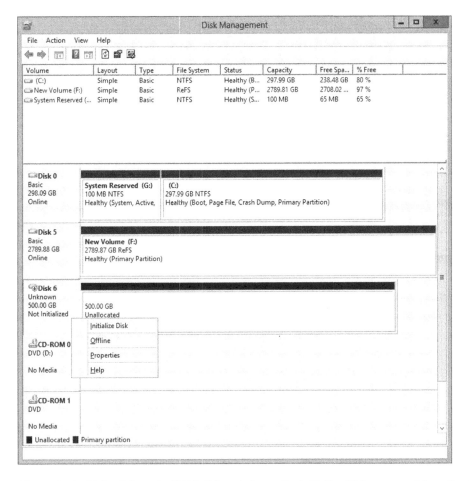

Figure 2-16. *Right click on the iSCSI disk and choose the Initialize Disk command from the shortcut menu*

5. Specify the type of partition that you wish to use for the iSCSI target.

6. Click OK.

7. Right click on the unallocated space and choose the New Simple Volume command from the shortcut menu (see Figure 2-17). As you look at the figure, you will notice that the options to create other volume types are grayed out. As you will recall, I previously stated that it is a good idea to use a RAID 1+0 volume. In this case, the RAID structure is being handled at the hardware level on the iSCSI target. As such, there is no need to choose anything beyond a simple volume at this point in the process.

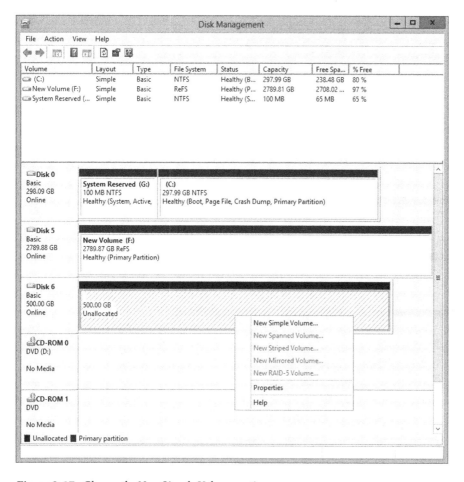

Figure 2-17. *Choose the New Simple Volume option*

8. When the New Simple Volume Wizard opens, click Next to bypass the wizard's Welcome page.

9. Click Next to accept the default volume size.

10. Choose the Do Not Assign a Drive Letter or Drive Path option.

11. Click Next.

12. Format the volume using the NTFS file system.

13. Click Next.

14. Click Finish

15. When the formatting process completes, close the Disk Management console.

Building a Failover Cluster

Now that we have installed Windows Server onto our cluster nodes and created an iSCSI target, it is time to build a failover cluster. The procedure described below assumes that the servers are running Windows Server 2012 R2 and that they have been attached to the iSCSI target. It also assumes that the Hyper-V role has already been installed onto each cluster node.

The procedure that I am about to show you will do two things. First, it will install the Failover Clustering feature. Second, it will configure the failover cluster. Once the failover cluster has been created and configured, there will still be a little bit of work left to do in order to make the cluster use our iSCSI target. There is also a procedure that will need to be performed in order to make the virtual machines fault tolerant.

Deploying the Failover Cluster Feature

Installing the Failover Clustering feature is a simple process that doesn't work much differently from deploying any other feature. To install the necessary feature, perform the following tasks on each of your failover cluster nodes:

1. Log in with administrative credentials and open the Server Manager.

2. Select the Add Roles and Features command from the Manage menu. This will cause the Add Roles and Features Wizard to launch.

3. Click Next to bypass the wizard's Welcome page.

4. Select the Role-Based or Feature-Based Installation option.

5. Click Next.

6. Verify that your server is selected.

7. Click Next.

8. The wizard should now display a list of server roles. We don't need to deploy any roles, so just click Next.

9. The wizard will now display a list of available features. Select the Failover Clustering feature (see Figure 2-18).

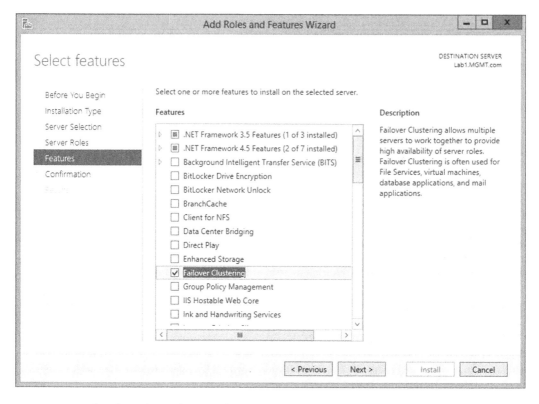

Figure 2-18. *Select the Failover Clustering feature*

10. If the wizard prompts you to install additional features, click the Add button.

11. Click Next.

12. Click Install.

13. When the installation process completes, click Close.

14. Repeat this procedure on each cluster node.

Checking the Hyper-V Virtual Switch

Before you begin the cluster creation process, it is a good idea to review your Hyper-V Virtual Switch configuration. Windows Server 2012 R2 does not require your cluster nodes to be completely identical to one another. However, if your cluster nodes are not 100% identical then Hyper-V may be using inconsistent virtual switch names. The Hyper-V virtual switch names must be identical across your cluster nodes.

You can verify the name of the Hyper-V virtual switch that is in use on each cluster node by completing the following steps:

1. Open the Hyper-V Manager.

2. Click on the Virtual Switch Manager link within the Actions pane.

3. Check the name of your existing virtual switch. By default, the virtual switch should be named New Virtual Switch (see Figure 2-19). However, there are a few things that can cause the virtual switch to have a different name, including:

- The virtual switch has been manually assigned a different name.

- Multiple physical network adapters exist (a separate virtual switch is created for each physical network adapter).

- The network adapter has not been detected, or its driver is incorrect or missing. No virtual switch will be created unless a physical network adapter is detected.

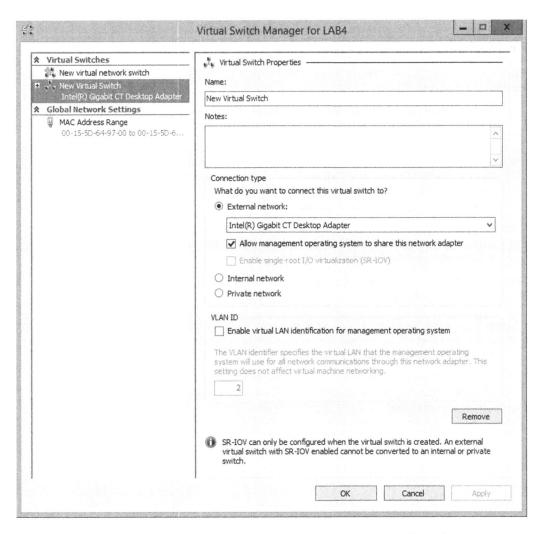

Figure 2-19. *By default, the Hyper-V virtual switch should be named New Virtual Switch*

4. As you check the name of the virtual switch on each cluster node, look for any inconsistencies. If a cluster node uses a virtual switch with a name that does not exactly match the virtual switch names used by the other cluster nodes, you can rename the virtual switch by clicking on it and then entering a new name into the Name field.

5. If your server hardware does not match exactly, then you could run into a situation in which one or more cluster nodes contain extra Hyper-V virtual switches. This happens because a virtual switch is automatically created for each network adapter that is authorized for use with Hyper-V. The easiest way to deal with virtual switches that exist on some, but not all, of your nodes is to simply remove them. To do so, click on the virtual switch and then click the Remove button.

6. Click OK to close the Virtual Switch Manager.

Now it's time to construct our failover cluster. In order to do so, there are three pieces of information that you will need to have on hand.

- **The names of your cluster nodes.** As you will recall, each cluster node was assigned a name. You will have to specify these names during the cluster creation process.

- **A cluster name.** Just as each Windows server has a computer name, the cluster is also assigned a name. This name makes it possible to communicate with the cluster as a cohesive unit, rather than having to communicate with each cluster node individually. The name that you choose must be unique and must not match the name used by any of your cluster nodes.

- **A cluster IP address.** Just as the cluster requires a unique name, it also requires a unique IP address. The IP address that you choose must be different from the address used on any of the cluster nodes.

To create the failover cluster, complete the following steps on one of the cluster nodes (you do not have to repeat these steps for each node).

1. Open the Server Manager on one of your cluster nodes.

2. Select the Failover Cluster Manager option from the Tools menu. This will cause the Failover Cluster Manager to open.

3. Click on the Create Cluster link. This link is located within the Failover Cluster Manager's Actions pane (see Figure 2-20). This will cause Windows to launch the Create Cluster Wizard.

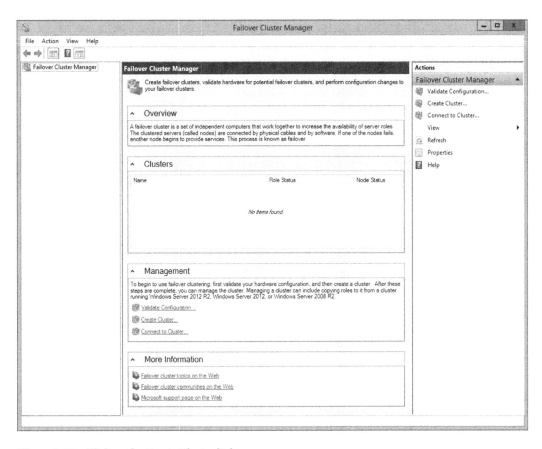

Figure 2-20. *Click on the Create Cluster link*

4. Click Next to bypass the wizard's Welcome page.

5. Enter the names of all of your cluster nodes (see Figure 2-21).

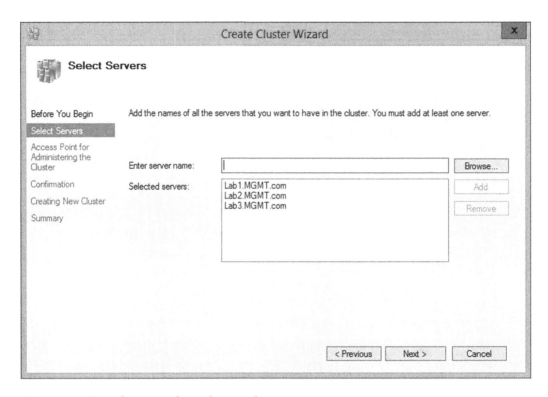

Figure 2-21. *Enter the names of your cluster nodes*

6. Click Next.

7. Enter the name that you have chosen to use for the cluster (see Figure 2-22). This must be a unique NetBIOS name that does not match the name of any of the cluster nodes.

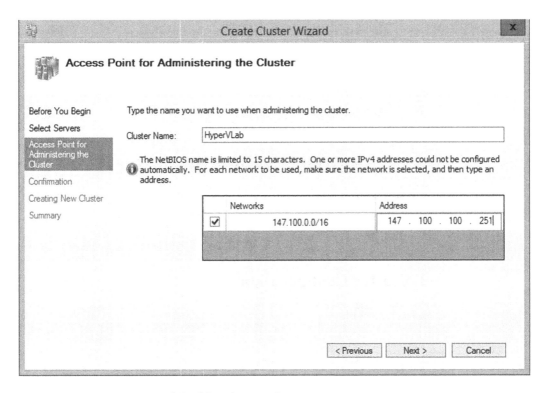

Figure 2-22. *Enter a name and IP address for your cluster*

8. Enter the IP address that you want to assign to the cluster. This must be a unique IP address that does not match any address currently in use on your network.

9. Click Next.

10. Take a moment to verify the information shown on the Confirmation page and click Next.

11. Verify that the cluster was created successfully and click Finish.

12. Upon returning to the main Failover Cluster Manager page, click on the Validate Cluster link. This will launch the Validate a Configuration Wizard.

13. Click Next to bypass the wizard's Welcome page.

14. Select the Run All Tests (Recommended) option.

15. Click Next.

16. Click Next again to begin running the tests.

17. When the tests complete, take a few minutes to review the report (see Figure 2-23). It is completely normal and acceptable for some warnings to be present, but there should not be any errors. You can click on the View Report button to see more detailed results.

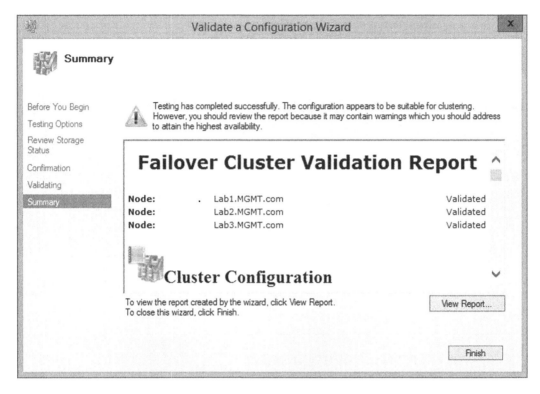

Figure 2-23. *Make sure that the report does not contain any errors*

18. Click Finish.

Fault Tolerance for Virtual Machines

Up to this point, we have created a failover cluster consisting of a series of Hyper-V servers. Even so, the cluster isn't quite ready to use. Before the cluster will be able to protect a virtual machine, a couple of things have to happen. First, the cluster must be made aware of our iSCSI target. That way, protected virtual machines can be stored on a storage device that is accessible to all of the cluster nodes.

The other thing that has to happen is that our virtual machines have to be manually designated as being fault tolerant. Obviously, we haven't created or migrated any virtual machines yet, but I will show you what the process looks like.

Connecting the Cluster to the iSCSI Target

The next thing that we have to do in order to get our cluster ready to use is to configure our failover cluster to treat the iSCSI target as a cluster-shared volume. Depending on the type of storage that you are using, there is a chance that the volume will automatically be made available to the cluster. If not, however, you can add the volume to the cluster by completing the following steps:

1. Open the Server Manager on one of the cluster nodes (you do not have to repeat this process on each individual node).

2. Select the Failover Cluster Manager option from the Tools menu to open the Failover Cluster Manager.

3. Navigate through the Failover Cluster Manager's console tree to Failover Cluster Manager ➤ <your cluster name> ➤ Storage ➤ Disks.

4. Check to see if your shared storage volume has already been added to the cluster. If it has been added to the cluster and the disk is being used as Available Storage, as it is in Figure 2-24, you are done. If it is listed as Quorum Witness instead of as Available Storage, or if the volume was not added to the cluster, you have additional work to do:

    - If the disk is listed as a Quorum Witness instead of as Available Storage, continue on and complete steps 5 and 6.

    - If your shared storage volume was not automatically added to the cluster, skip step 5 but complete step 6.

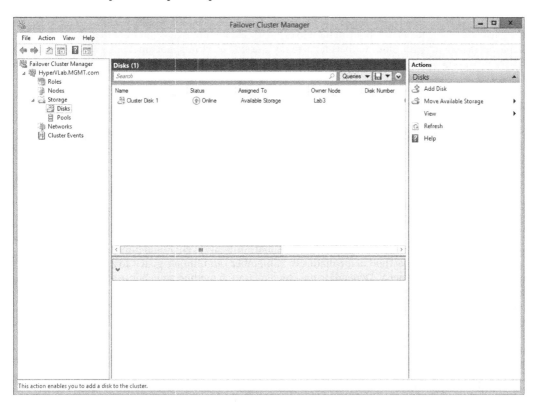

Figure 2-24. *The shared storage volume was added to the cluster automatically*

■ **Note**   If your cluster disk is not displayed, try rebooting your cluster nodes.

---

5. If the disk is listed as a Quorum Witness, then you need to detach the iSCSI storage, delete and rebuild the cluster, and reattach the iSCSI storage (these steps must be performed in this order). Then, complete step 6 to manually add the storage to the cluster.

6. If your shared storage volume was not automatically added to the cluster, or if you had to detach the storage and rebuild the cluster in step 5, complete the following steps to manually attach your storage volume:

    a. Click the Add Disk link, found in the Actions pane.

    b. Select your iSCSI target for inclusion in the cluster (if it is not already selected) and click OK.

    c. Check the Failover Cluster Manager console to see if the iSCSI target is displayed. It may take a couple of minutes for the disk to appear. You can try refreshing the console if the disk does not appear within a reasonable amount of time.

    d. Verify that the iSCSI target is listed as being online.

    e. Click on your iSCSI target disk and then click Add to Cluster Shared Volumes.

The cluster is now ready to use, but you have to explicitly tell Windows that you want to make your virtual machines fault tolerant. Since we haven't actually created any virtual machines yet, I will walk you through the process and then show you how to make the virtual machine fault tolerant.

Creating a Virtual Machine

There are a number of different ways in which you can create a Hyper-V virtual machine. Some of the tools that are capable of creating virtual machines are the Hyper-V Manager, the Failover Cluster Manager, PowerShell, and System Center Virtual Machine Manager (which I will talk about in the next chapter).

For the purposes of this chapter, I am going to show you how to create a virtual machine using the Hyper-V Manager console. In the real world, if you wanted to create a fault-tolerant virtual machine, you would typically use the Failover Cluster Manager or System Center Virtual Machine Manager. However, there is a good reason why I am using the Hyper-V Manager.

The reason why I am using the Hyper-V Manager is because it doesn't have any native functionality for making virtual machines fault tolerant. Yes, you read that correctly. Even though this probably sounds counterproductive, there is a method to the madness. Remember, our ultimate goal is to migrate virtual machines from VMware to Hyper-V. Depending on which migration method you choose to use, your VMware virtual machines may not be fault tolerant when the migration completes. You need to know how to make those virtual machines fault tolerant. If I were to create a virtual machine using the Failover Clustering Manager, the new virtual machine would automatically be made fault tolerant and I would never get the chance to show you how to manually implement fault tolerance. As such, the plan is to create a virtual machine using the Hyper-V Manager. After doing so, we will pretend that the newly created virtual machine is a VMware virtual machine that has recently been migrated, and I will show you how to make it fault tolerant.

Before I show you how to create a new virtual machine, there is one more thing that I want to point out. Even if you already know how to create a Hyper-V virtual machine, I recommend reading through this section because there are some storage considerations that I am going to point out along the way.

With that said, you can create a virtual machine by completing the following steps:

1. Open the Hyper-V Manager on one of your cluster nodes.

2. Click the New link, located within the Actions pane.

3. Choose the Virtual Machine option (see Figure 2-25). This will cause Windows to launch the New Virtual Machine Wizard.

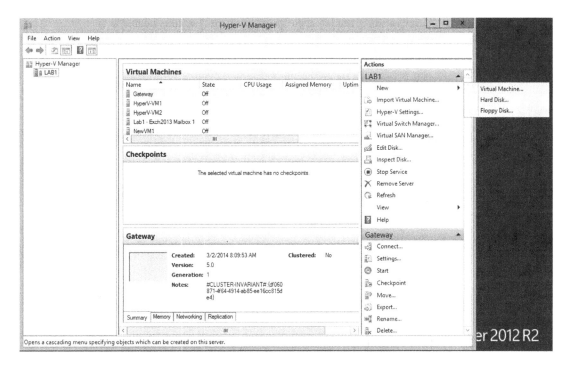

Figure 2-25. *Choose the New and Virtual Machine options*

4. Click Next to bypass the wizard's Welcome page.

5. Enter a name for the new virtual machine. It is worth noting that the name you enter only impacts the way that Hyper-V identifies the virtual machine. The virtual machine's Windows computer name will not automatically be configured to match the virtual machine name. Once an operating system is installed, you should assign a computer name that is identical to the virtual machine name.

6. Select the Store the Virtual Machine in a Different Location check box.

7. Hyper-V does not have an equivalent to the VMware datastore. As such, you must enter a path to where you want the virtual machine to reside. Hyper-V will create a folder within the specified path, and will store the virtual machine components in the folder. Since the virtual machine will eventually be made fault tolerant, we need to store the virtual machine on our iSCSI target (which is now recognized as a cluster-shared volume). Windows uses a special path for cluster-shared volumes in order to allow the volume to be accessed in a consistent way from each cluster node. That path is C:\ClusterStorage. C:\ClusterStorage is a logical path that points to the storage that you previously added to your cluster. Regardless of any mappings that might have been assigned to the cluster-shared volume, you can't store anything directly in C:\ClusterStorage, but you can store data on the volume within it. Enter C:\ClusterStorage in the Location field (see Figure 2-26), but do not click Next.

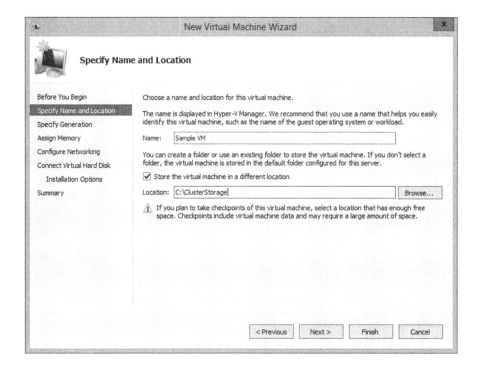

Figure 2-26. *Enter C:\ClusterStorage into the Location field*

8. Click Browse.

9. Select the volume that you want to use for virtual machine storage. The default volume name is Volume1.

10. Click Select Folder.

11. Click Next.

12. Choose the virtual machine generation that you want to use (see Figure 2-27). Virtual machine generations were discussed in the previous chapter.

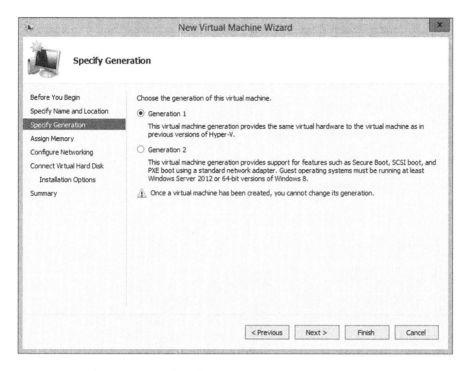

Figure 2-27. *Choose the virtual machine generation*

13. Click Next.

14. Enter the amount of startup memory that you want to assign to the virtual machine.

15. If you want the virtual machine to use dynamic memory, select the Use Dynamic Memory for this Virtual Machine check box and then populate the various memory-related fields.

16. Click Next.

17. Select the Hyper-V virtual switch to which you wish to connect the virtual machine.

18. Select the Create a Virtual Hard Disk option (this option should be selected by default).

19. Enter a name for the virtual hard disk that you are creating.

20. Verify that the location points to your cluster-shared volume.

21. Enter the desired size for your virtual hard disk (see Figure 2-28).

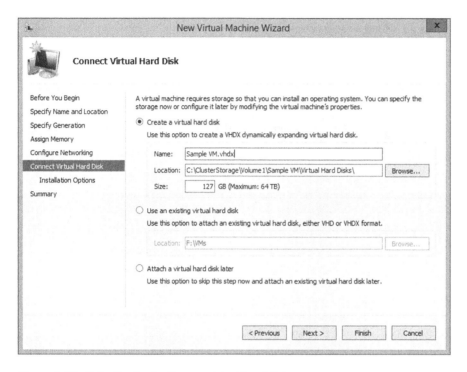

Figure 2-28. *Enter the size for the new virtual hard disk*

22. Click Next.

23. Choose the option that you want to use for installing an operating system onto the new virtual machine.

24. Click Next.

25. Verify the summary information for the new virtual machine.

26. Click Finish to create the virtual machine.

Once the new virtual machine has been created, it will appear within the Hyper-V Manager (see Figure 2-29). At this point, we can power up the virtual machine and install an operating system. Although the virtual machine exists on a cluster node, the virtual machine is not yet fault tolerant.

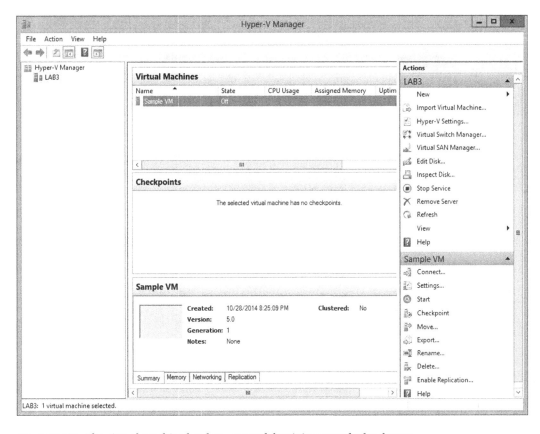

Figure 2-29. *The virtual machine has been created, but it is not yet fault tolerant*

Enabling Fault Tolerance for Your Virtual Machine

Now that the virtual machine has been created, we need to make it fault tolerant. We have created the virtual machine on the cluster-shared volume, so the virtual machine is already in the appropriate location. If the virtual machine were not stored on a cluster-shared volume, we could perform a storage migration as a way of moving the virtual machine to the appropriate storage location. In Hyper-V, you can perform a storage migration by right clicking on a virtual machine and selecting the Move command from the shortcut menu. This will bring up the Move Wizard. The wizard's second page asks you what kind of move you want to perform. You can choose the Move the Virtual Machine's Storage option and then follow the prompts.

Assuming that the virtual machine resides on a cluster-shared volume, you can make the virtual machine fault tolerant by defining the virtual machine as a clustered role. You can accomplish this by completing these steps:

1. Open the Server Manager on one of your cluster nodes.

2. Select the Failover Cluster Manager command from the Tools menu.

3. When the Failover Cluster Manager opens, navigate through the console tree to Failover Cluster Manager ➤ *<your cluster>* ➤ Roles (see Figure 2-30).

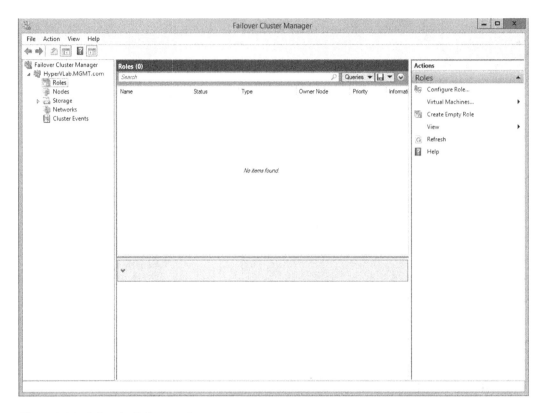

Figure 2-30. *Select the Roles container*

4. Click on the Configure Role link. This will cause Windows to launch the High Availability Wizard.

5. Click Next to bypass the wizard's Welcome page.

6. You should now be looking at the Role Selection page. Select the Virtual Machine option (see Figure 2-31).

Figure 2-31. *Select the Virtual Machine option*

7. Click Next.

8. You should now see a list of all of the virtual machines that are running on nodes within the cluster. Select the virtual machine (or virtual machines) that you want to make fault tolerant (see Figure 2-32).

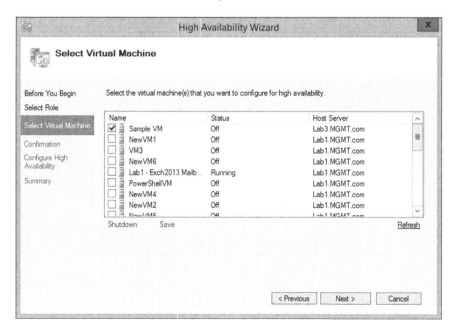

Figure 2-32. *Select the virtual machine that you want to make fault tolerant*

9. Click Next.

10. Verify that the Confirmation page lists the correct virtual machine.

11. Click Next.

12. Verify that Windows has successfully made the virtual machine highly available.

13. Click Finish.

14. You should now see the virtual machine listed within the Failover Cluster Manager.

As you look at Figure 2-33, you will notice that the Failover Cluster Manager offers much of the same functionality as the Hyper-V Manager does. You can start, stop, configure, and even build virtual machines from within the Failover Cluster Manager. Of course, this raises the question of which tool you should be using.

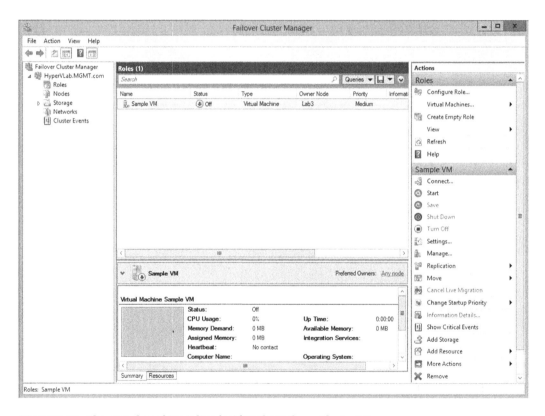

Figure 2-33. *The virtual machine is listed within the Failover Cluster Manager*

The general rule of thumb is that fault-tolerant virtual machines should be managed through the Failover Cluster Manager, while virtual machines that are not fault tolerant should be managed through the Hyper-V Manager.

Moving On

In this chapter, you have gotten to work a bit with the Hyper-V Manager and with the Failover Cluster Manager. If you think back to Chapter 1, however, you will recall that I mentioned that there was another management tool called System Center Virtual Machine Manager. In the next chapter, you will learn how to install System Center Virtual Machine Manager, attach it to your Hyper-V cluster, and then use the Virtual Machine Manager console to manage virtual machines.

CHAPTER 3

■ ■ ■

An Introduction to System Center Virtual Machine Manager

So far in this book, we have been using the Hyper-V Manager and the Failover Cluster Manager as our primary management tools for Hyper-V. As I mentioned in the first chapter, however, these tools tend to be inadequate for managing larger Hyper-V Deployments. In this chapter, I want to introduce you to another management tool called System Center Virtual Machine Manager. We will be using System Center Virtual Machine Manager quite a bit in the coming chapters.

What Is System Center Virtual Machine Manager?

System Center Virtual Machine Manager (VMM) is a Microsoft product that is sold separately from Windows Server. It allows for the centralized management of multi-server Hyper-V deployments. It also provides functionality for creating private or hybrid clouds and for automating the creation of virtual machines. For the purposes of this book, I will be treating VMM solely as a management and migration tool.

In most cases, it is possible to manage a Hyper-V deployment without investing in VMM. It does make virtual machine management easier, but the Hyper-V Manager (which is included with Hyper-V) has everything that you need for basic virtual machine management. Of course, this assumes that the basic management of virtual machines is the ultimate goal.

In our case, we are doing more than just trying to create and manage a few virtual machines. Our ultimate goal is to be able to establish coexistence between Hyper-V and VMware, and eventually migrate some virtual machines from vSphere to Hyper-V. Unless you are going to invest in a third-party migration utility (which I will discuss later, in Chapter 6), VMM is an absolute requirement for achieving this goal. That being the case, my aim in this chapter is to show you how to deploy VMM and how to bring your newly constructed Hyper-V cluster under its management.

Because we are going to be spending so much time throughout the rest of the book working with VMM, I want to jump right into the installation process. I realize that if you are new to System Center, you might not really have a solid understanding of what VMM is or why it is so important.

The first thing that you should know about VMM is that it is similar to vCenter. Just as vCenter allows for the management of multiple vSphere servers, VMM allows for the management of multiple Hyper-V servers.

The second thing that you should know is that VMM is a multi-platform management tool. Yes, VMM is a Microsoft product, and its primary function is Hyper-V Management, but there is more to it than that. VMM can also manage vSphere servers (and VMware virtual machines). It can even manage Citrix XenServer!

I plan to talk more about VMM as we go along. For right now, however, I want to help you to get VMM up and running.

In a large organization you may want to run VMM on a dedicated physical server. VMM also requires a SQL Server database. In a large organization you may want to use a dedicated SQL Server (or, more likely, a clustered SQL Server deployment). For smaller deployments, however, it is perfectly acceptable to run VMM within a Hyper-V virtual machine. Since our ultimate goal is to migrate from vSphere to Hyper-V, I don't recommend installing VMM onto a vSphere virtual machine.

Important Things to Remember:

- VMM is an add-on product that is not included with Hyper-V.

- VMM is an essential tool for managing large Hyper-V deployments.

- VMM is also capable of managing VMware environments and XenServer environments, but has some limitations.

You can use VMM to build private clouds and hybrid clouds.

The System Center Virtual Machine Manager Components

VMM is an enterprise application. Like any other enterprise-class application, it needs to be able to scale as the organization grows. The way that Microsoft accomplishes this is by taking a modular approach to the VMM architecture.

Entire books have been written about VMM, so, a comprehensive discussion on architecture is far beyond the scope of this book. Even so, there are a few major components that you need to be aware of prior to installing VMM.

The first thing that you need to know about is the core Virtual Machine Manager Server. Virtual Machine Manager Server is the heart and soul of VMM. It is the component that does all of the heavy lifting. This is the part that runs jobs and that coordinates communications across all of the VMM and Hyper-V servers.

Another critical component is the previously mentioned SQL Server database. The database stores everything from VMM configuration data to virtual machine profiles and service templates.

Yet another major component is the System Center Virtual Machine Manager console. The VMM console is the primary management interface that is used for managing not only VMM, but also Hyper-V and your virtual machines. We are going to be spending a lot of time working within this console over the next few chapters. On a side note, the VMM console is built on top of Windows PowerShell. As such, VMM can be fully managed at the command line using PowerShell. Although PowerShell-based management is largely beyond the scope of this book, know that it is also possible to manage Hyper-V through PowerShell.

One last component that you need to be aware of is the Virtual Machine Manager Library Server. The VMM library serves as a collection of virtual server resources. Some of the things that can be included within the library are virtual hard disks and virtual machine templates. Library resources are often file based (for instance, a virtual hard disk is usually a VHD or VHDX file). As such, the Virtual Machine Manager Library Server could be thought of as being somewhat similar to a specialized file server.

Important Things to Remember:

- The Virtual Machine Manager Server is the main VMM component.

- The VMM console is the primary management tool that is used for managing not only VMM, but also Hyper-V and your virtual machines.

- The VMM library serves as a collection of virtual server resources such as templates, ISO files, and virtual hard disks.

The Deployment Process

Now that I have given you a brief introduction to VMM, I want to walk you through the deployment process. As previously explained, VMM is a multi-tiered application, and it is possible to install the various components on separate servers. For the purposes of this book, however, I am going to be installing all of the VMM components onto a single Hyper-V virtual machine.

The Prep Work

There are a few things that need to be done prior to installing VMM. First, install Windows Server 2012 R2, assign the server an appropriate name, and join the server to your management domain.

This part of the process has been known to cause some problems and confusion for people in the past. Let me explain why.

One of the most common Hyper-V architectures involves creating a management domain whose sole purpose is to manage the Hyper-V servers. There is typically one or more completely separate Active Directory forests that exist at the virtual machine level.

With that said, you may recall that it is OK to install VMM into a Hyper-V virtual machine. In doing so, the natural tendency is to join the virtual machine to the virtual machine forest rather than to the management forest. Doing so, however, will cause a lot of problems later on when you attempt to bring your Hyper-V servers under management. As such, make sure to join the VMM server to the management domain.

■ **Caution**   Be sure to join the VMM server to the hypervisor management domain, not to the domain where your virtual machines reside. Otherwise, you will be unable to use VMM to manage Hyper-V.

Another thing that you will need to do before you begin the installation process is to create a RunAs account. A RunAs account is an Active Directory account that has domain admin privileges. The need for a RunAs account has to do with the way that VMM works.

When you perform a management task, the task is usually executed on a Hyper-V server, even though you initiated the task from the VMM console. That being the case, VMM treats most management actions as jobs. A job cannot run unless the VMM has permission to run the job (usually on a remote Hyper-V server). This is where the RunAs account comes into play. The RunAs account is created within the management forest and exists for the sole purpose of running management jobs.

We will be making extensive use of the RunAs account throughout this book. You must create a dedicated RunAs account. You cannot simply use the built-in Administrator account. You can create a RunAs Account by completing these steps:

1. Log on to a domain controller within your management domain using administrative credentials.

2. Open the Server Manager.

3. Select the Active Directory Users and Computers command from the Tools menu. This will cause the Active Directory Users and Computers console to open.

4. Navigate through the console tree to Active Directory Users and Computers ➤ *<your domain>* ➤ Users (see Figure 3-1).

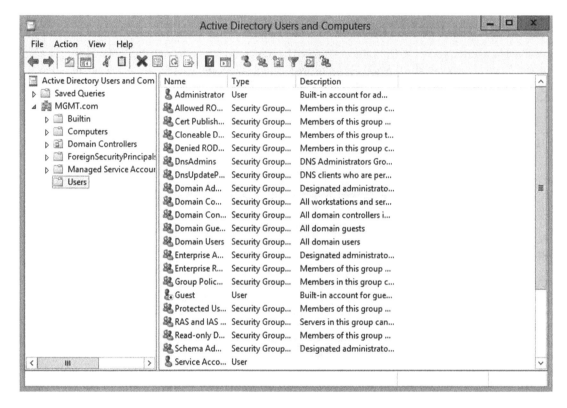

Figure 3-1. *Navigate through the console tree to Active Directory Users and Computers ➤ <your domain> ➤ Users*

5. Right click on the Users container and select the New ➤ User commands from the shortcut menus.

6. Enter the details for your RunAs account (see Figure 3-2). For the purposes of this book, I am naming my RunAs account RunAs.

Figure 3-2. *Enter the details for your RunAs account*

7. Click Next.

8. Enter and confirm a password for your RunAs account (see Figure 3-3).

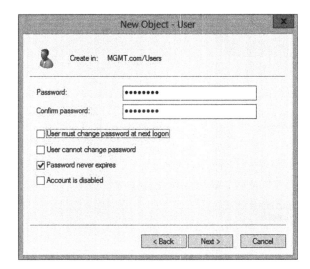

Figure 3-3. *Enter and confirm a password for the account*

9. Deselect the User Must Change Password at Next Logon check box.

10. Select the Password Never Expires check box. It is worth noting that you will receive an error message at the end of the account creation process if your group policy settings prohibit the use of non-expiring passwords.

11. Click Next.

12. Click Finish.

13. When you are returned to the main Active Directory Users and Computers screen, right click on the newly created RunAs account and select the Properties command from the resulting shortcut menu.

14. When Windows displays the account's properties sheet, select the Member Of tab.

15. Click Add.

16. Enter Domain Admins into the Enter the Object Names to Select field.

17. Click OK.

18. Verify that the RunAs account is a member of the Domain Admins group and the Domain Users group (see Figure 3-4).

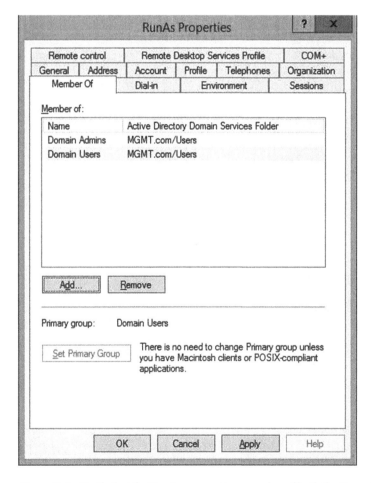

Figure 3-4. *Verify that the RunAs account is a member of both the Domain Admins group and the Domain Users group and click OK*

19. Click OK.

Once you have created the RunAs account, there are a few more things that you will need to do in order to get your server ready. First, I recommend running Windows Update and installing all of the available updates. My experience has been that the deployment process seems to go more smoothly if the server is fully patched prior to installing VMM.

You are also going to need to install some prerequisite software. First, install version 4.5.x of the .NET Framework. The .NET Framework is included with Windows Server, but it must be manually installed. You can complete this process by performing the following steps:

1. Open the Server Manager.

2. Select the Add Roles and Features command from the Manage menu. This will cause Windows to launch the Add Roles and Features Wizard.

3. Click Next to bypass the wizard's Before You Begin screen.

4. Select the Role-Based or Feature-Based Installation option.

5. Click Next.

6. Make sure that your server is selected within the server pool.

7. Click Next.

8. You should see a list of server roles. We don't need to add any roles, so click Next.

9. You should now see a list of the available features. Select the .NET Framework 4.5 Feature if it is not already selected (see Figure 3-5). If you are prompted to add any additional features, click Add Feature.

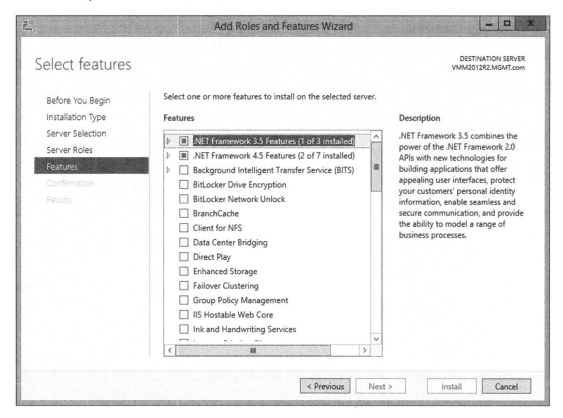

Figure 3-5. *Select the .NET Framework 4.5 Feature if it is not already selected*

10. Click Next.

11. You will now see a confirmation screen. Take a moment to verify that you are about to install the .NET Framework 4.5 Feature and then click Install.

12. When the installation process completes, click Close.

One last thing that you are going to need to install is the Windows Assessment and Deployment Kit for Windows 8.1. It is important to use the Windows 8.1 version, because the Windows 7 and Windows 8 versions won't work. You can download the Windows 8.1 version of the kit at: http://www.microsoft.com/en-US/download/details.aspx?id=39982.

As you install the Windows Assessment and Deployment Kit, you must make sure to install the Windows Preinstallation Environment feature as well as the Deployment Tools. You can complete this process by performing the following steps.

1. When the download process completes, run the ADSETUP.EXE file.

2. Choose the Install the Assessment and Deployment Kit to this Computer option.

3. Accept the default path.

4. Verify that your server has sufficient disk space available. The installation process requires about 5.7 GB (see Figure 3-6).

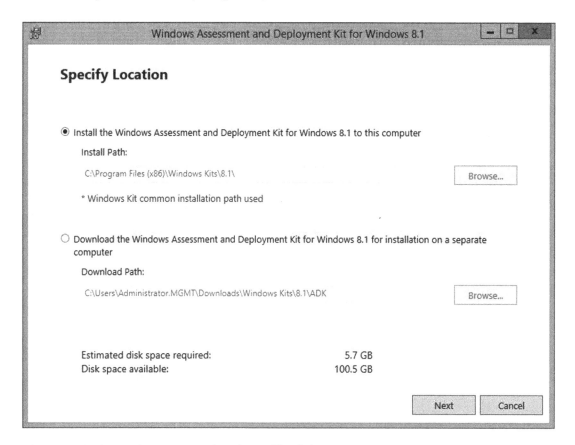

Figure 3-6. *Make sure that your server has plenty of free disk space*

5. Click Next.

6. Decide whether or not you wish to join Microsoft's Customer Improvement Program.

7. Click Next.

8. Accept the license agreement.

9. Make sure the Windows Preinstallation Environment (Windows PE) option and the Deployment Tools options are selected (see Figure 3-7). If any additional options are selected, it is OK to leave them selected.

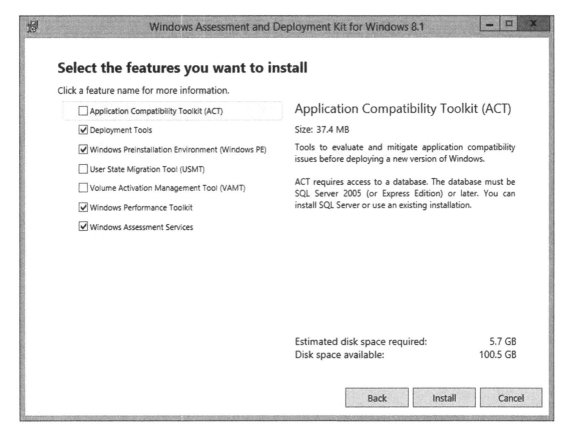

Figure 3-7. *Make sure the Windows Preinstallation Environment (Windows PE) option and the Deployment Tools options are selected*

10. Click Install.

11. When the installation process completes, click Close.

System Requirements and Scalability

The system requirements for System Center 2012 R2 Virtual Machine Manager vary widely depending on the components that you plan to install and the number of hosts that you intend to manage. For the purposes of this book, I am going to be using a single virtual machine to run all of the required roles, plus the SQL Server database. In a production environment, it is a good idea to run the database on a clustered SQL Server deployment rather than running it directly on the VMM server. The exception is that it is acceptable to run the SQL Server database locally if you have a small virtualization infrastructure.

Microsoft bases the VMM hardware requirements primarily on the number of hosts that need to be managed. The environment that I am building for this book is fairly small, so I am basing it on the hardware requirements that Microsoft has established for organizations that need to manage fewer than 150 hosts. Those requirements are shown in Table 3-1.

Table 3-1. *Virtual Machine Manager Hardware Requirements*

Component	Minimum	Recommended
Processor	Pentium 4 (x64) running at 2 GHz	Dual processor, dual core, 2.8 GHz (X64)
RAM	4 GB	4 GB
Hard Disk Space (without a local database)	2 GB	40 GB
Hard Disk Space (with local SQL Server deployment)	80 GB	150 GB

Keep in mind that these requirements are only for VMM. They do not take SQL Server into account. The SQL Server requirements vary depending on the version of SQL Server that you use, but typically only the database engine will be required. The following SQL Server versions are supported:

- SQL Server 2012, 64-bit Standard or Enterprise RTM or SP1

- SQL Server 2008 R2, 64-bit Standard, Enterprise, or Datacenter with SP2 or 3

Although it is easy to focus on the requirements for the Virtual Machine Manager Server, you may also want to consider the requirements for the management console. The management console can be installed on a separate machine so that you don't have to manage VMM directly from the server console. I'm not going to be deploying the VMM console separately in this book, but if you did opt to perform a separate deployment (and you have fewer than 150 hosts), Table 3-2 shows the hardware requirements.

Table 3-2. *Virtual Machine Manager Console Hardware Requirements*

Component	Fewer than 150 Hosts	More than 150 Hosts
Processor	Pentium 4, 1GHz	Pentium 4, dual processor, 2 GHz
RAM	2 GB	4 GB
Hard disk space	2 GB	4 GB

If you plan to manage more than 150 hosts, or if you plan to perform a tiered deployment, then you will need to check Microsoft's official system requirements. You can find the requirements for System Center 2012 R2 Virtual Machine Manager (as well as for all of the other System Center 2012 R2 products) at: http://technet.microsoft.com/en-us/library/dn281925.aspx.

Installing System Center 2012 R2 Virtual Machine Manager

Now that all of the prep work is done, we can install VMM. I am not going to explicitly cover the steps for installing SQL Server because the SQL Server installation process can vary widely depending on which version you install. As such, the instructions below assume that you have already installed a supported SQL Server instance, either locally or on a dedicated server.

To install System Center 2012 R2 Virtual Machine Manager, complete the following steps:

1. Log in to your VMM server using Domain Admin credentials. Do not log in using the RunAs account.

2. Insert your System Center 2012 R2 installation media and run `Setup.exe`.

3. When the System Center 2012 R2 Virtual Machine Manager splash screen appears, click on the Install link (see Figure 3-8).

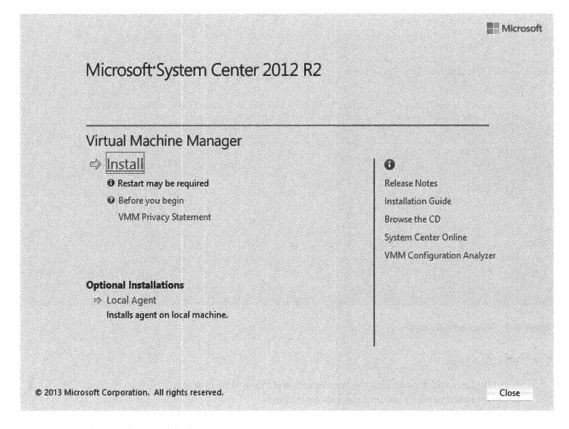

Figure 3-8. *Click on the Install link*

4. After a brief file copy process, Windows will launch the Microsoft System Center 2012 R2 Virtual Machine Manager Setup Wizard. The wizard's initial screen will ask you which components you wish to install. If you are performing a consolidated deployment (like I am), select both options (VMM Management Server and VMM console), as shown in Figure 3-9.

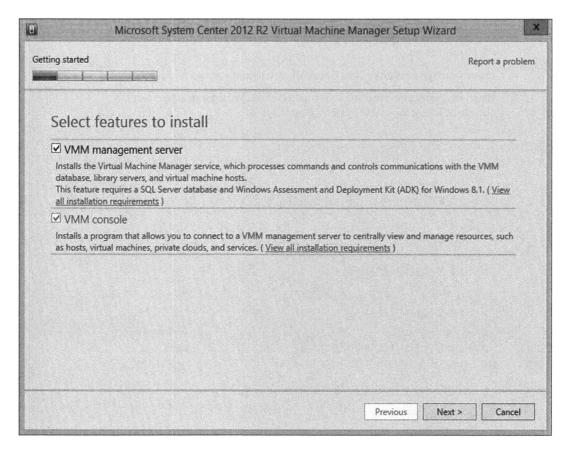

Figure 3-9. *Select both features*

5. Click Next.

6. Windows will now display the wizard's Product Registration screen. Enter your product key into the space provided.

7. Click Next.

8. When prompted, accept the software's license agreement.

9. Click Next.

10. You will now see a prompt asking if you wish to participate in Microsoft's Customer Experience Improvement Program. Make your selection and click Next.

11. You will now see a screen asking you to specify the desired installation path. It's OK to accept the default path, but take a moment and verify the amount of free disk space on your chosen path. The amount of free disk space is displayed within the Setup Wizard (see Figure 3-10).

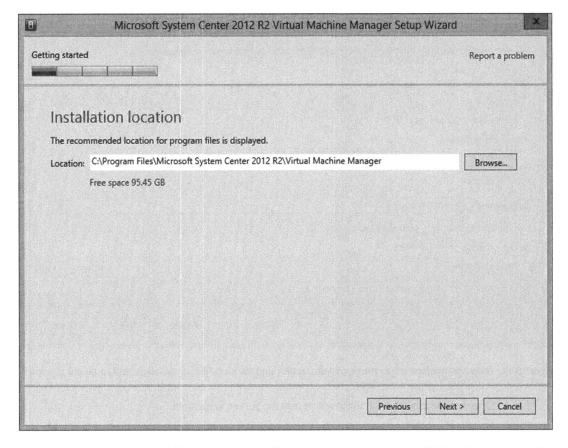

Figure 3-10. The Setup Wizard displays the amount of free space on the volume where VMM is about to be installed

12. Click Next.

13. The wizard will now perform a prerequisite check. Assuming that you have followed the previously outlined steps, the test should succeed.

14. You will now be taken to the wizard's Database Configuration screen (see Figure 3-11). This is the screen that is used to connect VMM to SQL Server. Establishing database connectivity tends to be the most error-prone part of the configuration process. The key to making this process work is to make sure that your VMM server is able to perform DNS resolution for the database server. It's also a good idea to make sure that there are no firewall rules getting in the way.

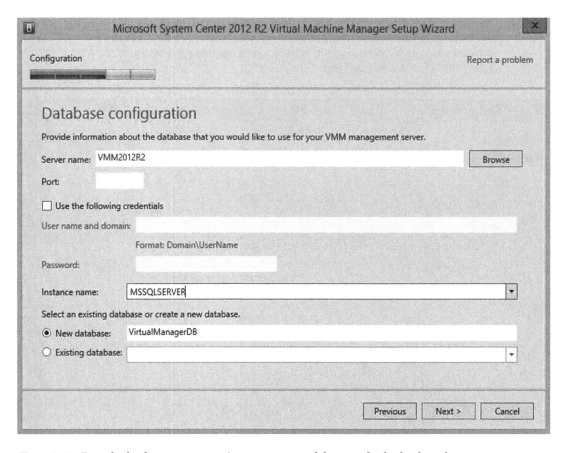

Figure 3-11. *Enter the database server name, instance name, and the name for the database that you want to create*

15. Enter the name of your database server into the Server Name field.

16. Click on the down arrow on the Instance Name field and then select the SQL Server instance that you want to use.

17. Make sure that the New Database option is selected.

18. Verify that the new database name is set to VirtualManagerDB.

19. Click Next.

20. The next screen that you will see asks you to enter the name of a service account that you will use for VMM. The prompt goes on to explain that if VMM is to be made highly available then you will need a domain account. For our purposes, it's OK to go ahead and select the Local System Account option. Remember, I installed VMM in a virtual machine and can achieve high availability at the hypervisor if desired. However, if you think that there is a chance that you could ever require application-level high availability, then it is better to go ahead and create an Active Directory user account now and enter it into the space provided. The account can be a basic user account. You do not have to assign it administrative credentials.

21. As a best practice, you should store your encryption keys in the Active Directory. Doing so reduces the chances that the keys could be lost. This is required for highly available deployments, but is recommended for all deployments. To do so, select the Store My Keys in Active Directory check box (see Figure 3-12).

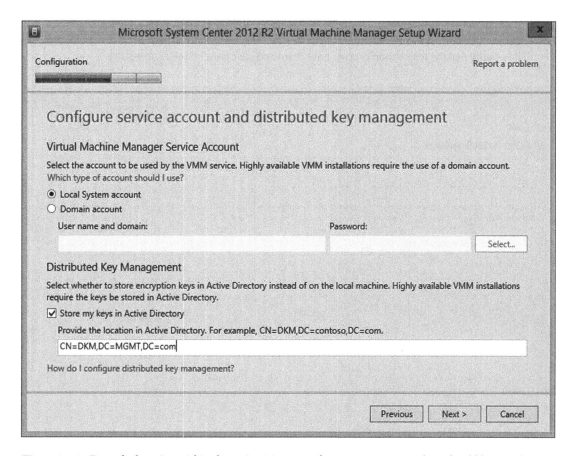

Figure 3-12. *Enter the location within the Active Directory where your encryption keys should be stored*

22. Enter the location within the Active Directory where you want your keys to be stored. This is usually going to be the distinguished name for your domain, plus a container for key storage. For instance, if your management domain is named MGMT.com and you wanted to store your keys in a container named DKM, then you would use CN=DKM,DC=MGMT,DC=com (see Figure 3-12).

23. Click Next.

24. The following screen lists the firewall ports that are used by VMM. You can modify the ports, but doing so greatly increases the difficulty of troubleshooting any problems that might occur, so it is best to use the default ports. Take a moment to write down the ports that are being used so that you can make sure that your firewalls are not blocking any of them.

25. Click Next.

26. You should now see a screen asking you to create a new library share. Click Next to accept the defaults.

27. The Setup Wizard will now display a summary of the installation options that you have chosen. Take a moment to verify that the information that is being displayed is correct.

28. Click Install.

29. Verify that the installation process has completed successfully (see Figure 3-13).

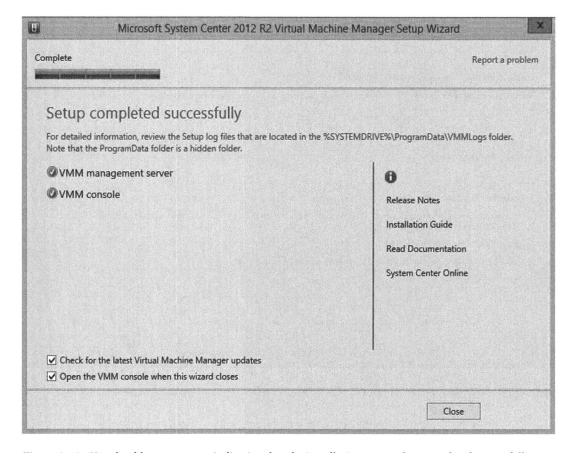

Figure 3-13. *You should see a message indicating that the installation process has completed successfully*

30. Click Close.

The Virtual Machine Manager Console

As a part of the installation process, VMM places an icon on the server's desktop that can be used to launch the VMM console. Upon doing so, you will see a login screen that asks for your server name and your credentials (see Figure 3-14).

Figure 3-14. *The login screen asks for your server name and your credentials*

Assuming that the VMM console is being run directly from the same server that is also running the Management Server component, the server name should be populated automatically, as it is in the previous figure. If you are logged into the server using administrative credentials, you should be able to use your current Microsoft Windows session identity rather than manually specifying a set of credentials. You can log in by clicking on the Connect button.

If the Connection Fails

System Center 2012 Virtual Machine Manager had a tendency to display an error message after an attempted login. This problem has largely been fixed in System Center 2012 R2 Virtual Machine Manager, but I want to show you the error and the fix in case you are using the 2012 version or in case you happen to encounter the problem in 2012 R2.

The error that I am referring to indicates that the VMM console is unable to connect to the Virtual Machine Manager Server or that the server did not respond. You can see what the actual error message looks like in Figure 3-15.

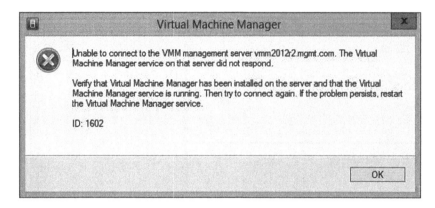

Figure 3-15. *This error message is sometimes displayed in response to the login process*

This error occurs as a result of a problem with the System Center Virtual Machine Manager Service. To fix the problem, perform the following steps:

1. Enter SERVICES.MSC at the server's Run prompt.

2. When the Service Control Manager opens, scroll through the list of services until you locate the System Center Virtual Machine Manager service.

3. Right click on the System Center Virtual Machine Manager service and select the Start command from the shortcut menu (see Figure 3-16).

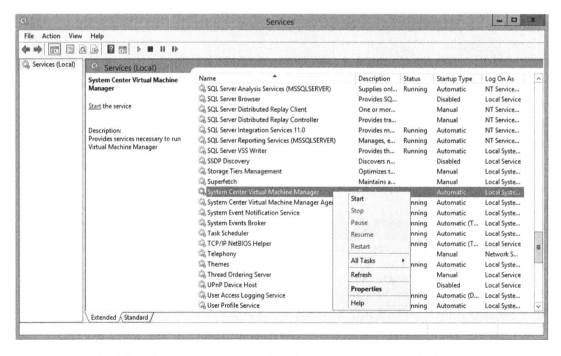

Figure 3-16. *Right click on the System Center Virtual Machine Manager service and select the Start command from the shortcut menu*

4.   Verify that the service starts. Once the service is running, you should be able to log into VMM.

An Overview of the Virtual Machine Manager Console

I don't want to try to turn this chapter into a deep dive that goes into every conceivable aspect of using VMM. After all, entire books have been written on that particular topic. Even so, we are going to be spending quite a bit of time using VMM over the next few chapters, so I do want to take a few minutes to show you around the console a bit.

You can see what the VMM console looks like in Figure 3-17. The console is divided into a series of panes. Currently, the upper right pane lists managed computers. These are computers that VMM has been made aware of and that have been brought under management. As it stands right now, the VMM server is the only system that is under management.

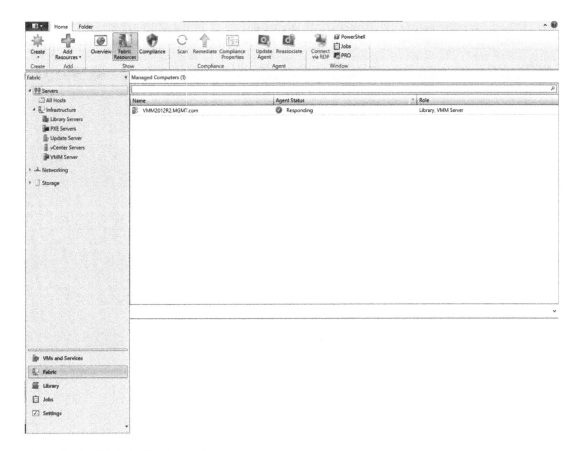

Figure 3-17. *This is the VMM console*

Computers are brought under management by installing a VMM agent. You will learn how to do this in the next chapter. For right now, though, you will notice that the console shows the agent status for each computer, as well as the roles that have been installed.

The Fabric Workspace

The next thing that I want to show you is the pane in the lower left portion of the console. The options shown in this pane are known as workspaces. In Figure 3-17, the Fabric workspace is selected. The console's functionality changes depending on the workspace that is selected. The Fabric workspace, for instance, is used for managing host servers, virtual networks, and storage (among other things).

The VMs and Services Workspace

Over the next few chapters, we will be spending a lot of time working in the Fabric workspace, and in the VMs and Services workspace. The VMs and Services workspace (see Figure 3-18) is the primary interface that you will use for managing virtual machines.

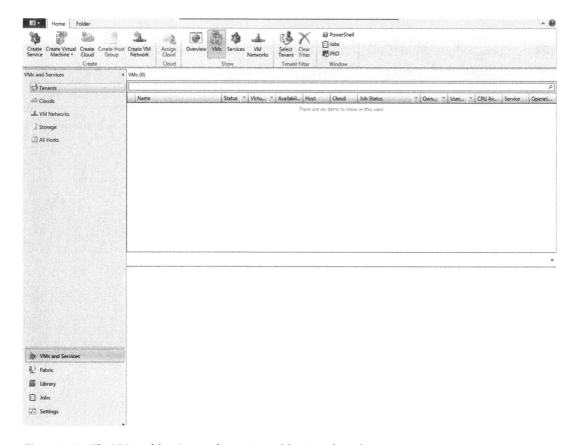

Figure 3-18. *The VMs and Services workspace is used for virtual machine management*

Earlier, I mentioned that in spite of its name, VMM can be used for more than just virtual machine management. It actually allows you to construct and manage private clouds (or even multiple private clouds). As you might have noticed in the previous figure, the VMs and Services tab exposes VMM's private cloud and multi-tenant capabilities.

The Library Workspace

The three remaining workspaces are a little bit less relevant to this book, but I will show you what they are. The Library workspace (see Figure 3-19) is used to store library objects. There are many different types of library objects that can be defined, but the best example is probably virtual machine templates. You can use a virtual machine template to automate the creation of a virtual machine. This capability is especially useful in private cloud environments in which you want to allow a non-administrator to create virtual machines under very controlled conditions.

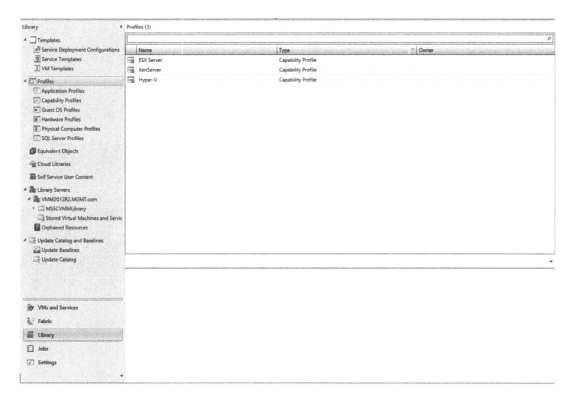

Figure 3-19. *The Library tab is used to store virtual machine templates and other types of library objects*

The Jobs Workspace

The next workspace that you need to know about is the Jobs workspace (see Figure 3-20). Earlier, I explained that VMM is a multi-tier application and that it is possible to install the VMM server and the management console on separate servers. Because the management console can reside on a machine by itself, most management actions are treated as jobs. These jobs are initiated by the management console, but run on the VMM server. The Jobs workspace lists all of the recent jobs. You can also use this workspace to cancel or restart a job.

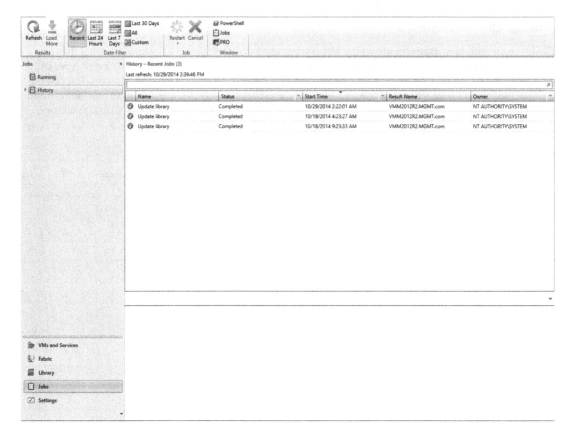

Figure 3-20. *The Jobs workspace lists all of the recent jobs*

The Settings Workspace

The last workspace used by VMM is the Settings workspace (see Figure 3-21). The Settings workspace is used to configure most of VMM's internal settings. For example, you can use the Settings workspace to configure VMM's database connection, the RunAs account, any administrative settings, and even some remote control settings.

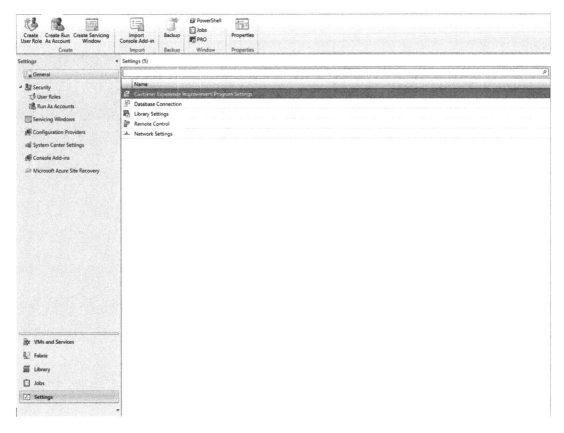

Figure 3-21. *The Settings workspace is used to configure VMM's internal settings*

Moving On

Now that we have gotten VMM up and running, we have all of the necessary infrastructure in place to begin transitioning away from VMware.

My plan for the next chapter is to show you how to use VMM as a cross platform management tool. I will show you how to connect VMM to both Hyper-V and to your VMware environment. I will also show you how to perform some basic management tasks, and then I will explain some of the limitations that you will encounter when using VMM for VMware management.

Once we get the VMM tier into Hyper-V and VMware, the real fun begins. In Chapter 5, I will be walking you through a full-blown virtual machine migration from VMware to Hyper-V.

CHAPTER 4

■ ■ ■

Using Virtual Machine Manager as a Cross-Platform Management Tool

In the last chapter, we set up System Center Virtual Machine Manager. Even so, our VMM server really doesn't do much yet. As such, this chapter is all about putting Virtual Machine Manager (VMM) to work. The main goal of this chapter is to show you how to connect Virtual Machine Manager to both Hyper-V and vSphere and to demonstrate how to use it as a cross-platform management tool. We will start out by bringing our virtualization hosts under management by deploying the required agents. As we go along, I will show you some techniques for using VMM to manage your virtualization infrastructure.

Bringing Hyper-V Under Management

The first thing that needs to be done after bringing a new VMM server online is to bring your Hyper-V infrastructure under management. This is a fancy way of saying that we need to configure VMM to recognize the existence of our Hyper-V servers and give it the authority to interact with our virtualization infrastructure.

The way that we accomplish this is by deploying an agent to each of our Hyper-V servers. This agent enables communication between Hyper-V and VMM. However, the agent does not provide the necessary permissions. We will be assigning permissions to our VMM server by way of the RunAs account that we created previously.

Some Advice About Virtual Machine Manager Agents

One thing that I want to quickly point out before we get started is that the VMM agent is server specific. Suppose for a moment that you were to deploy VMM and then bring Hyper-V under management. Now let's pretend that something happened to the server and you decided to uninstall and reinstall VMM. The previously deployed agents would not work with the new VMM deployment because the agents were registered to the old deployment.

In this type of situation, you would need to open the Control Panel on all of the managed hosts and use the Remove Program option to remove the existing VMM agent. You could then bring the servers back under management. In some cases it is possible to use a check box within the Add Resources Wizard to overwrite an existing agent without having to manually uninstall it first.

Bringing a Standalone Hyper-V Server Under Management

The first thing that I want to show you is how to bring a standalone Hyper-V server under management. This is a non-clustered Hyper-V server that typically belongs to a trusted Active Directory domain (although not always). In this case, the server that I will be bringing under management is named Lab4, and the server is a member of the management domain that I set up in one of the previous chapters.

To bring a Hyper-V Server under management, follow these steps:

1. Open the VMM console.

2. Select the Fabric workspace.

3. Click on the Add Resources button on the ribbon (see Figure 4-1)
   This will cause the Add Resources Wizard to open.

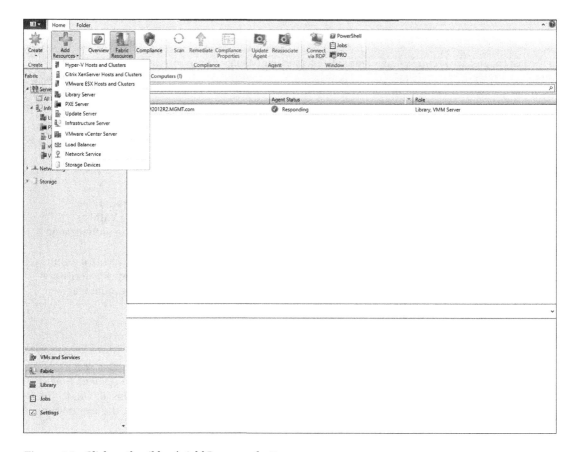

Figure 4-1. *Click on the ribbon's Add Resources button*

4. Select the Hyper-V Hosts and Clusters option. This will launch the Add Resources link.

5. Choose the Windows Server Computers in a Trusted Active Directory Domain option.

6. Click Next.

7. Choose the Manually Enter the Credentials option (see Figure 4-2).

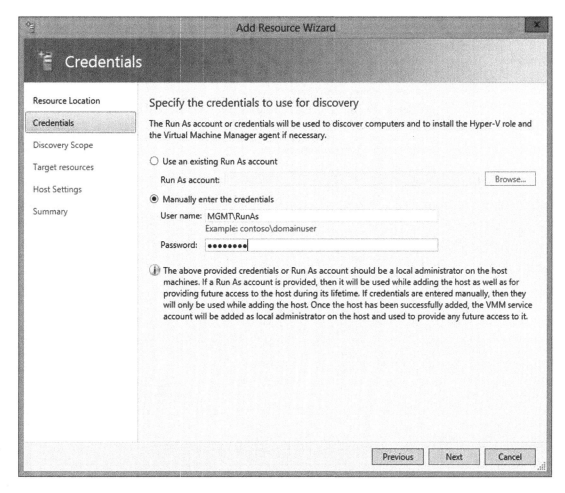

Figure 4-2. *Select the option to manually enter the credentials*

8. Enter the credentials for the RunAs account that you created in Chapter 1.

9. Click Next.

10. Choose the option to Specify Windows Server Computers by names.

11. Enter the name or IP address of the Hyper-V server that you want to add (see Figure 4-3).

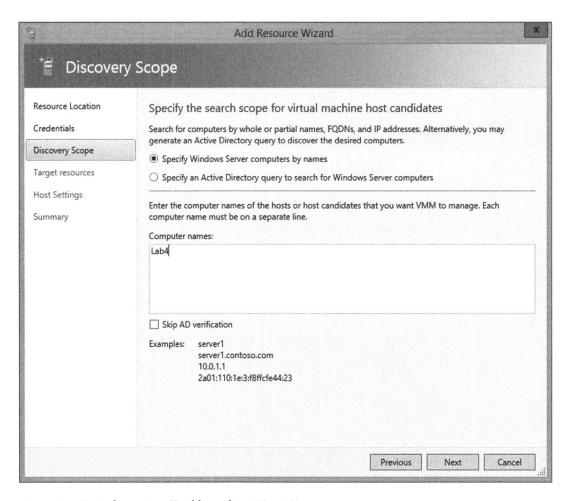

Figure 4-3. *Enter the name or IP address of your Hyper-V server*

12. Click Next.

13. Select the check box corresponding to the Hyper-V server that you want to add.

14. Click Next.

15. Verify that the All Hosts group is selected and click Next.

16. Take a moment to verify the summary information and click Finish.

17. When the job completes, you should see the Hyper-V server listed within the Virtual Machine Manager console (see Figure 4-4).

Figure 4-4. *The Hyper-V server has been added to the console*

Bringing a Clustered Hyper-V Deployment Under Management

Now that I have shown you how to bring a standalone Hyper-V server under management, I want to show you the procedure for bringing a Hyper-V cluster under management. The procedure is largely the same as what you have already seen, but this time we need to take failover clustering into account.

To bring a clustered Hyper-V deployment under management, follow these steps:

1. Use the Failover Cluster Manager to verify that your cluster is online. If you have been following along and completing the steps that I have described thus far, then your cluster should be online. However, this procedure will fail if the cluster happens to be offline, so it is a good idea to check the cluster's status just to be sure.

2. Open the VMM console.

3. Select the Fabric workspace.

4. Click on the Add Resources button on the ribbon.

5. Select the Hyper-V Hosts and Clusters option. This will launch the Add Resources link.

6. Choose the Windows Server Computers in a Trusted Active Directory Domain option.

7. Click Next.

8. Choose the Manually Enter the Credentials option.

9. Enter the credentials for the RunAs account that you created in Chapter 1.

10. Click Next.

11. Choose the option to Specify Windows Server Computers by names.

12. Enter the name or IP address of your Hyper-V cluster. Do not enter the names or IP addresses of the individual cluster nodes (see Figure 4-5).

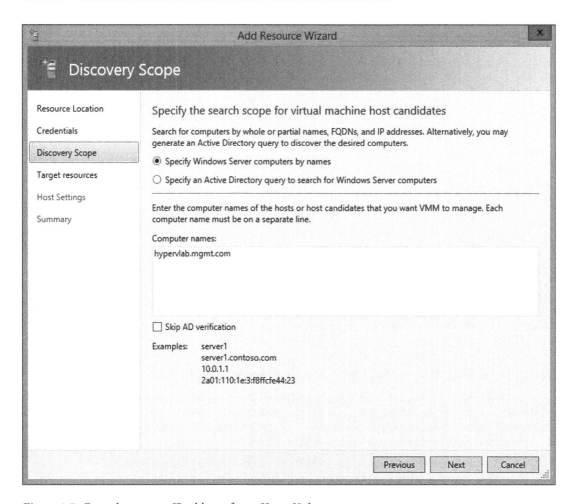

Figure 4-5. Enter the name or IP address of your Hyper-V cluster

13. Click Next.

14. Select the check box corresponding to the clustered Hyper-V deployment that you want to add (see Figure 4-6).

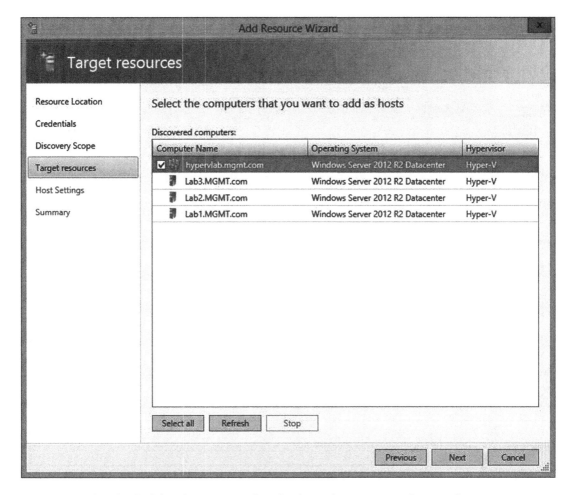

Figure 4-6. *Select the check box that corresponds to the cluster that you want to bring under management*

15. Verify that all of the cluster nodes are listed beneath the cluster.

16. Click Next. Depending on the software version you are using, you may see a warning message telling you that if the Hyper-V role is not enabled on your servers then it will be added. If you see this message, click Yes to continue.

17. Verify that the All Hosts group is selected and click Next.

18. Take a moment to verify the summary information and click Finish.

19. When the job completes, you should see the clustered Hyper-V deployment listed within the VMM console (see Figure 4-7).

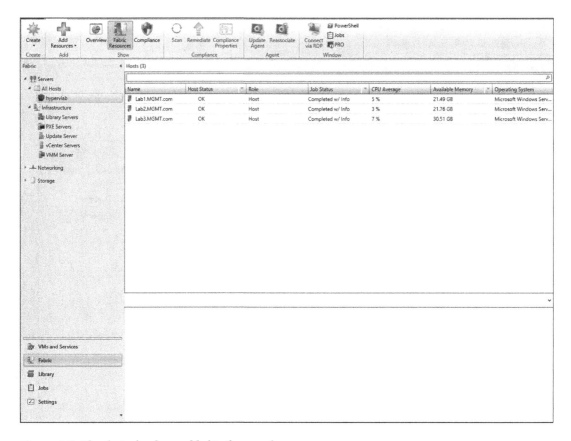

Figure 4-7. *The cluster has been added to the console*

20. Although the cluster has been added, there is the possibility that it is not yet being fully managed. The individual cluster nodes might not yet have been provisioned with the agent needed to bring them under management. To find out whether or not this is the case, select the VMs and Services tab, expand All Hosts, and expand the Hyper-V cluster (HyperVLab, in my case).

21. Check to see if the hosts within the cluster are listed as Pending under the Host Status column. If the hosts are pending, complete the remaining steps in this section. Otherwise, you are done.

22. Right click on a host that has a status of Pending and select the Add Host to Cluster command from the shortcut menu. This will cause the Add to Host Cluster dialog box to be displayed.

23. Click the Browse button.

24. Select the Enter a User Name and Password option. Do not specify your RunAs account.

25. Enter the credentials for an account that has domain admin permissions.

26. Click OK.

27. Click OK again.

28. Verify that the Pending status goes away. If the Pending status remains after a few seconds, check the Jobs workspace to find out what went wrong.

29. Add the remaining hosts to the cluster.

VMware Management

As previously discussed, System Center 2012 R2 Virtual Machine Manager can be used as a tool for managing VMware environments (it can also manage Cisco XenServer environments). Now that we have brought our Hyper-V servers under management, I want to show you how to do the same thing with your VMware servers. Configuring VMM to manage VMware is actually a prerequisite for the VM migration method that I will be showing you later in this book. For right now, though, there are two things that I want to do. First, I want to show you how to connect VMM to VMware. Second, I want to show you some techniques for using VMM to manage your VMware environment.

VMware's Take on Virtual Machine Manager

Before I begin showing you how to link VMM to vSphere, I need to point out that VMware actively discourages their customers from using VMM. In fact, VMware even published a document named "Limitations of Managing VMware vSphere with MS System Center Virtual Machine Manager 2012." You can find this document at: www.vmware.com/files/pdf/getthefacts/vmw-limitations-of-managing-vSphere-with-MS-SCVMM.pdf.

The VMware document refers to System Center 2012, not 2012 R2. Even so, I think that the spirit of the document still holds true. That being the case, I want to briefly summarize the VMware document in an effort to give you a balanced picture of the management process by including VMware's position.

According to the VMware document, "SCVMM 2012 offers only rudimentary management capabilities for VMware environments and introduces unnecessary complexity, overhead, and frustration for vSphere administrators." The document goes on to say that "administrators will continue to rely on native VMware interfaces for many common management and configuration tasks." Some of the tasks that are listed include:

- Configuring vSphere hosts, clusters, and resource pools

- Provisioning storage and networking

- Deploying Linux VMs from templates

- Installing VMware Tools

- Hot expanding virtual disks and other vSphere-specific VM capabilities.

VMware summarizes the statements made in the document by stating that "vSphere administrators will find that SCVMM 2012—

1. Increases complexity while adding little value

2. Is not a 'single pane of glass interface,' vCenter is still required

3. Adds new overhead, delivers little benefit

4. Degrades operational efficiency, frustrating administrators"

My Take on Using Virtual Machine Manager for vSphere Management

Contrary to what you might have expected, I am not going to attempt to discredit this VMware document, aside from pointing out that it refers to an older version of Virtual Machine Manager and that new features and capabilities exist in the newer version. Even so, I think that VMware is exactly right—at least within a certain context.

The VMware document that I have been discussing tries to make the case that vCenter is a better tool for VMware management than VMM is. Of course it is. It is perfectly logical that a native VMware tool would do a better job of managing vSphere than a third-party tool would. However, you have to understand that the document in question seems to be geared toward shops that are using only VMware, not a mixture of VMware and Hyper-V.

For organizations that are using a mixture of Hyper-V, vSphere, and possibly even XenServer, VMM is an excellent management tool. Yes, there are some VMware functions that will still have to be performed through vCenter, but when it comes to day-to-day management, VMM acts as a cross-platform, single-pane-of-glass interface for managing multiple hypervisors.

Connecting Virtual Machine Manager to Your VMware Deployment

Now that I have addressed some of the pros and cons of using VMM for VMware management, I want to show you how to link VMM 2012 R2 to your VMware deployment.

My Lab Setup

Let's start out by talking about some prerequisites. If you have been following along with the first three chapters then you should already have a clustered Hyper-V deployment in place. You should also have System Center 2012 R2 Virtual Machine Manager installed and connected to your clustered Hyper-V servers. Everything that I am going to be discussing throughout the next two chapters is based on the premise that these requirements have been met.

On the VMware side of things, I have an ESX 5.0 server that is hosting some virtual machines. I also have a vCenter server being used to manage my vSphere Server. I have created a datacenter that I simply named Datacenter, and I have placed my ESX 5.0 server into that datacenter.

In the interest of being completely honest with my readers, there are a few things that I want to point out.

First, my vCenter server is actually running as a Hyper-V virtual machine. vCenter is an absolute requirement for managing vSphere through System Center 2012 R2 Virtual Machine Manager. Unfortunately, I did not have a physical server that I could dedicate to running vCenter, so I chose to run it within a VM. The reason why I placed vCenter onto a Hyper-V virtual machine instead of into a VMware virtual machine is that our goal is to migrate the VMware virtual machines to Hyper-V, and I didn't want to risk breaking anything by running vCenter on a VMware virtual machine.

As for the virtual machines themselves, I have three of them. Each of the virtual machines is running Windows Server 2012 R2 and also has the VMware Tools installed. I have named these virtual machines VMware VM 1, VMware VM 2, and VMware VM 3. I chose these particular names as a way of making it really obvious which virtual machines are running in the VMware environment. While this might seem trivial right now, it will be important when we begin the migration process in the next chapter.

Another thing that I need to point out is that ESX 5.5 is not officially supported for use with VMM. It is possible to manage an ESX 5.5 server using VMM 2012 R2, but Microsoft discourages the practice. That's why

I am going to be using ESX 5.0 (5.1 is supported, too). If you try to use VMM to manage an ESX 5.5 server, then there are two main issues (at least within the context of this book) that you will run into:

- You won't be able to securely communicate with the ESX server because you won't be able to import the required certificate.

- The migration process will fail. The next chapter covers a migration technique that does work for ESX 5.5 servers.

I will talk more about these issues as we go along.

Using the RunAs Account

As you may recall, there was a section back in the first chapter where I walked you through the process of creating a RunAs account. We briefly used the RunAs account earlier in this chapter to link VMM to our Hyper-V hosts. In actuality, however, we could have accomplished that task without using a dedicated Active Directory account. When it comes to linking VMM to VMware, though, the RunAs account becomes really important. The connection between the two environments will fail unless you have an Active Directory account that you can use as a RunAs account. So with that said, let's go ahead and configure vCenter to use our RunAs account.

1. Open the vSphere Web Client on your vCenter server.

2. Log in as Administrator@vsphere.local.

3. Click on the Administration tab.

4. Click on Single Sign On.

5. Click on Configuration (see Figure 4-8).

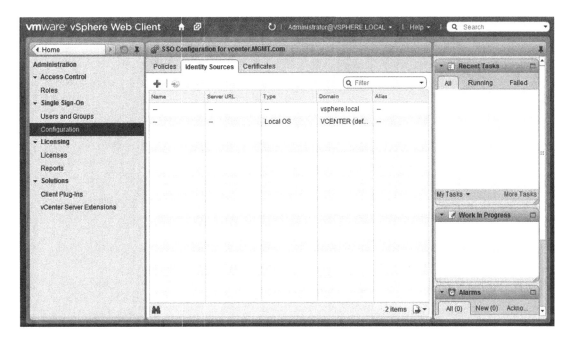

Figure 4-8. *Click on Configuration*

6. Select the Identity Sources tab.

7. Click on the green plus-sign icon. This will cause the Add Identity Source dialog box to be displayed.

8. Select the Active Directory (Integrated Windows Authentication) option.

9. Enter the name of your Windows management domain into the Domain Name field (see Figure 4-9).

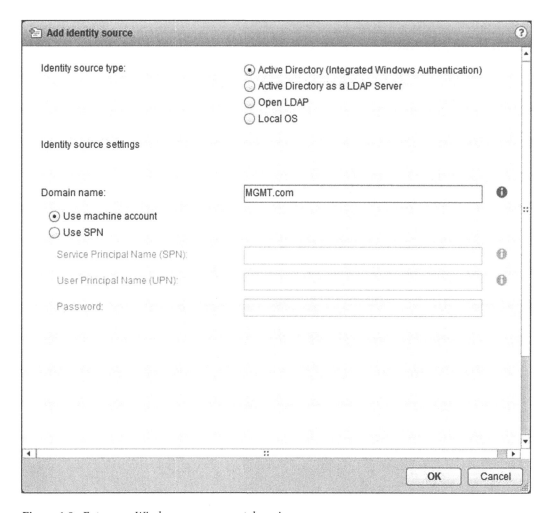

Figure 4-9. Enter your Windows management domain name

10. Click OK to add the Windows domain to vCenter as an identity source.

11. Go back to the vSphere Web Client's Home screen.

12. Click on the vCenter tab.

13. Click on vCenter Servers.

14. Click on your vCenter server.

15. Select the Manage tab.

16. Select the Permissions category.

17. Click on the green plus sign (see Figure 4-10). This will cause the Add Permissions window to appear.

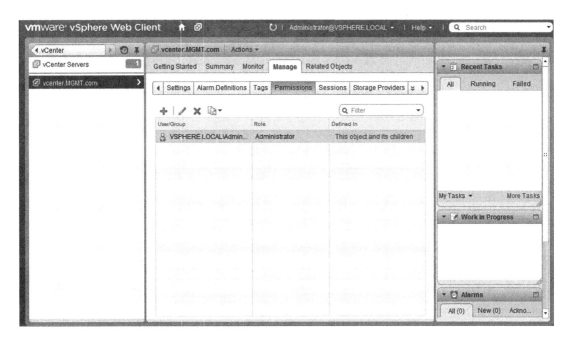

Figure 4-10. *Click on the green plus sign to open the Add Permissions window*

18. When the Add Permission window opens, click the Add button.

19. Select your Windows domain from the Domain drop-down list. By default, this drop-down list will display the fully qualified domain name of your vCenter server rather than that of a Windows domain, so you must manually select the Windows domain.

20. Select your RunAs account from the list of Active Directory user accounts (see Figure 4-11).

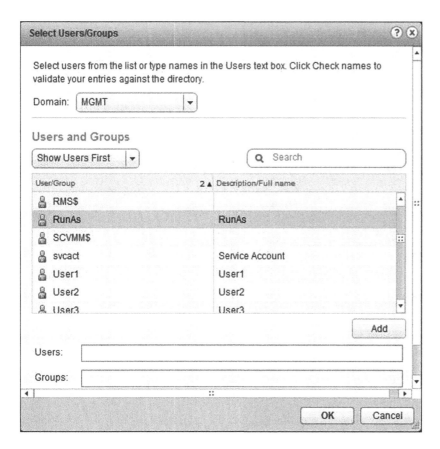

Figure 4-11. *Select your RunAs account*

21. Click the Add button.

22. Click OK to close the list of accounts.

23. When you are returned to the Add Permission window, verify that your RunAs account is listed.

24. Select the Administrator option from the Assigned Role list (see Figure 4-12).

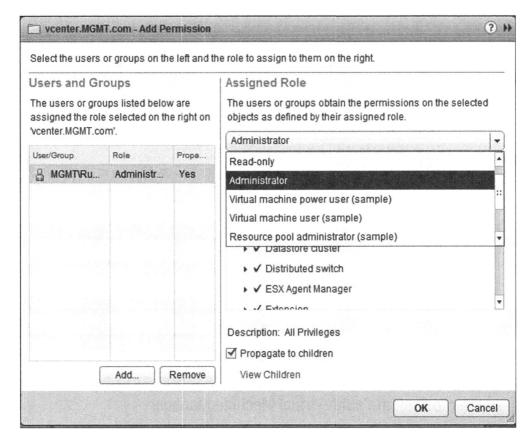

Figure 4-12. *Select the Administrator role*

25. Click OK.

26. Verify that the RunAs account appears on the Permissions tab (see Figure 4-13).

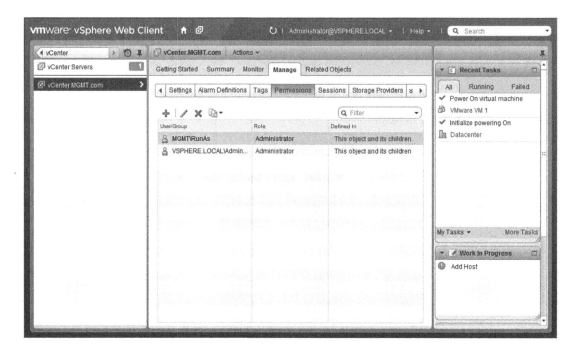

Figure 4-13. *Make sure that the RunAs account is listed on the Permissions tab*

Linking vCenter to System Center Virtual Machine Manager

Now that the RunAs account is in place, we need to link the vCenter server to VMM. This will make it possible to view and manage our VMware virtual machines using VMM.

To establish connectivity from VMM to vSphere, complete these steps:

1. Log in to your VMM server using domain administrator credentials.

2. Open the VMM console.

3. Select the Fabric workspace.

4. Right click on the vCenter Servers container and select the Add VMware vCenter Server command from the shortcut menu (see Figure 4-14). This will cause Windows to launch the Add VMware vCenter Server dialog box.

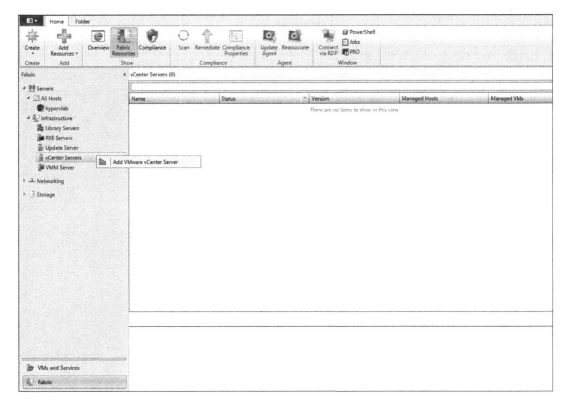

Figure 4-14. *Right click on the vCenter Servers container and choose the Add VMware vCenter Server command from the resulting shortcut menu*

5. Enter the name or IP address of your vCenter server into the Computer Name field.

6. Now you need to tell VMM which account you want to use as a RunAs account. Even though you have already created and used your RunAs account, VMM refers to this process as creating a RunAs account. Begin the process by clicking the Browse button.

7. When the Select a RunAs Account dialog box appears, click the Create Run As Account button. This will cause Windows to open the Create Run As Account dialog box.

8. Enter a name for the RunAs account that you are creating.

9. Enter an optional description of the account.

10. Enter the name of your RunAs account. This name must be entered in domain\account format. For example, I am entering the name as MGMT\RunAs.

11. Enter and confirm a password for the account.

12. Click OK (see Figure 4-15).

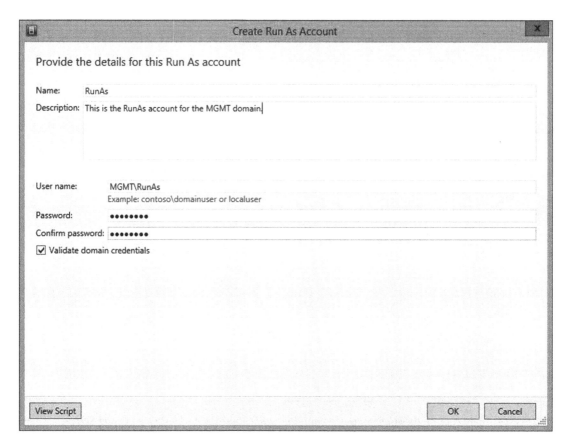

Figure 4-15. *You must enter the information for your RunAs account*

13. Select your RunAs account from the list of Available accounts (see Figure 4-16).

Figure 4-16. *Select your RunAs account*

14. Click OK.

15. Verify that the Communicate with VMware ESX Hosts in Secure Mode check box is selected. There are three important points to make note of just below the check box. These points include:

    • In secure mode, a certificate and public key are required for each ESX host that is being managed by a vCenter server. The instructions in this chapter and the next chapter are based on the use of secure mode, but secure mode will not work if you are going to be using ESX 5.5 servers.

    • VMM initially provides limited management of newly imported ESX hosts. I will show you how to remove this limitation later.

    • Adding a vCenter server does not automatically add ESX hosts to VMM. You must add the vCenter server and then use the Add VMware ESX Hosts and Clusters Wizard to add ESX hosts and clusters.

16. Click OK.

17. Windows will now display an Import Certificate dialog box. Click the Import button.

18. When the import job completes, verify that the vCenter server has been added to the vCenter Servers container (see Figure 4-17). You may have to refresh the console to see the change.

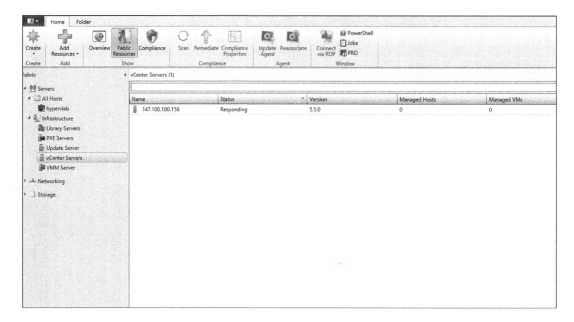

Figure 4-17. *Make sure that your vCenter server has been added to the vCenter Servers container*

Adding VMware Hosts

If you look at the previous figure, you will notice that although we have added a vCenter server, the console isn't displaying any VMware hosts or virtual machines. As such, we need to add our VMware hosts. The procedure for doing so will only work if you have already connected VMM to vCenter.

You can add VMware hosts to VMM by completing these steps:

1. Open the VMM console.

2. Select the Fabric workspace.

3. Click the Add Resources button, which is found in the ribbon.

4. Choose the VMware ESX Hosts and Clusters option from the drop-down list (see Figure 4-18). This will launch the Add Resources Wizard.

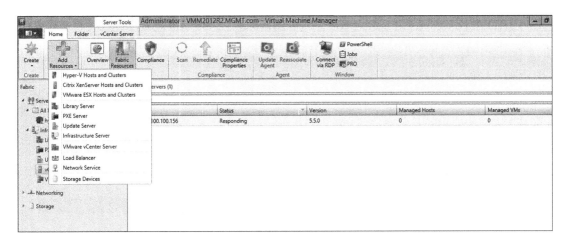

Figure 4-18. *Select the VMware ESX Hosts and Clusters option*

5. Click the Browse button.

6. Select your RunAs account. This must be the same RunAs account that you used to attach to the vCenter server.

7. Click OK.

8. Click Next.

9. Select the check box that corresponds to the VMware server that you want to manage (see Figure 4-19). If you plan to manage multiple servers, you can select multiple check boxes.

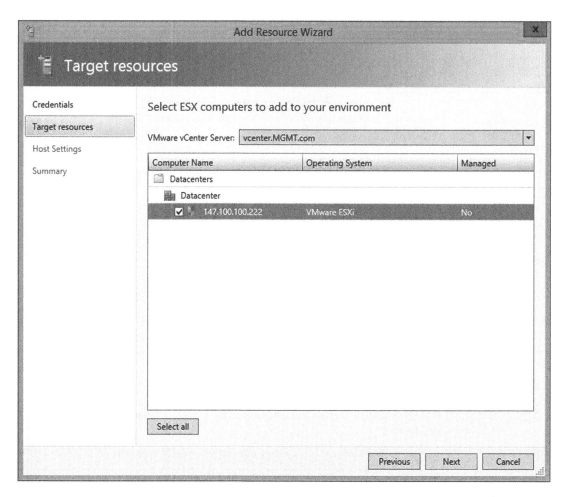

Figure 4-19. *Select the VMware servers that you want to manage*

10. Click Next.

11. Select the host group to which you want to add the previously selected VMware servers.

12. Click Next.

13. Take a moment to verify the information shown on the Summary page to make sure that it is correct.

14. Click Finish.

The Verification Process

You should now be able to manage both your Hyper-V virtual machines and your VMware virtual machines through VMM, although your VMware management capabilities will be limited for now. Before we move forward, however, it is a good idea to make sure that your VMware resources are accessible through the VMM console.

To verify that your VMware environment can now be managed through VMM, complete these steps:

1. Wait for the job to finish and then close the Jobs window.

2. Select the vCenter Servers container and make sure that the correct number of managed hosts and managed VMs are being displayed (see Figure 4-20). Initially, you probably won't see all of your VMware resources. It can take some time for all of the virtual machines to be discovered. You will need to periodically refresh the console in order to bring it up to date.

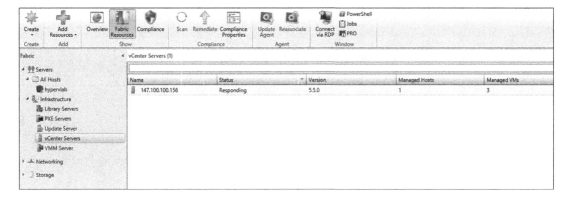

Figure 4-20. *Make sure that the correct number of Managed Hosts and Managed VMs are displayed*

3. Select the VMs and Services workspace.

4. Expand the host group that you specified earlier and verify that your VMware server is listed (see Figure 4-21). As you can see in the figure below, all of my servers reside in the All Hosts group. HyperLab is a Hyper-V cluster. Lab1, Lab2, Lab3, and Lab4 are all Hyper-V servers, but 147.100.100.222 is a VMware ESX server.

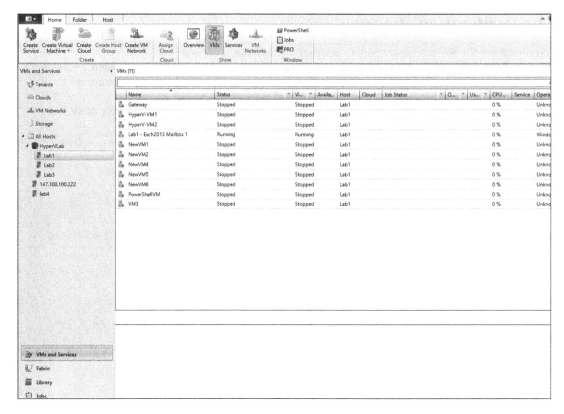

Figure 4-21. *Make sure that your VMware servers are visible*

5. Select the listing for your VMware server and make sure that you can see your VMware virtual machines (see Figure 4-22).

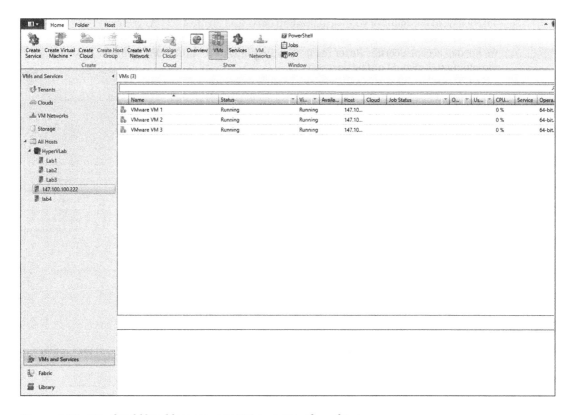

Figure 4-22. *You should be able to see your VMware virtual machines*

Importing a Security Certificate

So far we have attached our VMware servers to VMM and verified connectivity. However, there is one more thing that we have to do before we are ready to begin managing our VMware environment through VMM.

When we established connectivity to vCenter, one of the steps in the configuration process involved verifying that the Communicate with VMware ESX Hosts in Secure Mode check box was checked. The fact that we chose to use secure mode means that we have to accept a certificate for the host before we can fully manage our VMware environment. Fortunately, this process is easier than it sounds. However, in order for this process to work, we will need to create a second RunAs account. Thankfully, we can do that as a part of the certificate-import process.

Accepting a Certificate

To accept a certificate for the host, complete the following steps:

1. Within the VMM console, go to the Fabric workspace.

2. Select the All Hosts container (you must be in the Fabric workspace for the next step to work).

3. Take a look at the status of your virtualization hosts (see Figure 4-23). As you can see in the figure, our VMware host has a status of OK (Limited). This means that we need to accept a certificate for the host. If the status were simply OK, then the remaining steps would not be necessary.

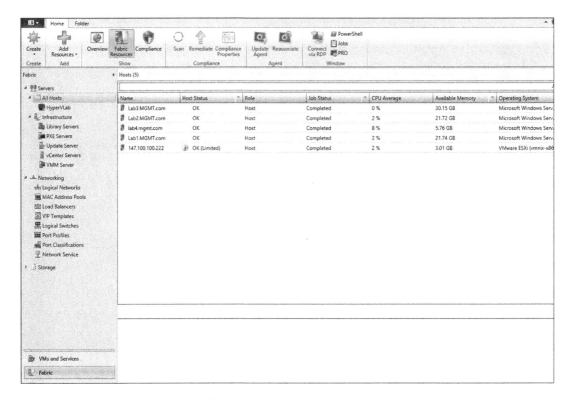

Figure 4-23. *Check the status of your VMware servers*

4. Right click on your VMware server and choose the Properties command from the shortcut menu. This will cause the server's properties sheet to be displayed.

5. Select the Management tab.

6. Click the Browse button. This will cause Windows to display the Select a Run As Account dialog box.

7. Click the Create Run As Account button. After doing so, you will see the Create Run As dialog box.

8. Enter ESX Root as the name of the new RunAs account.

9. Enter root as the username (this must be lower case).

10. Enter and confirm the password that is used by the root account on your ESX server (see Figure 4-24).

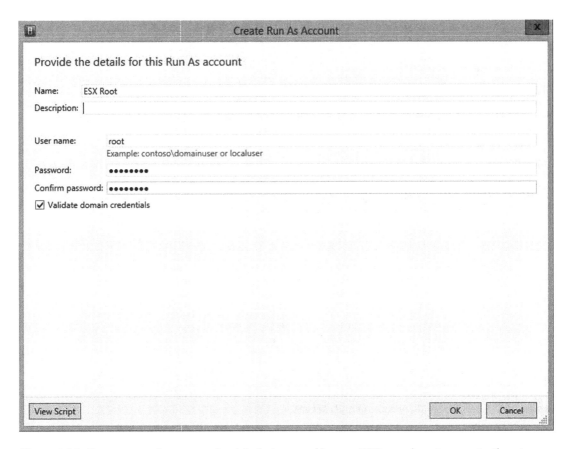

***Figure 4-24.** You must use the same credentials that are used by your ESX server's root account; otherwise, this process will not work*

11. Click OK.

12. You should now be returned to the Select a Run As Account dialog box. Select your newly created ESX Root account and click OK (see Figure 4-25). You will now be returned to the Management tab on the Properties dialog box for your VMware server.

Figure 4-25. *Select the ESX Root account and click OK*

13. Click on the Retrieve button. This will cause a certificate thumbprint to be retrieved from the VMware server. Make sure that a certificate thumbprint is displayed (see Figure 4-26).

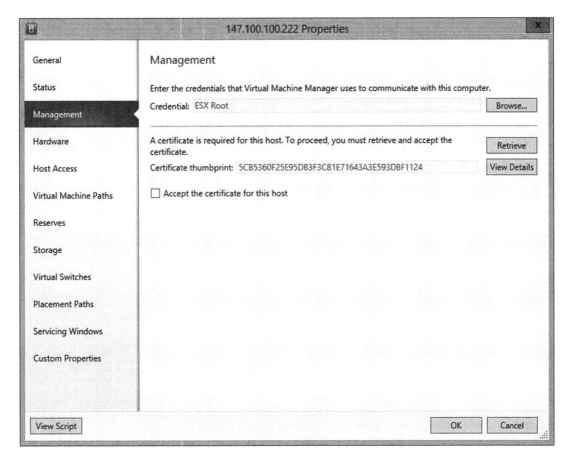

Figure 4-26. *Make sure that the certificate thumbprint is displayed*

14. Click View Details to view the certificate details.

15. Click OK to close the certificate details.

16. Select the Accept the Certificate for this host check box (if it is not already selected).

17. Click OK.

18. Verify that your VMware server now displays a host status of OK (see Figure 4-27).

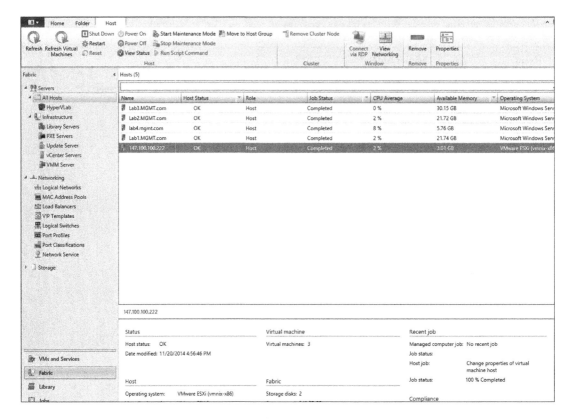

Figure 4-27. *Make sure that your VMware server displays a host status of OK*

What Went Wrong?

It is worth noting that this procedure sometimes fails and results in an error message citing an invalid username and password. If this happens, then there are two things that you can do. The first thing that I recommend doing is to make absolutely sure that your RunAs account has credentials that match those of the RunAs account used by your ESX server. If you need to check and possibly modify these credentials, then follow these steps:

1. Select the Settings workspace within the VMM console.

2. Select the Run As Accounts container.

3. Right click on your ESX Root account and select the Properties command from the shortcut menu (see Figure 4-28).

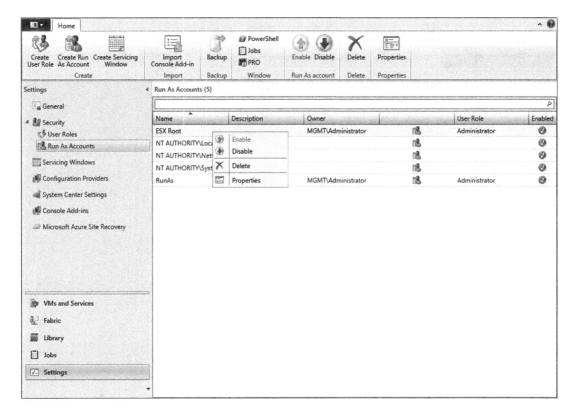

Figure 4-28. *Right click on your ESX Root account and select the Properties command from the shortcut menu*

4. Verify your account credentials and click OK (see Figure 4-29).

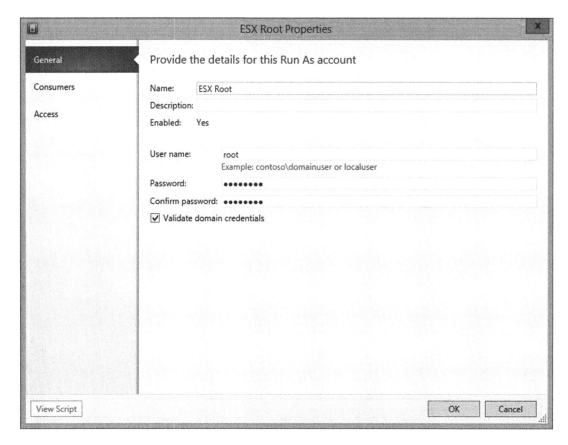

Figure 4-29. Make any necessary modifications to the ESX Root account and click OK

    5.   Try importing the certificate again.

Another reason why this procedure sometimes fails is because ESX version 5.5 is not officially supported. My screen captures in this chapter are all based on the use of ESX 5.0. Version 5.1 is supported, but 5.5 is not.

My experience has been that although ESX 5.5 is not officially supported, VMM works relatively well for managing ESX 5.5 hosts and the virtual machines residing on them. However, there are a couple of important caveats:

- The certificate-import process does not work for ESX 5.5 servers (I will show you a workaround in a moment).

- The migration process described in Chapter 5 does not work for virtual machines residing on ESX 5.5 servers (there is a workaround in Chapter 6).

If you are running ESX 5.5, or if you are experiencing problems importing a certificate, then you can work around the problem by removing the requirement for communicating with ESX hosts in secure mode. To do so, complete these steps:

    1.   In the VMM console, select the Fabric workspace.

    2.   Select the vCenter Servers container.

3. Right click on your vCenter server and select the Properties command from the shortcut menu.

4. When the Properties dialog box opens, deselect the Communicate with VMware ESX Hosts in Secure Mode check box (see Figure 4-30).

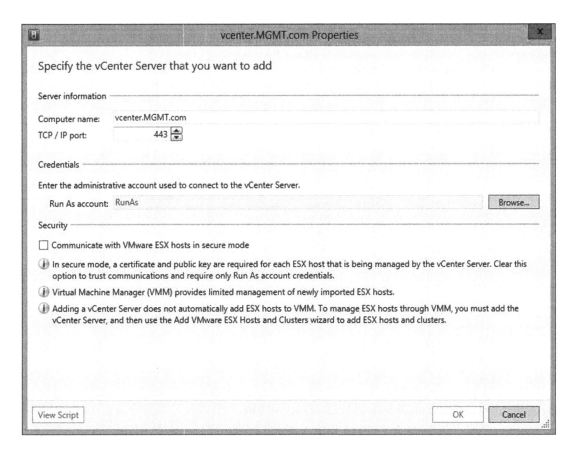

Figure 4-30. *Deselect the Communicate with VMware ESX Hosts in Secure Mode check box*

5. Click OK.

VMware Management Techniques

Connecting VMM to your VMware environment is the first step in the migration process, but there is no rule that says that you have to begin the migration immediately. If you haven't had a lot of experience with using VMM, you might want to spend some time getting used to the console before you attempt a migration. With that in mind, I want to spend the rest of this chapter showing you some ways that you can manage your VMware environment using VMM.

A Single Pane of Glass

As I explained in one of the earlier chapters, one of the primary advantages to using VMM is that it gives you a single-pane-of-glass interface for managing your virtualization infrastructure. Although VMware disputes the "single pane of glass" concept, it is important to remember that the VMware document that I discussed earlier does not address multi-hypervisor environments.

In the previous section, you saw that it is possible to display your VMware servers alongside your Hyper-V servers, and I also showed you how to access your VMware virtual machines. But what about displaying VMware and Hyper-V virtual machines through a single pane of glass?

It is actually really easy to get a consolidated view of all your VMs, regardless of what hypervisor they reside on. All you have to do is to select the host group (in my case, All Hosts) in which the host servers reside. As you can see in Figure 4-31, all of the virtual machines are displayed, regardless of where they reside.

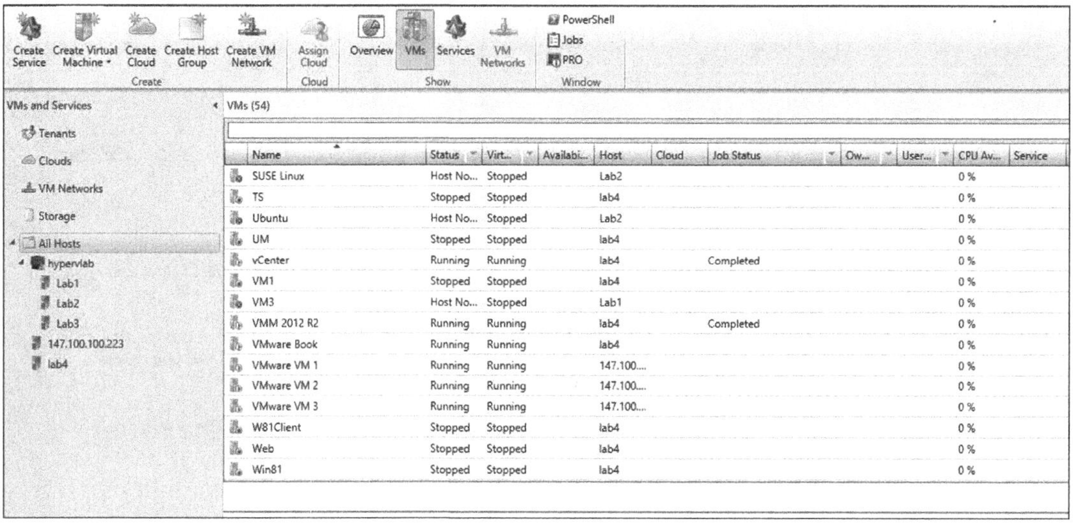

Figure 4-31. *VMware VMs are displayed alongside Hyper-V VMs*

Remember earlier when I said that I was naming my VMware virtual machines VMware VM? I did that as a way of making it easier to track the virtual machine migration process in the next chapter. If you look at the figure above, however, you can see that if it were not for me naming the VMware virtual machines in this way, the Host column would be the only way to initially differentiate between the virtual machines that are running on VMware and the virtual machines running on Hyper-V.

Even the virtual machine summary data is displayed in a consistent manner across hypervisors. To show you what I mean, take a look at Figure 4-32. This figure shows a Hyper-V virtual machine. You can see that the VM is hosted on a server named Lab4.mgmt.com, which is a Hyper-V server. You can also see the virtual machine's status, the number of virtual processors being used, the memory consumption, the logical network in use, the job status, the storage consumption, and the daily CPU performance. I got all of this information simply by clicking on a running Hyper-V virtual machine.

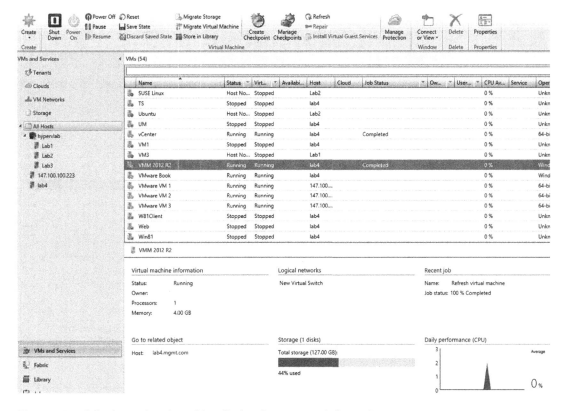

Figure 4-32. *Selecting a virtual machine displays its summary information*

Now take a look at what happens when I select a VMware virtual machine (see Figure 4-33). All of the same summary information is displayed. You will also notice that the VMware logical network vSwitch0 is displayed, even though the VMM server hasn't been manually connected to that switch.

Figure 4-33. *This is the summary information for a VMware virtual machine*

Creating New VMs

In the last chapter, I showed you how to create a virtual machine by using the Hyper-V Manager. As I explained then, I wanted to show you the basics of how the virtual machine creation process works. In real life, however, you probably won't be using the Hyper-V Manager to create virtual machines. Instead, you have a couple of other options.

If your goal is to create highly available Hyper-V virtual machines, then you can create those virtual machines through the Failover Cluster Manager. However, one of our goals is to completely consolidate the management process (as much as we can, anyway). As such, the tool of choice for virtual machine creation is the VMM console.

Under normal circumstances, the virtual machine creation process within the VMM console is really similar to the process of creating a virtual machine using the Hyper-V Manager. Even so, you have to remember that we are no longer operating exclusively within a Hyper-V environment. We are now using VMM as a management console for both VMware and Hyper-V. That being the case, I want to show you how the virtual machine creation process works.

For the purpose of this discussion, I am going to be creating a couple of virtual machines—one on the Hyper-V cluster and another on the VMware server. That way, you can see the similarities and differences that exist.

Before I show you the process, I need to point out that, although I am going to be creating these virtual machines manually, you are not limited to manual VM creation. VMM allows you to build template virtual machines that you can use for VM creation.

Creating a Hyper-V Virtual Machine

You can create a Hyper-V virtual machine using VMM by following these steps:

1. Open the VMM console.

2. Select the VMs and Services workspace.

3. Select your preferred host container. For the purposes of this book, I will be using the All Hosts container.

4. Right click on the host container and select the Create Virtual Machine command from the shortcut menu (see Figure 4-34). This will cause Windows to launch the Create Virtual Machine Wizard.

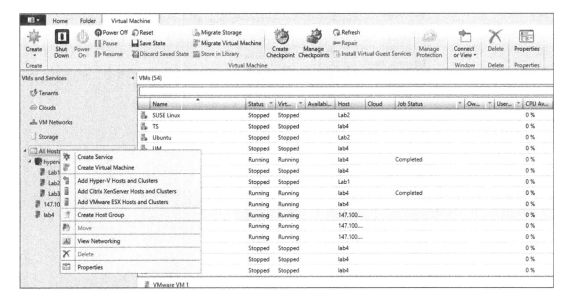

Figure 4-34. *Right click on the host container and select the Create Virtual Machine command from the shortcut menu*

5. The wizard's initial page asks if you want to use an existing virtual machine, VM template, or virtual hard disk, or if you would prefer to create the new virtual machine with a blank virtual hard disk. Choose the option to use a blank virtual hard disk.

6. Click Next.

7. Enter a name for your new virtual machine.

8. Enter a description of the virtual machine that you are creating.

9. Select a virtual machine generation.

10. Click Next.

11. Select the Hyper-V compatibility profile check box (see Figure 4-35).

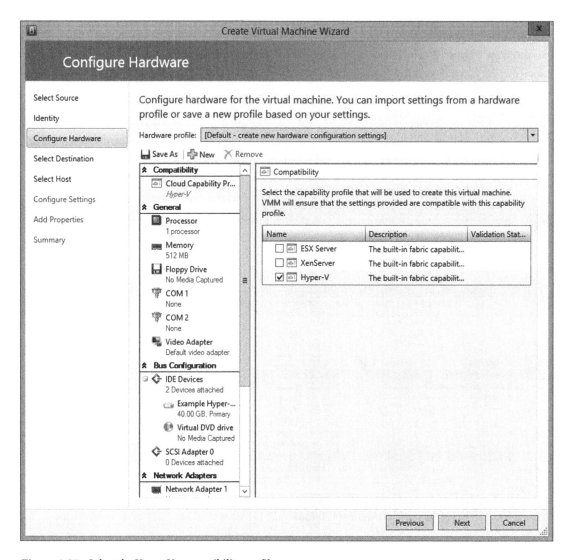

Figure 4-35. Select the Hyper-V compatibility profile

12. Make any required changes to the hardware allocations.

13. Click Next.

14. Select your host container.

15. Click Next.

16. Select the Hyper-V host on which you wish to create the virtual machine
    (see Figure 4-36). Generally, the host with the highest star rating is the most
    suitable for hosting the virtual machine, but this is not always the case.
    I will talk about the star ratings in detail in a later chapter.

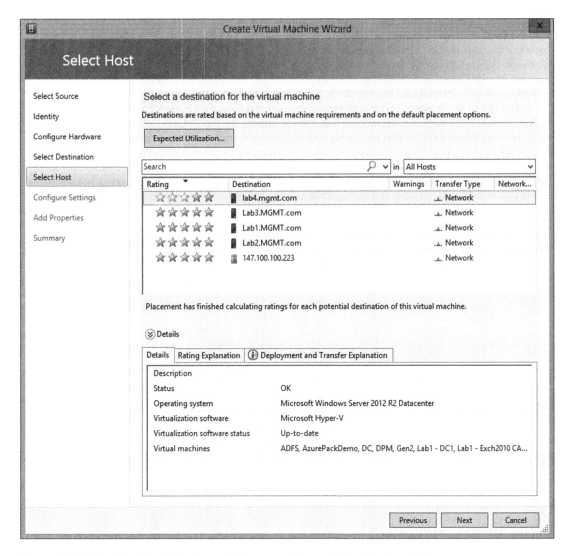

Figure 4-36. *Select the Hyper-V host on which you want to create the virtual machine*

17. If necessary, configure the storage path, virtual network, and machine resources for the virtual machine.

18. Click Next.

19. Select the virtual switch to which you want to connect the new virtual machine.

20. Click Next.

21. Specify the automatic startup and stop actions (if necessary) and then specify the operating system that you plan to install on the new virtual machine.

22. Click Next.

23. Review the settings for the virtual machine.

24. Click Create.

Creating a VMware Virtual Machine

I have to admit that the first time that I ever tried to create a VMware virtual machine using VMM, I assumed that the procedure was largely the same as for creating a Hyper-V virtual machine. I thought that I would be able to use the Create Virtual Machine Wizard to create the virtual machine and then simply select the VMware host as the destination. Unfortunately, things aren't quite that intuitive.

As you saw in the section on creating a Hyper-V virtual machine, the Create Virtual Machine Wizard asks you to specify the virtual machine generation. If you choose the Generation 1 virtual machine option, you will receive an error stating that the virtualization software doesn't support virtual hard disks on IDE bus (see Figure 4-37). However, if you try to create a Generation 2 virtual machine, you will receive an error stating that you can't create a Generation 2 virtual machine because the host is running an older operating system (see Figure 4-38).

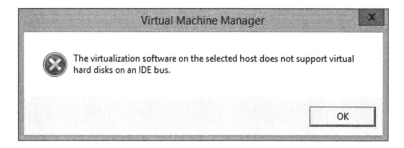

Figure 4-37. *This is what happens if you try to create a Generation 1 VM on a VMware host*

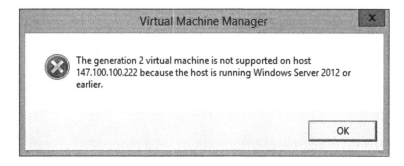

Figure 4-38. *This is what happens if you try to create a Generation 2 VM on a VMware host*

As if those errors weren't problematic enough, you can't use VMM to create a virtual machine on a VMware host if that host is still under limited management. If you attempt this, you will receive the following error message:

> Host is not available for placement because it is in a state that has limited management functionality. To use an ESX host for placement you must configure the security settings of the host to enable full management.

The easiest method of using VMM to create a VMware virtual machine involves using an existing VMware virtual machine as a model. My advice is to use vCenter and create one or more virtual machines that can be used as templates. That way, you don't have to worry about the complications of trying to clone production virtual machines.

Preparing Your Template VMs

If your template virtual machines are running Windows, then you will want to run SYSPREP on the virtual machines as a way of removing machine-specific information, such as the computer name or IP address. This should be done before making any virtual machine clones.

Using SYSPREP

SYSPREP must never be run on a production VM. SYSPREP puts the operating system into a state that allows for safe cloning by removing machine-specific data. If you run SYSPREP on a production VM, you will destroy the VM in the process.

In case you are wondering, when you generate a clone from a sysprepped VM, the clone will have Windows partially installed. You will be asked a few simple questions (such as your time zone and the administrator password), and then the operating system installation process will be completed.

You can SYSPREP a VM by completing the following steps:

1. Open the VMware virtual machine's console.

2. Log in to Windows (remember, SYSPREP only works with Windows).

3. Enter the SYSPREP command at the server's Run prompt.

4. Depending on the version of Windows that you are running, File Explorer may open. If so, double click on the SYSPREP icon to launch SYSPREP.

5. Choose the Enter System Out of Box Experience (OOBE) option (see Figure 4-39).

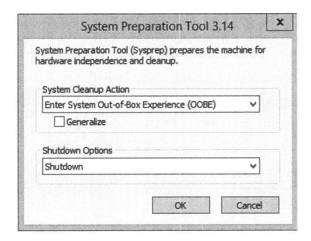

Figure 4-39. *Configure SYSPREP to Enter System Out of Box Experience*

6. Set the Shut Down option to Shut Down (do not use Reboot).

7. Click OK.

8. Close the virtual machine console.

Cloning a VM

Now that you have run SYSPREP on a virtual machine, it is time to create a new virtual machine by cloning your existing VM. To do so, follow these steps:

1. Open the VMM console.

2. Click on the VMs and Services workspace.

3. Click on the All Hosts container (or the host container within which you want to create the VM).

4. Right click on the host container and select the Create Virtual Machine command from the shortcut menu. This will cause Windows to launch the Create Virtual Machine Wizard.

5. When the wizard's initial page appears, choose the option to Use an Existing Virtual Machine, VM Template, or Virtual Hard Disk (see Figure 4-40).

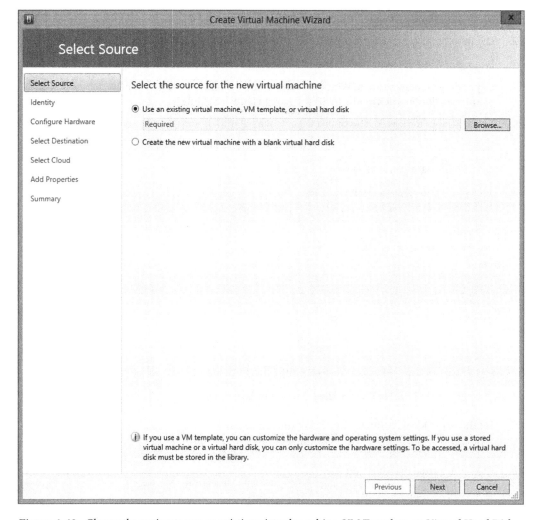

Figure 4-40. *Choose the option to use an existing virtual machine, VM Template, or Virtual Hard Disk*

6. Click Browse.

7. Select the virtual machine from which you want to base the new virtual machine.

8. Click OK.

9. Click Next.

10. Enter a name for the virtual machine that you are creating.

11. Enter an optional description for the new VM.

12. Click Next.

13. You should now see the Configure Hardware page (see Figure 4-41). Normally, you would select the hypervisor that will host the VM and then make any necessary adjustments to the hardware allocation. However, a lot of the hardware configuration options (but not all of them) are grayed out because you are cloning an existing virtual machine. Go ahead and make any desired hardware allocation changes.

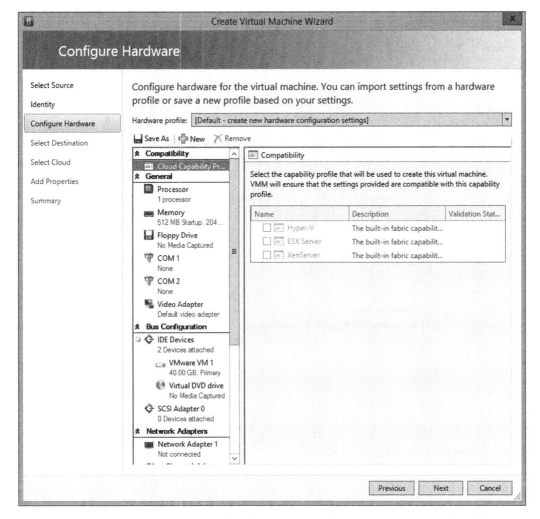

Figure 4-41. *Most of the options are greyed out because we are cloning an existing virtual machine*

14. Click Next.

15. Choose the option to place the virtual machine on a host.

16. Click Next.

17. Select a VMware host to use for virtual machine placement (see Figure 4-42). Notice in the figure that the VMware host is the only host server that has been assigned a star rating.

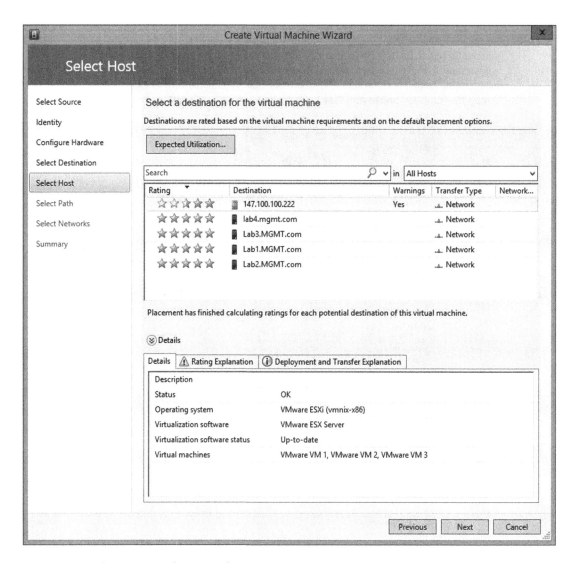

Figure 4-42. *Select a VMware host to use for placement*

18. Click Next.

19. Select the VMware datastore to use for virtual machine placement
     (see Figure 4-43).

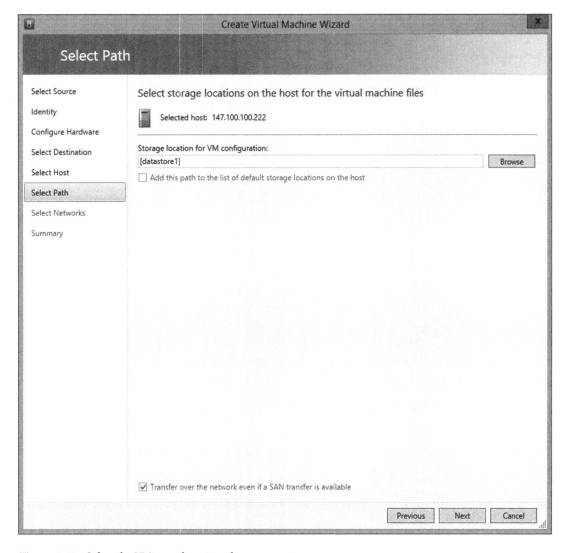

Figure 4-43. *Select the VMware datastore that you want to use*

20. Click Next.

21. Select the VMware network, virtual switch, port classification, and VLAN to use
     (see Figure 4-44).

Figure 4-44. *Select the virtual machine network to which you want to connect the new virtual machine*

22. Click Next.

23. Take a moment to review the virtual machine summary.

24. Click the Create button to create the new virtual machine.

25. After the virtual machine creation completes, the new virtual machine should be listed among the other VMware virtual machines (see Figure 4-45).

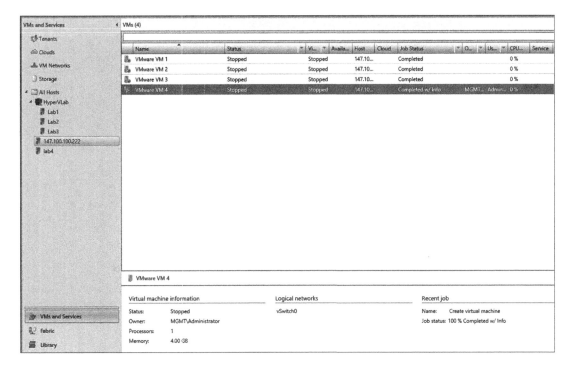

Figure 4-45. *The new VMware virtual machine has been created*

26. Right click on the newly created virtual machine and choose the Power On command from the shortcut menu.

27. After the virtual machine starts, right click on the virtual machine and select the Connect or View ➤ Connect Via Console commands from the shortcut menu.

28. At this point, you may see a prompt telling you that you need to install the VMware ActiveX control. If you receive this prompt, click Yes to install the control, then follow the prompts to complete the installation.

29. When the console opens, follow the guest operating system's prompts to complete the deployment of the operating system (see Figure 4-46). As previously mentioned, this involves answering a few simple questions. The screen that you see in the figure is the screen that is initially shown (based on the use of Windows Server 2012 R2) when you open the new virtual machine's console for the first time.

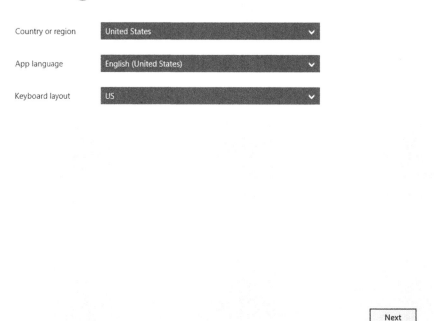

Figure 4-46. *You will need to answer a few simple questions to complete the deployment of the guest operating system*

Moving On

In this chapter, my primary goal was to show you how to connect your Hyper-V and VMware environments to VMM. Hopefully, along the way you have started getting a feel for how to manage the two environments. If not, though, don't worry. I'm not done yet.

Over the next two chapters I am going to show you two different methods for migrating virtual machines to Hyper-V. Chapter 5 will focus on migrating ESX 5.1 and earlier VMs, while Chapter 6 will use an alternative technique that is suitable for VMware ESX 5.5 virtual machines (this technique also works with older virtual machines).

Once I am done talking about virtual machine migrations, I am going to spend the last two chapters of the book giving you something of a crash course on using VMM for the day-to-day management of your virtual machines.

CHAPTER 5

Using System Center Virtual Machine Manager for Virtual Machine Migrations

Over the last couple of chapters, we have put quite a bit of time and effort into setting up centralized management through System Center Virtual Machine Manager (VMM). Now, it's time for the main event. In this chapter, I am going to show you how to perform a VMware-to-Hyper-V migration.

Given how much work was involved in connecting our two environments to VMM, I'm sure that some of you are expecting the migration process to be absolutely grueling. Oddly enough, however, the migration is actually really simple. The whole process is wizard based, and you can initiate a migration in less than five minutes' time.

So, here is my plan for this chapter. I know that some of you only bought this book because you wanted to learn how to perform a virtual machine migration. That being the case, I am going to jump right into explaining what you need to do to prepare a VM for migration, and then I will show you the migration process itself. Once I have done that, I am going to spend some time covering a few troubleshooting techniques. When I do, I will also explain what is really going on behind the scenes during the migration process.

Some Important Things to Know

Although it might be tempting to jump right in and attempt a virtual machine migration (or a V2V migration, as Microsoft calls it), you can't. If you attempt a migration right now, it will fail. There are a few things that you are going to need to do in order to get your virtual machines ready before you can begin the migration process. There are also some important things that you need to know before you begin.

Supported Versions of VMware

The first thing that you need to know is that System Center 2012 R2 Virtual Machine Manager is not officially supported for use with ESX 5.5. As I explained in the previous chapter, you can usually get away with connecting ESX 5.5 to VMM and using VMM for various management tasks. However, you cannot use VMM to migrate virtual machines that currently exist on an ESX 5.5 server. If you do, the migration process will fail.

Likewise, VMM does not support converting VMware workstations. If you have VMware Workstation, then you will have to find another conversion method—the technique that I am about to show you won't work.

VMM supports migrating virtual machines that are hosted on the following versions of VMware:

- ESX / ESXi 4.1

- ESX / ESXi 5.1

If you need to convert virtual machines that are running on an older version of VMware, you might try using an older version of VMM. VMM 2012 originally supported ESX / ESXi 3.5 Update 5 and ESX / ESXi 4.0. However, that support was removed with Service Pack 1. VMM 2012 R2 has never supported any version of VMware older than ESX / ESXi 4.1.

If the virtual machines that you want to migrate are currently running on ESX 5.5, there are a couple of things that you can do. One option is to move the virtual machines to an older version of ESX. As previously mentioned, ESX 5.1 is supported. For the purposes of this chapter, I am going to be using ESX 5.0.

My recommendation is that if you are currently running ESX 5.5 then you should skip ahead to the next chapter. In Chapter 6, I'm going to show you an alternative method for migrating your VMware virtual machines. This method works really well for ESX 5.5 servers.

The Resulting Downtime

The next thing that you need to know before preparing for the migration is that this is not a live migration. In other words, we won't be able to use vMotion or Hyper-V Live Migration to move a running virtual machine from VMware to Hyper-V. Unfortunately, things just don't work this way. Virtual machines have to be shut down and completely disconnected from the network in order for the migration to succeed.

Another thing that I want to point out before I move on is that the migration process can be very time consuming. I performed several virtual machine migrations before sitting down to write this chapter because I wanted to make sure that the technique that I wrote about was solid. What I found was that it took about 2.5 hours to migrate a 40 GB virtual machine.

Obviously, your hardware is going to make a big difference. The hardware in my lab is not super fast, but it isn't painfully slow either. Regardless of your hardware, you should expect the migration process to take a long time to complete.

Storage Provisioning

The reason why the migration process takes a long time is because VMM uses thick provisioning. If you are creating a brand-new Hyper-V virtual machine from scratch, you have the option of choosing whether you want to use thin or thick provisioning. Conversely, if you are using VMM to migrate a virtual machine from VMware to Hyper-V, then the Hyper-V virtual machine will have thick provisioning regardless of whether the source virtual machine used thin or thick provisioning. This is why the migration process takes so long. VMM has to construct a Hyper-V-compatible virtual hard disk as a part of the migration process.

While I am on the subject of storage, I need to mention that VMM does not support converting VMware virtual machines that have virtual hard disks connected to an IDE bus. Keep in mind that this refers to the storage bus that is used within the virtual machine. It has nothing to do with physical storage.

Key Points to Remember:

- ESX / ESXi 5.5 is not supported. If you have ESX 5.5, then use the technique described in the next chapter.

- ESX / ESXi 4.0 and older versions of VMware are not supported.

- VMware Workstation is not supported.

- This is not a live migration. The virtual machines will have to be powered down to be migrated.

- Migrations are time consuming. It can take several hours to migrate a virtual machine.

- Virtual hard disks created on the Hyper-V server as a part of the migration are thick provisioned. This behavior cannot be changed, so you are going to need plenty of available storage space.

- VMM does not support converting VMware virtual machines whose virtual hard disks are connected to an IDE bus (within the virtual machine).

Preparing for the Migration

Now that I have talked about the prerequisites for migration, it is time to begin preparing our virtual machines. The first thing that you probably need to know about the migration process is that you can only migrate one VM at a time using the method that I am going to show you. As such, you will probably want to wait to do the prep work for a VM until just before you plan to migrate that VM.

There are several tasks that you will need to complete in preparation for the virtual machine migration. These tasks include:

- Backing up your virtual machines

- Removing the VMware Tools

- Making note of any static IP addresses

- Disconnecting from the VMware virtual switch

- Disabling any antivirus software that is running on the VM

- Shutting down the VM

I will talk about each of these items in the sections that follow.

Backing Up Your Virtual Machines

The procedure that we are going to be using for virtual machine conversion is relatively safe. Even so, it is important to make a backup of your virtual machines before moving forward.

As you might have guessed, there are a lot of things that can go wrong in a virtual machine conversion, such as a power failure or virtual hard disk corruption. Even so, VMM does a pretty good job of protecting you against catastrophic loss. The VMware virtual machine is left intact. Hence, the virtual machine is not moved to the Hyper-V server, but rather copied there. After the migration completes, your original VMware virtual machine will remain on the VMware server, and a duplicate virtual machine will exist on the Hyper-V server.

So, why the need for the backup? Well, as you have already seen, there is quite a bit of prep work that needs to be done prior to the migration. Some of these tasks alter the original virtual machine (such as disconnecting the network or removing the VMware Tools). Admittedly, these are not major modifications, but as a best practice you should make a backup prior to any virtual machine modifications.

Removing the VMware Tools

Once you have created a backup of the virtual machine that you will be migrating, the next thing that you need to do is to remove the VMware Tools from the virtual machine. You can accomplish this by performing these steps:

1. Open the vSphere Web Client.

2. Navigate through the console to *<your vCenter Server>* ➤ *<your datacenter>* ➤ Discovered Virtual Machines ➤ *<the virtual machine that you want to migrate>*.

3. Click on the Launch Console link (see Figure 5-1).

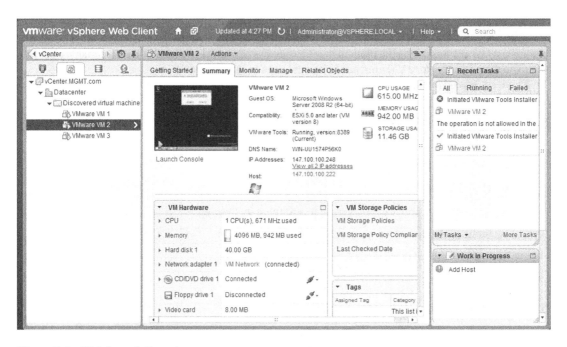

Figure 5-1. *Click Launch Console*

4. Log in to the virtual machine using an account that has administrative permissions.

5. The procedure for removing the VMware Tools varies depending on the guest operating system that is being used. Assuming that the VM is running Windows Server 2012 R2, open the Control Panel.

6. Click on Programs.

7. Click on Uninstall a Program.

8.   Select VMware Tools from the list of installed programs (see Figure 5-2).

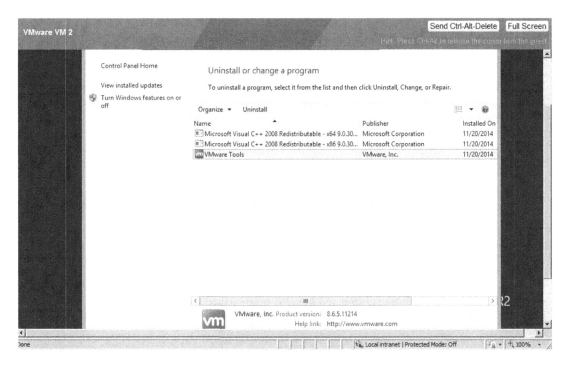

Figure 5-2. *Select VMware Tools from the list of installed applications*

9.   Click Uninstall.

10.   When Windows asks if you want to uninstall the program, click Yes.

11.   When the removal is complete, click Yes to reboot the virtual machine.

Making Note of Any Static IP Addresses

Making note of any static IP addresses is probably the most commonly overlooked step in the entire process. Obviously, this is a non-issue if the virtual machine that you are converting is using a dynamically assigned IP address. However, if the VM is using a static IP address, you will need to make note of the address so that you can reassign the address to the VM after the conversion process has completed.

Disconnecting from the Virtual Network

The next thing that we have to do before migrating a virtual machine is to disconnect the virtual machine from its VMware virtual network. The reason why this has to be done is because we are going to be attaching the virtual machine to the Hyper-V virtual network. Although it might seem as though VMM would be smart enough to disconnect the virtual machine from the VMware virtual network automatically as a part of the migration process, you do have to manually disconnect the virtual machine. If you fail to do this then the migration wizard will display the following error message:

No Available Connector to the Selected VM Network Can Be Found. Ensure Host NICs Have Connection to the Fabric Network on Which VM Network Is Created.

Fortunately, it is easy to sever the virtual machine's network connection. The entire process can be completed through the VMM console. To disconnect the virtual machine from its network, complete the following steps:

1. Open the VMM console.

2. Select the VMs and Services workspace

3. Select the All Hosts container (or the container containing your VMware virtual machines).

4. Right click on the VMware virtual machine that you want to migrate and select the Shut Down option. If you receive an error message indicating that the virtual machine cannot be shut down, then you can open the console and manually shut down the guest OS.

5. After the virtual machine has been shut down, right click on the virtual machine and select the Properties command from the shortcut menu. This will cause the virtual machine's properties sheet to be displayed.

6. Select the Hardware Configuration tab (see Figure 5-3).

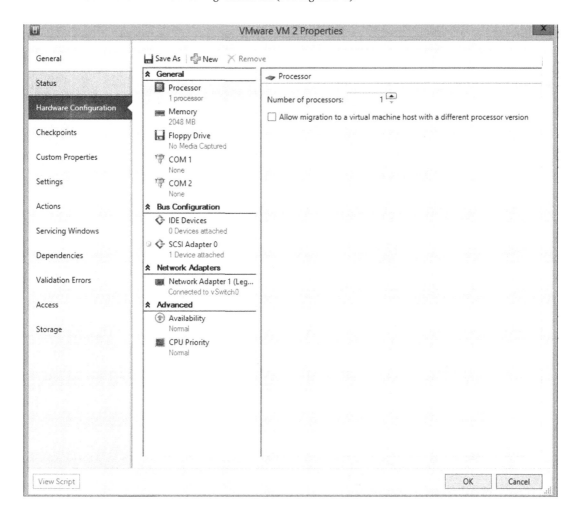

Figure 5-3. *Select the Hardware Configuration tab*

7. Click on the Network Adapter.

8. Select the Not Connected option (see Figure 5-4). You may want to make note of the previous connection just in case you need to revert the virtual machine back to the way it was.

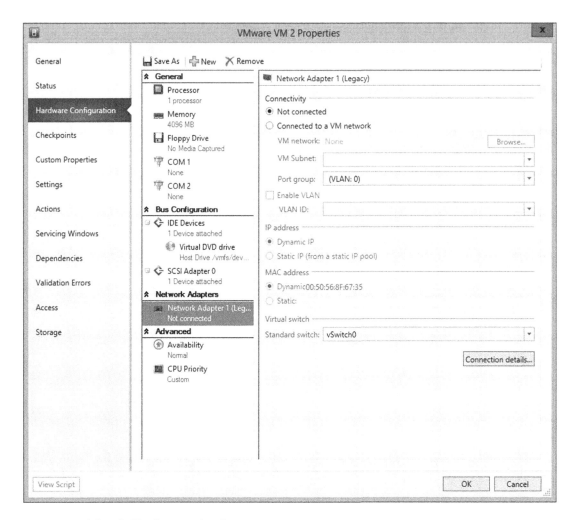

Figure 5-4. Select the Not Connected option

9. If any additional network adapters exist, you must set those adapters to a state of Not Connected.

10. Click OK.

Uninstalling Your Antivirus Software

The next thing that you should do is uninstall your antivirus software. Doing so isn't an absolute requirement. After all, the virtual machine is shut down during the conversion process. However, I would recommend removing your antivirus software anyway.

Why should you bother? Remember what I said about how the migration process works? VMM builds a Hyper-V virtual hard disk that is based on the contents of the VMware virtual hard disk. It is possible that when you boot the newly created Hyper-V virtual machine your antivirus software will interpret the new virtual hard disk structure as being the result of a malware attack and attempt to take some form of corrective action.

It would be a shame to have an otherwise successful migration ruined by your antivirus software. In my opinion it's best to remove the antivirus software ahead of time so as to eliminate any chance that it will cause problems. You can easily install the software onto the new VM after the migration completes.

Shutting Down the Virtual Machine

The last step in the prep work is to shut down the virtual machine that you are going to be migrating. This is an absolute requirement. You cannot convert a running virtual machine.

Converting a Virtual Machine

Now that all of the prep work is done, it is time to migrate our virtual machine. As previously mentioned, the migration process is relatively simple (but time consuming). You can perform the migration by completing these steps:

1. Open the VMM console.

2. Click on the VMs and Services workspace.

3. Select the All Hosts container.

4. Click on the ribbon's Create Virtual Machine tile. Sometimes a bug in VMM keeps this option from being displayed. If this occurs, just click on the Fabric workspace and then go back to the VMs and Services workspace.

5. Choose the Convert Virtual Machine option from the resulting menu (see Figure 5-5). This will cause Windows to launch the Convert Virtual Machine Wizard.

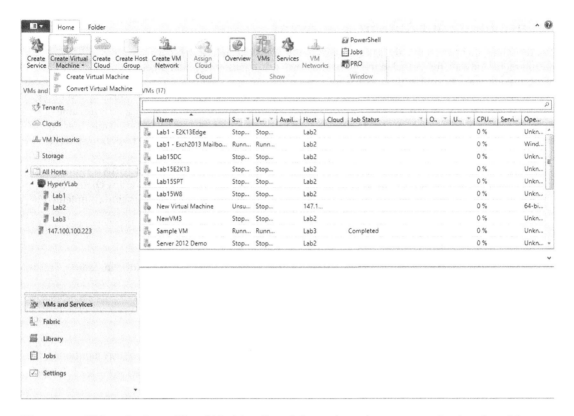

Figure 5-5. *Click on the Create Virtual Machine tile and choose the option to convert the virtual machine*

6. The wizard's initial page asks you to select the virtual machine that you wish to convert. Although you can type in the virtual machine's name, it is easier to click the Browse button. This will cause Windows to display the Select Virtual Machine Source dialog box.

7. The Select Virtual Machine Source dialog box only displays VMware virtual machines (see Figure 5-6). If the virtual machine that you want to migrate is not listed, you should check to make sure that the virtual machine has been shut down. Select the virtual machine that you want to convert. You can only select one virtual machine at a time.

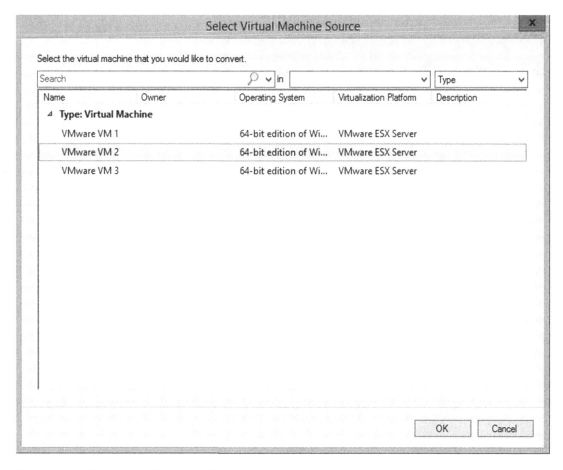

Figure 5-6. *Select the virtual machine that you want to convert*

8. Click OK.

9. You should now be returned to the main Convert Virtual Machine Wizard page. Click Next to continue.

10. Verify the virtual machine name. You can take this opportunity to change the virtual machine name if necessary.

11. Enter an optional description of the virtual machine.

12. Click Next.

13. Specify the number of virtual processors that you want to assign to the virtual machine once it has been migrated to Hyper-V (see Figure 5-7).

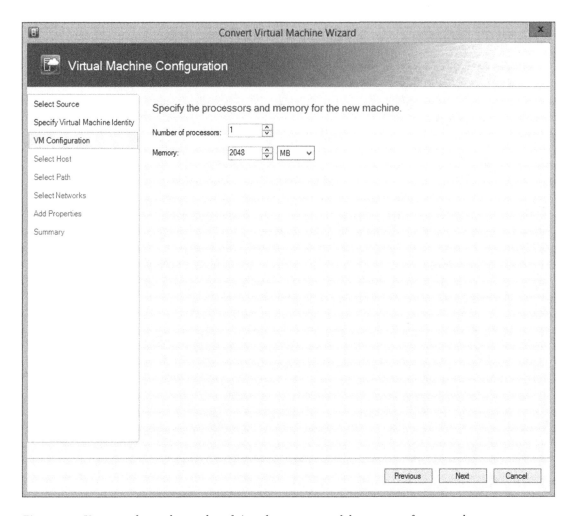

Figure 5-7. You must choose the number of virtual processors and the amount of memory that you want to assign to the virtual machine once it has been migrated to Hyper-V

14. Specify the amount of memory that you would like to assign to the virtual machine within Hyper-V.

15. Click Next.

16. Select the Hyper-V server on which you would like to host the virtual machine (see Figure 5-8). You have to be careful with making your selection because VMware servers also appear on the list. I am going to spend some time talking about the star ratings in a later chapter. Generally speaking, the more stars that appear next to the Hyper-V server, the better suited that server is for hosting the VM.

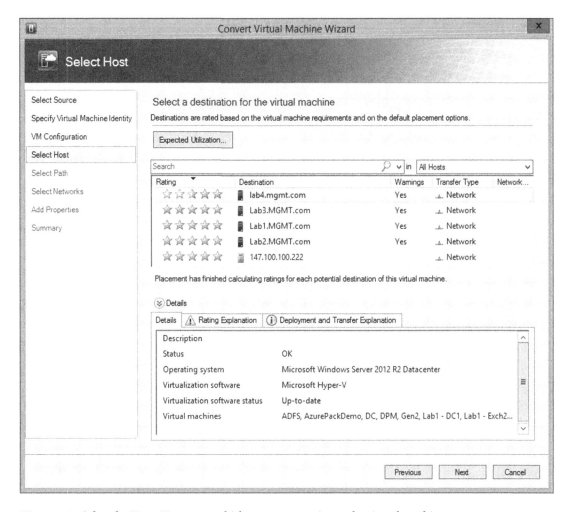

Figure 5-8. *Select the Hyper-V server to which you want to migrate the virtual machine*

17. Click Next.

18. Select the storage path where you want to place the virtual machine. If your ideal storage path is not listed when you click the Browse button, just go with the default location (as long as it has enough free storage space). You can always perform a storage migration later on. I will show you how to do so at the end of the next chapter.

19. Click Next.

20. You must now select either the virtual machine network or the Hyper-V virtual switch that you want to attach the virtual machine to after the migration completes. You can do this by selecting a virtual machine network from the VM Network drop-down list and / or by selecting a Hyper-V virtual switch from the Virtual Switch drop-down list (see Figure 5-9).

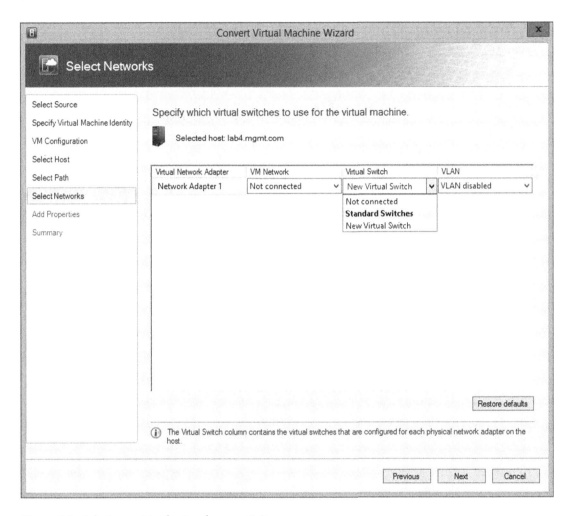

Figure 5-9. *Select your virtual network connectivity*

21. If necessary, select your VLAN identification from the VLAN drop-down list.

22. Click Next.

23. Choose an action to take when the host server starts. By default, virtual machines never automatically start when the host is booted, but you can change that behavior if desired (see Figure 5-10).

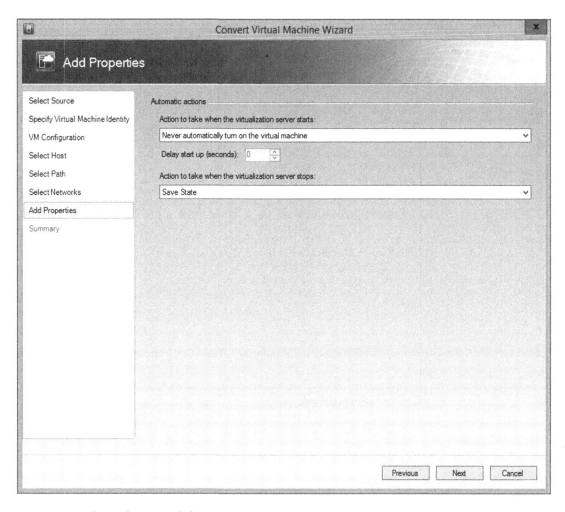

Figure 5-10. *Choose the startup behavior for the virtual machine*

24. Choose the action to take when the host server is shut down. By default, the virtual machine is placed into a saved state, but you can opt to turn off the virtual machine or to shut down the guest OS instead. I personally recommend going with the shut-down option.

25. Click Next.

26. Take a moment to review the summary information that is displayed (see Figure 5-11).

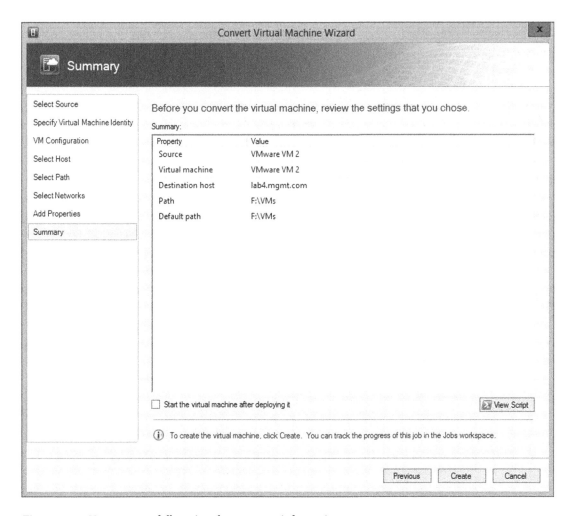

Figure 5-11. *You must carefully review the summary information*

27. Select the Start the Virtual Machine after Deploying It check box if you want the virtual machine to automatically start after it is created.

28. Click Create.

29. You can monitor the migration process through the Jobs window (see Figure 5-12).

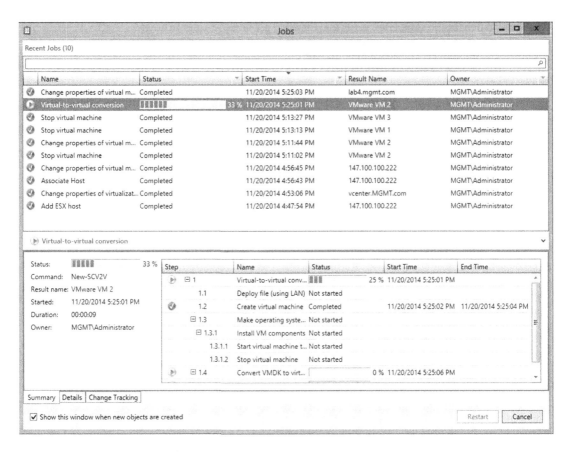

Figure 5-12. *You can monitor the migration's progress through the Jobs window*

30. When the job completes, verify that there are not any errors or warnings (see Figure 5-13). If you do run into problems, look at the troubleshooting techniques I cover later in this chapter.

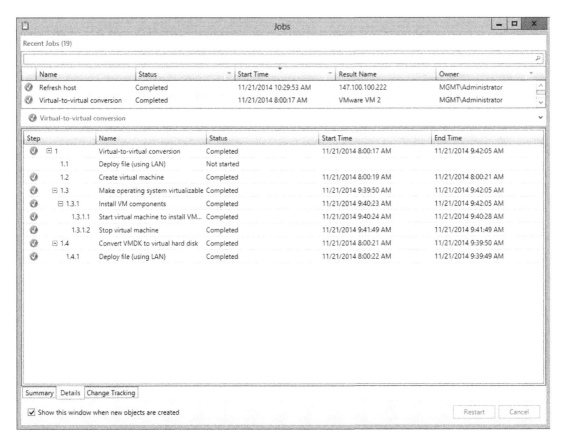

Figure 5-13. *Verify that the conversion has completed without any errors or warnings*

You can use the Summary tab in the Jobs window to verify the newly created virtual machine's configuration is correct (see Figure 5-14).

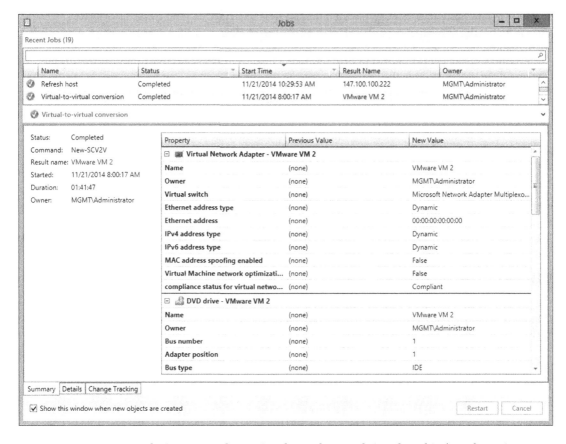

Figure 5-14. *You can use the Summary tab to review the newly created virtual machine's configuration*

What's Really Going On?

Hopefully your virtual machine migration went smoothly, but if not, the troubleshooting process requires that you know a little bit about what is going on behind the scenes.

There are quite a few moving parts involved in the migration process. There is, of course, a VMware ESX / ESXi server, a vCenter Server, a Hyper-V server, and a VMM server. If you look back at Figure 5-13, you can begin to get a feel for how these components interact with one another and the steps that are performed by VMM as a part of the migration process. The basic steps include:

1. Deploying file using LAN

2. Converting virtual machine

3. Making operating system virtualizable

4. Installing VM components

5. Starting virtual machine to install VM components

6. Stopping virtual machine

7. Converting VMDK to virtual hard disk

8. Deploying file using LAN

Keep in mind that these steps do not occur in the order listed by VMM (the order listed above). You can look at the time stamps shown in Figure 5-13 to get a better sense of the order in which the steps are performed.

Essentially, what happens is that BITS (Background Intelligent Transfer Service) is used to copy the contents of the VMDK file from the ESX / ESXi server to the Hyper-V server. This process results in the creation of a VHD file on the Hyper-V server. Although this results in a copy of the virtual machine being made on the Hyper-V server, the Hyper-V virtual machine is not yet usable because the virtual machine thinks that it is running on VMware.

This being the case, the newly created virtual hard disk is mounted on the Hyper-V host. The BITS service pulls the system registry hive from the VHD and copies it to the VMM server. The VMM server then corrects the system hive to allow the virtual machine to boot in a Hyper-V environment and uses BITS to pass the system hive back to the virtual hard disk.

As such, the success of the operation is based on the use of BITS. BITS is used to transfer files using HTTPS. The VMM server must be able to establish an HTTPS session with both the VMware server and the Hyper-V server.

What Went Wrong?

Now that I have shown you the migration process and given you a brief explanation of what is happening behind the scenes, I want to spend some time talking about some of the most common problems that you are likely to encounter and how to fix them.

Error 2940

One error that you might encounter is error 2940 (see Figure 5-15). This error states that VMM is unable to complete the requested file transfer because an HTTP connection to the VMware server could not be established.

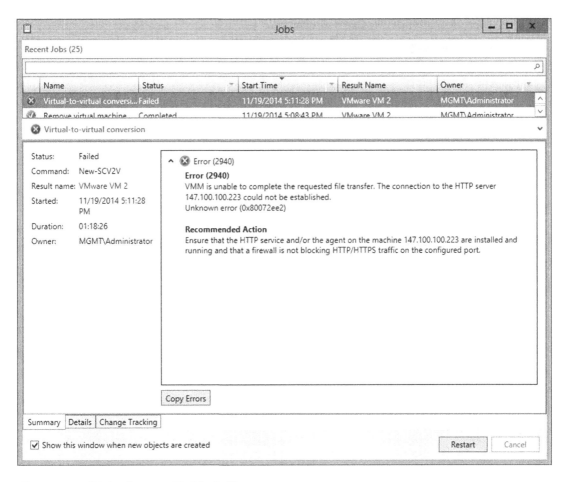

Figure 5-15. *This is what error 2940 looks like*

If you receive this error, the first thing that you should do is to make sure that you are not trying to convert a VMware virtual machine that is residing on an ESX / ESXi 5.5 server. As previously mentioned, ESX / ESXi 5.5 is not supported, and attempting a conversion from this version of VMware will result in error 2940.

So, what if you are using a supported version of ESX / ESXi and you still get this error? In that case, there are a few things that you can check. First, check to make sure that there are no firewall rules that are blocking HTTP or HTTPS traffic on any of the servers involved. You can access the Windows Firewall through the System and Security section of the Control Panel.

VMware ESX / ESXi also has its own firewall that is enabled by default. The VMware firewall isn't usually a problem, but if you get desperate you can disable it (I don't recommend doing this unless you have no choice). To do so, you will need to complete the following steps:

1. From the VMware console, press F2 and enter your credentials.

2. Scroll to the Troubleshooting Options and press Enter.

3. Select the Enable ESXi Shell option and press Enter.

4. Press the Escape key to return to the main console screen.

5. Press Alt–F1 to open the console window.

6. Enter your credentials.

7. When you arrive at the shell, enter this command:

    ```
    Esxcli network firewall set --enabled false
    ```

8. Type Exit and press Enter to close the shell.

Most Common Causes of Error 2940:

- Trying to convert a VM that resides on an ESX / ESXi 5.5 server

- Firewall blocking ports 80 and 443

Error 2912

Perhaps the most commonly encountered error when migrating a virtual machine from VMware to Hyper-V using VMM is error 2912. This is a generic error that basically states that "an internal error has occurred" (see Figure 5-16).

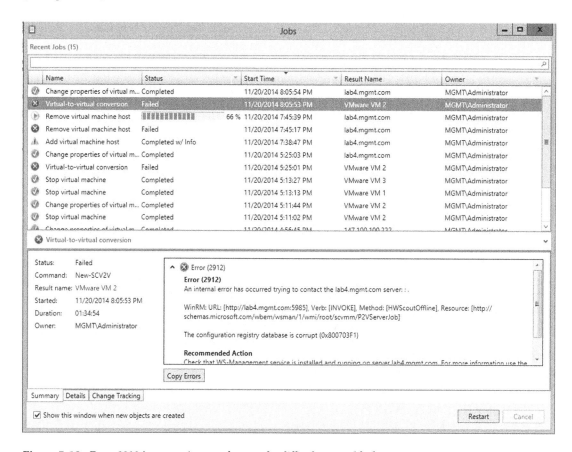

Figure 5-16. *Error 2912 is a generic error that can be difficult to troubleshoot*

Error 2912 can be surprisingly tough to troubleshoot for three main reasons:

- Error 2912 is a generic, catch-all error.

- The error details often contain inaccurate and misleading information.

- There are a lot of different things that can cause error 2912.

Lesson number one when troubleshooting error 2912 is to never trust the descriptive text that is displayed beneath the error. Let me show you what I mean. If you look back at Figure 5-16, you will see a particularly daunting error message with accompanying text that indicates that the registry is corrupt. In actuality, this error was caused by a missing certificate. The registry was fine.

The most common causes of error 2912 include:

- A missing or invalid certificate

- A port conflict

- A service problem (especially related to BITS or WS-Management)

- A missing agent

I will discuss each of these causes in the following sections.

Certificate Problems

Earlier in this chapter, I talked about how BITS is used for transferring data between servers as a part of the migration process. BITS uses HTTPS, which requires a certificate in order to be used for SSL encryption. The first BITS transfer occurs between the virtual machine manager and the VMware server. That transfer usually succeeds. The second BITS transfer occurs between VMM and the Hyper-V host. If the host certificate is missing (or is invalid) this second transfer will fail, resulting in a 2912 error. You can check for the presence of the required certificate by completing the following steps:

1. Log on to the VMM server using administrative credentials.

2. Enter the MMC command at the server's Run prompt. This will launch the Microsoft Management Console.

3. Select the Add / Remove Snap-In command from the console's File menu.

4. Select the Certificates snap-in (see Figure 5-17).

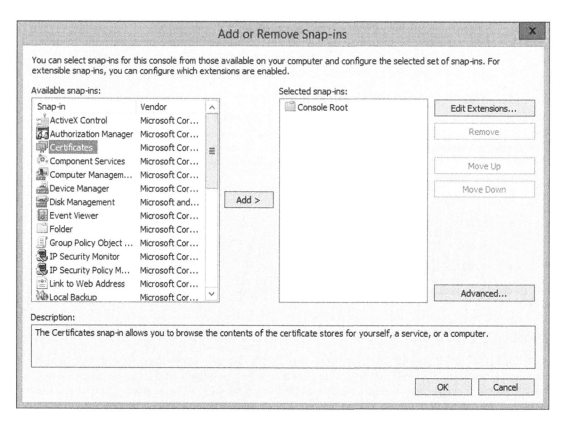

Figure 5-17. *Select the Certificates snap-in*

5. Click Add.

6. Select the Computer Account option.

7. Click Next.

8. Select the Local Computer option.

9. Click Finish.

10. Click OK.

11. Navigate through the console tree to Console Root ➤ Certificates (Local Computer) ➤ Trusted People ➤ Certificates.

12. Check for the existence of a certificate that matches the name of the Hyper-V server that you are trying to use as a migration destination (see Figure 5-18).

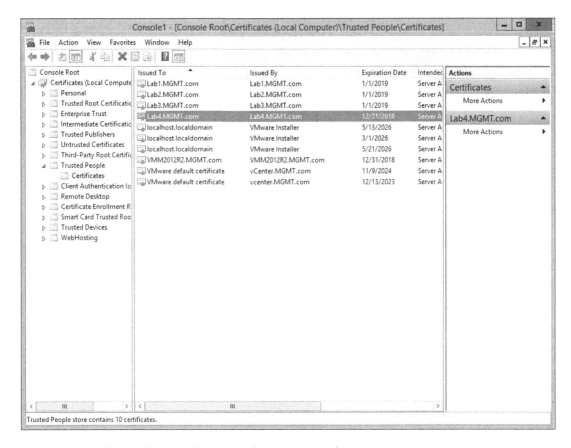

Figure 5-18. *Make sure that a certificate exists for your Hyper-V host*

If the certificate does not exist, you can fix the problem by removing the Hyper-V host from VMM (right click on the host and select Remove from the shortcut menu). After doing so, you can re-add the host by following the instructions found in Chapter 4.

If at some point along the way the host was already removed and re-added, then it is possible that there could be a certificate mismatch. If you suspect that to be the problem, you should remove the Hyper-V host, manually delete the certificate, and then re-add the host.

Port Conflicts

As previously explained, the migration process depends heavily on the use of BITS. For all practical purposes, BITS can be thought of as a Web server. However, BITS can break down if there is another service running on the host that uses common Web server ports (especially port 443).

I recommend checking to make sure that the World Wide Publishing Service is not running on your VMM server. If that service is running, a port conflict is likely to be the cause of your problem. To check for the existence of this service, complete the following steps:

1. Enter the Services.msc command at the server's Run prompt.

2. Check for the existence of the World Wide Publishing Service (see Figure 5-19).

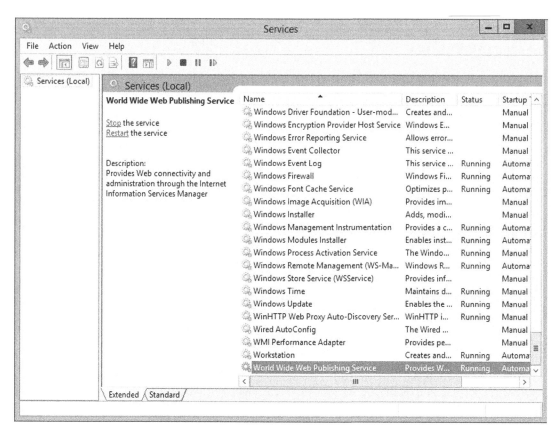

Figure 5-19. *Check to see if the World Wide Publishing Service exists on your VMM server*

The absence of the World Wide Publishing Service does not guarantee that no port conflict exists, but if the World Wide Publishing Service does exist, a port conflict is very likely to be the problem.

A Service Problem

The World Wide Publishing Service is not the only service that can cause problems. There are three critical services that must be running on your destination Hyper-V host in order for the virtual machine migration to succeed. These services are:

- System Center Virtual Machine Manager Agent

- BITS Compact Server

- Windows Remote Management (WS-Management)

You can use the instructions in the previous section to verify the existence of these services. Each of the services listed here must not only exist, but also its status must be listed as Running. If a service is listed, but is not running, try right clicking on the service and selecting the Start command from the shortcut menu (see Figure 5-20).

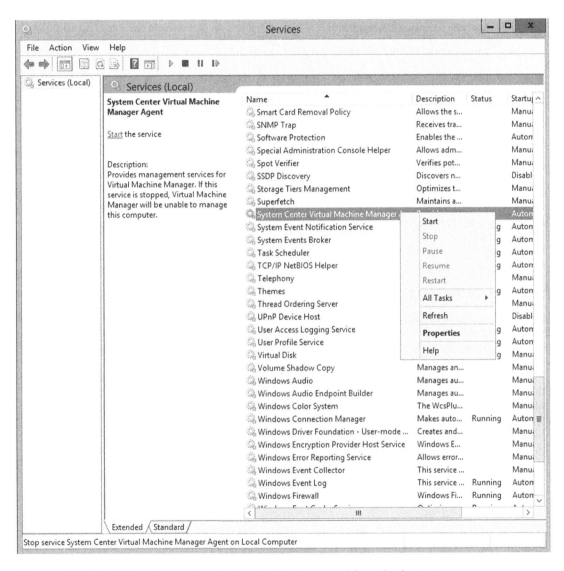

Figure 5-20. *Right click on the service and select the Start command from the shortcut menu*

Missing Agents

The previous section mentioned that the System Center Virtual Machine Manager Agent is a critical service. As the name implies, this service corresponds to the VMM agent. If the agent is missing, you should remove the host from VMM (along with any corresponding certificates) and then re-add the host according to the instructions in the previous chapter.

Post-Migration Tasks

Hopefully by now you have been able to resolve any errors and complete a virtual machine migration from VMware to Hyper-V. After the migration completes, there are several post-migration tasks that need to be completed. Some of these tasks may include:

- Verifying hardware allocations

- Making the virtual machine fault tolerant

- Starting the virtual machine

- Checking to make sure that the Integration Services have been installed

- Checking to make sure that the correct IP address is being used and updating DNS host records if necessary

- Reinstalling your antivirus software

Not all of these tasks will apply to every situation, but generally speaking these are the things that you will need to do after the migration process has been completed.

I'm not going to get into a discussion of these tasks because I have already talked about most of them earlier in the book. Tasks such as verifying IP addresses and reinstalling antivirus software are largely self-explanatory.

Moving Forward

Hopefully, you have been able to use this chapter to migrate your virtual machines from VMware to Hyper-V. If not, don't worry. I am going to show you an alternate method in the next chapter. The biggest advantages to that method are that VMM isn't required and that the method works for migrating ESX / ESXi 5.5–based virtual machines.

Once I finish talking about migrations, there are a couple of other things that I plan to discuss later in this book, such as talking about ways of protecting your Hyper-V virtual machines against data loss. The other thing that I plan to discuss is day-to-day Hyper-V management. For that, I have written a chapter explaining how to perform all of the most common management tasks for Hyper-V.

CHAPTER 6

░ ░ ░

An Alternate Migration Method

In this chapter, I want to show you an alternative method for migrating VMware virtual machines to Hyper-V, using a tool called the Microsoft Virtual Machine Converter.

Which Tool Should You Use?

In the previous chapter, I showed you how to migrate virtual machines from VMware to Hyper-V using System Center Virtual Machine Manager (VMM). The method that I used works especially well if you have a large number of virtual machines within your VMware infrastructure, and if you want to take your time with the migration process. It establishes long-term coexistence between Hyper-V and VMware and allows both environments to be managed through a common interface. The two environments can coexist for as long as might be required.

For all practical purposes, the technique discussed in the previous chapter is the preferred method for migrating from VMware to Hyper-V. However, it is not the best method in every situation. There are at least two major disadvantages to using VMM as a virtual machine migration tool:

- VMM is required (which means that you have to purchase the required software licenses).

- The technique does not work for migrating virtual machines that are hosted on ESX / ESXi 5.5.

Thankfully, the Microsoft Virtual Machine Converter overcomes these and other limitations. There are several advantages to using the Microsoft Virtual Machine Converter, including:

- The tool is free.

- It works without VMM.

- It works for converting virtual machines residing on ESX / ESXi 5.5 servers (versions 5.1 and 4.1 are also supported).

- The Microsoft Virtual Machine Converter is really easy to set up and use.

So, given the advantages of using the Microsoft Virtual Machine Converter, it is easy to wonder why I would ever recommend using VMM as a migration tool. The reason for this is that VMM is the best tool for managing Hyper-V environments. If you have more than two or three Hyper-V servers then you really should be using VMM. Since VMM is the best tool for managing Hyper-V, and since it can also be used to manage VMware, it makes sense to use VMM as a migration tool.

One thing that I want to point out before I get started is that you don't necessarily have to decide between one migration tool and the other. There are some situations in which it might be better to use a combination of tools. Suppose, for instance, that you have VMM, but you also have some VMs running on ESX 5.5. You could use the Microsoft Virtual Machine Converter to migrate the virtual machines, while continuing to use VMM for virtual machine management.

Microsoft Virtual Machine Converter Features

Before I get started, I want to point out that the Microsoft Virtual Machine Converter is much more than just a simple migration tool. It has a number of features that you might find useful. For example, the tool works with Windows and Linux VMs, it has a PowerShell interface that allows for scripted conversions and can be used to enable migrations from VMware to Microsoft Azure. Here is the full list of standard features as stated by Microsoft (http://blogs.technet.com/b/scvmm/archive/2014/10/13/microsoft-virtual-machine-converter-3-0-is-now-available-for-download.aspx):

- Converts virtual disks that are attached to a VMware virtual machine to virtual hard disks (VHDs) that can be uploaded to Microsoft Azure

- Provides native Windows PowerShell capability that enables scripting and integration into IT automation workflows

- Supports the conversion and provisioning of Linux-based guest operating systems from VMware hosts to Hyper-V hosts

- Supports the conversion of offline virtual machines

- Supports the new virtual hard disk format (VHDX) when converting and provisioning in Hyper-V in Windows Server 2012 R2 and Windows Server 2012

- Supports the conversion of virtual machines from VMware vSphere 5.5, VMware vSphere 5.1, and VMware vSphere 4.1 hosts for Hyper-V virtual machines

- Supports Windows Server 2012 R2, Windows Server 2012, and Windows 8 as guest operating systems that you can select for conversion

- Converts and deploys virtual machines from VMware hosts to Hyper-V hosts on any of the following operating systems:

  - Windows Server® 2012 R2

  - Windows Server® 2012

  - Windows Server® 2008 R2 SP1

- Converts VMware virtual machines, virtual disks, and configurations for memory, virtual processor, and other virtual computing resources from the source to Hyper-V

- Adds virtual network interface cards (NICs) to the converted virtual machine on Hyper-V

- Supports the conversion of virtual machines from VMware vSphere 5.5, VMware vSphere 5.0, and VMware vSphere 4.1 hosts to Hyper-V

- Has a wizard-driven GUI, which simplifies performing virtual machine conversions

- Uninstalls VMware Tools before online conversion (online only) to provide a clean way to migrate VMware-based virtual machines to Hyper-V

- Supports Windows Server and Linux guest operating system conversion

- Includes Windows PowerShell capability for offline conversions of VMware-based virtual hard disks (VMDK) to a Hyper-V–based virtual hard disk file format (.vhd file)

My Approach

As I said at the beginning of this book, I want to keep things as simple as possible for the benefit of those who might not have a lot of experience with Hyper-V environments. That being the case, my approach to the migration process will be to use the tool's GUI to perform a direct migration from VMware to Hyper-V.

For the purposes of this chapter, I have created three virtual machines (VMware VM 1, VMware VM 2, and VMware VM 3), and those virtual machines are running on ESX 5.5. My Hyper-V servers are running Windows Server 2012 R2.

Preparing for the Virtual Machine Converter

Even though the Microsoft Virtual Machine Converter is easy to use, there is quite a bit of prep work that you will need to do prior to installing the tool. If you think back to the previous chapter, you will recall that VMM acted as an intermediary between the Hyper-V and VMware environments. In the case of the Microsoft Virtual Machine Converter, an intermediary is still required, but it will take the form of a dedicated server that is running the Microsoft Virtual Machine Converter software. In case you are wondering, this dedicated machine can be either physical or virtual.

For the purposes of this book, I am going to be installing the Microsoft Virtual Machine Converter onto a Hyper-V virtual machine. My virtual machine will be running Windows Server 2012 R2, but Windows Server 2012 and Windows Server 2008 R2 are also supported.

I realize that I have already walked you through the process of creating Hyper-V virtual machines in a couple of different ways in some of the earlier chapters. Even so, I am going to do a lot of hand holding in this chapter and walk you through the entire process, starting with the creation of the virtual machine. I am doing this because there is a lot that can go wrong, and I want to maximize your chances of success by showing you all of the steps involved in the setup process.

Building the Virtual Machine

For the sake of this chapter, I am going to try to keep things simple by using the Hyper-V Manager to build a non-clustered Hyper-V virtual machine. We will use this virtual machine to run the Microsoft Virtual Machine Converter. You can build the required virtual machine by completing these steps:

1. Open the Hyper-V Manager.

2. Click on New ➤ Virtual Machine. This will launch the New Virtual Machine Wizard.

3. Click Next to bypass the wizard's Welcome page.

4. Enter a name for the virtual machine. I am going to be calling my virtual machine MSVMC.

5. Select the Store the Virtual Machine in a Different Location check box.

6. Enter a path to a storage location that has enough free disk space to accommodate copies of the virtual machines that you will be converting (see Figure 6-1).

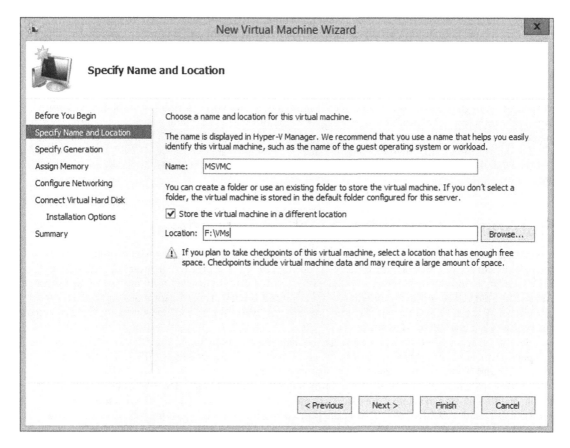

Figure 6-1. *You must place the virtual machine on a volume that has lots of free disk space*

7. Click Next.

8. Select your virtual machine generation. Either generation is acceptable for our purposes.

9. Click Next.

10. Enter the startup memory for the virtual machine. Microsoft doesn't specify the minimum amount of memory required by the Virtual Machine Converter. However, given the dependencies that are going to have to run on the server, I recommend setting the startup memory to 4096 MB or higher.

11. Click Next.

12. Connect your virtual machine to a Hyper-V virtual switch.

13. Click Next.

14. You must now set the size for the virtual hard disk. The default size is 127 GB, but that might not always be adequate. The virtual machine must have enough free space to accommodate a copy of all of the virtual machines that are being migrated. Virtual machines are migrated one at a time, so for now you will only need to accommodate a single virtual machine copy. Even so, you will need enough space to accommodate the largest VM that you plan on migrating. Don't forget that you will also need some extra space for the guest OS and the various components used by the migration software. The maximum virtual hard disk size that you can configure in Hyper-V is 64 TB (see Figure 6-2).

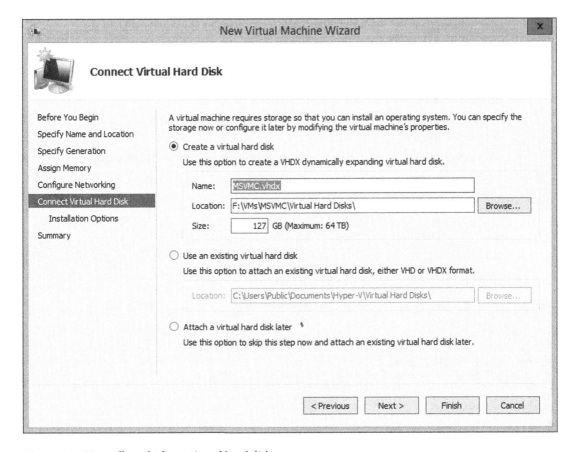

Figure 6-2. *You will need a large virtual hard disk*

15. Click Next.

16. Choose the option to install an operating system from a bootable CD / DVD ROM.

17. Insert your Windows Server installation DVD into the server's DVD drive.

18. Click Next.

19. Review your configuration and then click Finish.

20. Boot the virtual machine and then install and configure Windows Server.

Preparing Your Hyper-V Server

Before you will be able to perform a virtual machine migration using the Microsoft Virtual Machine Converter, you will need to create a file share on your Hyper-V server. This file share will act as a repository for the virtual machine files.

You don't have to worry about creating a share on the volume where your other Hyper-V virtual machines reside. For now, we just need to worry about getting the virtual machines to the Hyper-V server. I will show you how to move the virtual machines to a more appropriate storage location in Chapter 8.

You can create the necessary file share by completing the following steps:

1. Open File Explorer on your Hyper-V server and navigate to the location in which you want to create the share. Remember, this location needs to have enough free space to accommodate the virtual machines.

2. Right click within the window and choose the New ➤ Folder commands from the shortcut menu.

3. Give the folder a name. I am going to call the folder on my lab server VMware.

4. Right click on the VMware folder and choose the Properties command from the shortcut menu.

5. When the folder's properties sheet appears, select the Sharing tab (see Figure 6-3).

Figure 6-3. *Select the Sharing tab*

6. Click the Share button.

7. In a production environment you will obviously need to be careful regarding with whom you share the folder. Since every organization's permissions structure is different, I am going to make the folder an open share with no security. To do so, enter Everyone into the Name field.

8. Click Add.

9. Click on the Down arrow next to Read (in the Everyone row) and then choose the Read / Write option (see Figure 6-4).

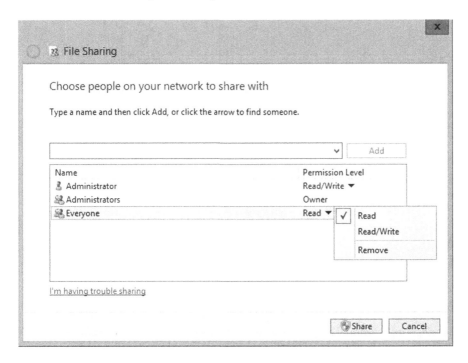

Figure 6-4. *Select the Read / Write option*

10. Click Share.

11. Make note of the share's UNC name (see Figure 6-5). In our example, the UNC path is \\Lab4\VMware.

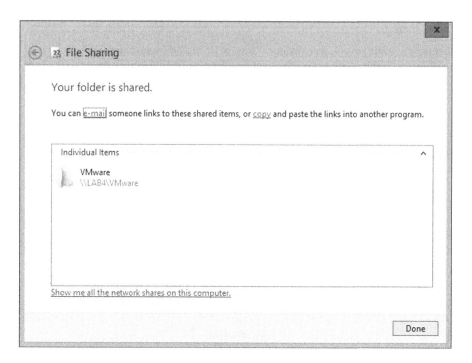

Figure 6-5. *Make a note of the share's UNC name*

12. Click Done.

13. Click Close.

Configuring Your Virtual Machine

Now it's time to begin configuring the virtual machine. There are several prerequisites that need to be fulfilled prior to your migrating any VMware virtual machines. I will walk you through the process of configuring the virtual machine. Before I do, however, it is important to install all of the available patches for Windows Server. Some Windows Server versions will produce an error during the feature-deployment portion of the procedure if Windows is not fully patched.

After patching the VM, you can install the prerequisite components onto the VM. The prerequisites include:

- Microsoft .NET Framework
  - Microsoft .NET Framework 3.5 and .NET Framework 4 if you install MVMC on Windows Server 2008 R2 SP1.
  - Microsoft .NET Framework 4.5 if you install MVMC on Windows Server 2012 or Windows 8.
- Background Intelligent Transfer Service (BITS) Compact Server
- Visual C++ Redistributable for Visual Studio 2012 Update 1

You can configure the VM and install the prerequisites by completing these steps:

1. Join the VM to your management domain. Instructions for joining a domain are found in Chapter 1.

2. Log in to your VM and open Server Manager.

3. Choose the Add Roles and Features command from the Manage menu. This will cause Windows to launch the Add Roles and Features Wizard.

4. Click Next to bypass the wizard's Welcome page.

5. Select either the Role-Based or Feature-Based Installation option.

6. Click Next.

7. Make sure that your virtual machine is selected within the server pool.

8. Click Next.

9. Click Next to bypass the Server Roles page.

10. When you reach the Select Features page, select the .NET Framework 3.5 feature.

11. Select .NET Framework 4.5.

12. Select the Background Intelligent Transfer Service (BITS) feature.

13. If you are prompted to install any additional features, click Install Feature.

14. Expand the Background Intelligent Transfer Service (BITS) container.

15. Select the Compact Server check box (see Figure 6-6).

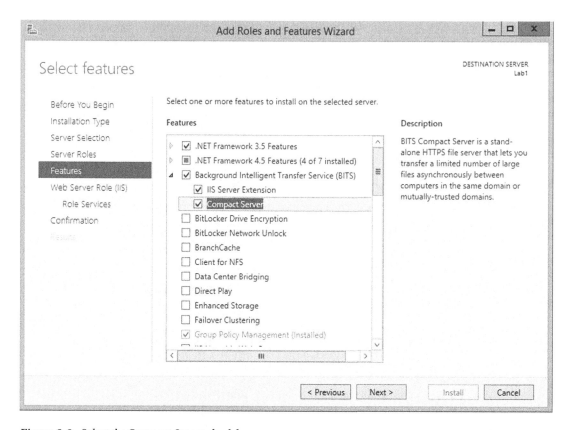

Figure 6-6. *Select the Compact Server check box*

16. Click Next.

17. When you see the Web Server Role (IIS) page, click Next.

18. Click Next on the Role Services page.

19. When you reach the Confirmation page, select the Restart the Destination Server Automatically if Required check box.

20. Click Install.

21. If prompted, click Yes to allow an automatic restart.

22. When the installation process completes, click Close.

23. Download Visual C++ Redistributable for Visual Studio 2012 Update 4 from

    www.microsoft.com/en-us/download/details.aspx?id=30679

    This component will allow Windows to run C++ applications that were built using Visual Studio 2012.

24. When the download completes, you will need to double click on the file in order to execute it.

25. When the installer launches, select the I Agree to the License Terms and Conditions check box (see Figure 6-7).

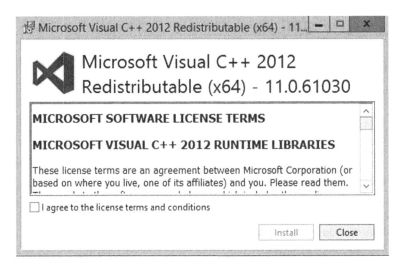

Figure 6-7. *Accept the license agreement and click Install*

26. Click Install.

27. When the installation completes, click Close.

Acquiring and Installing the Microsoft Virtual Machine Converter

Now that all of the prerequisites are in place, it is time to install the Microsoft Virtual Machine Converter. For the purposes of this book, I will be using version 3.0. You can deploy the Microsoft Virtual Machine Converter by completing these steps:

1. Download the Microsoft Virtual Machine Converter from

   `www.microsoft.com/en-us/download/details.aspx?id=42497`

2. When the download completes, double click on the `MVMC_Setup.MSI` file that you have downloaded. This will cause Windows to launch the Microsoft Virtual Machine Converter Setup Wizard.

3. Click Next to bypass the wizard's Welcome page.

4. Accept the terms of the license agreement.

5. Click Next.

6. Click Next to accept the default installation path.

7. Click Install.

8. When the installation process completes, click Finish.

Planning the Migration Logistics

The planning process for migrations based on the Microsoft Virtual Machine Converter is similar to what I discussed in the Chapter 5.

Migration Considerations

Here are some of the things that you must consider.

- Make a backup before you begin. The migration process is relatively safe and leaves the original VM intact on the VMware server. Even so, best practices mandate making a backup before attempting a migration.

- Make sure that ESX / ESXi servers are connected to a vCenter Server. vCenter is a requirement for VMware migrations using the Microsoft Virtual Machine Converter.

- Make note of your virtual machine's IP address. If the virtual machine uses a static IP address, there is a chance that you may have to manually enter it into the VM after the migration completes. You might also end up having to manually correct DNS host records for the VMs that you are converting. It just depends on how your organization is set up. If your Hyper-V virtual network exists in a different subnet than your VMware virtual network is in, you might not be able to reuse a virtual machine's previous IP address.

- Although not technically a requirement, I recommend uninstalling the antivirus software from a virtual machine before attempting a migration. The migration process tends to confuse certain types of antivirus software, which might interpret the new virtual hard disk structure as malware-related damage. The best way to keep that from happening is to simply remove the antivirus software before the migration and then put it back after the migration completes.

Planning for Running Virtual Machines

One of the big limitations that I talked about with regard to using VMM as a migration tool was that virtual machines had to be taken offline prior to the migration process. This limitation doesn't exist in the Microsoft Virtual Machine Converter. You can convert a virtual machine whether it is powered on or not. However, I would not recommend converting a running production virtual machine during business hours because there could be service interruptions during the migration.

If the virtual machine that you are converting is running, has Windows installed, and is using VMware Tools, then you will need to make sure that remote access through WMI is enabled on the VM. You must also be prepared to provide a set of administrative credentials for the VM as a part of the conversion process.

WMI is included with all modern Windows operating systems, but remote access has to be manually enabled. The exact steps for doing so will vary depending on the version of Windows that is running on the virtual machine. In the case of Windows Server 2012 R2, you can enable remote access for WMI by following these steps:

1. Log in to the VM using an account that has administrative privileges.

2. Open Server Manager.

3. Choose the Computer Management command from Server Manager's Tools menu. This will cause Windows to launch the Computer Management console.

4. Navigate through the console tree to Service and Applications ➤ WMI Control.

5. Right click on the WMI Control container and choose the Properties command from the shortcut menu (see Figure 6-8). This will cause the WMI Control Properties dialog box to open.

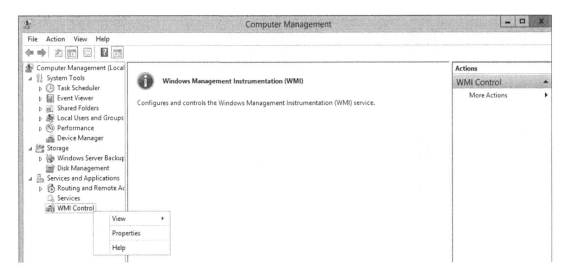

Figure 6-8. *Right click on the WMI Control container and select the Properties command from the shortcut menu*

6. Select the dialog box's Security tab.

7. Click the Security button.

8. When you perform the migration process later on, the Microsoft Virtual Machine Converter will prompt you to enter an account that has administrative access to the virtual machine. Whichever account you plan on using must have remote access through WMI. For the purposes of this book, I am going to be using the built-in Administrator account, but you can use any account you want so long as it has administrative permissions. If you choose to use an account other than the built-in account, click the Add button and add the account.

9. Select the account that you want to enable for remote access to the server.

10. Select the Allow check box for Remote Enable (see Figure 6-9).

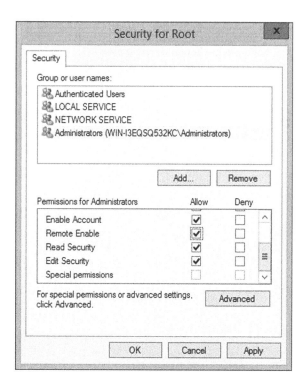

Figure 6-9. *Select the Allow check box for Remote Enable*

11. Click OK.

12. Click OK again.

13. If the Windows Firewall is running on the virtual machine then you will need to allow WMI traffic through the firewall. Depending on which Windows Server operating system version is running on the virtual machine, this may or may not require manual intervention. The easiest way to allow WMI traffic through the Windows Firewall is to open a Command Prompt window (not PowerShell) and enter: `NetSH Firewall Set Service RemoteAdmin Enable` (see Figure 6-10). If you look at the figure, you will notice that the command worked, but also that I received a message stating that this command has been deprecated. The reason why I chose to use this particular command is because it works in Windows versions both old and new.

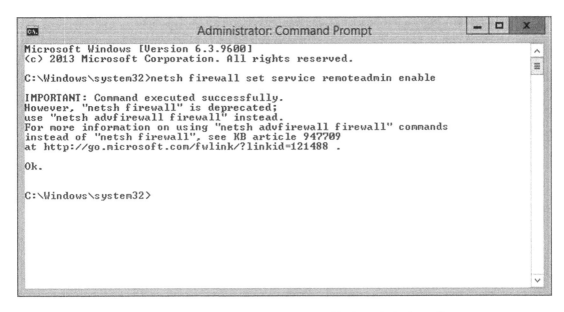

Figure 6-10. You can use the NetSh command to allow WMI traffic through the firewall

Another thing that you will have to think about ahead of time is the virtual machine's state. In other words, do you want to leave the virtual machine running after the migration? If so, then should the VM be running on the VMware server or on the Hyper-V server?

The Migration Process

As previously explained, the Microsoft Virtual Machine Converter will allow you to migrate virtual machines from VMware to Hyper-V. The software also makes it possible to migrate VMware virtual machines to Microsoft Azure, but Azure migrations are beyond the scope of this book.

As previously mentioned, I have set up a vSphere 5.5 server that is running three virtual machines (VMware VM 1, VMware VM 2, and VMware VM 3). Each of these virtual machines is running Windows Server 2012 R2 as a guest operating system and has VMware Tools installed. I am going to show you how to use the Microsoft Virtual Machine Converter to migrate these three virtual machines to a Windows Server 2012 R2 server that has the Hyper-V role installed. For the purposes of this demonstration, the virtual machines will be running during the migration.

Here is a walkthrough of a sample virtual machine migration:

1. Open File Explorer on the machine that will be coordinating the migration process.

2. Assuming that you used the default installation path, navigate to C:\Program Files\Microsoft Virtual Machine Converter.

3. Double click on MVMC.GUI.exe (the .EXE portion of the file name is hidden by default). This will launch the Microsoft Virtual Machine Converter.

4. Click Next.

5. You will now see a screen asking if you want to perform a virtual machine conversion or a physical machine conversion. Choose the Virtual Machine Conversion option.

6. Click Next.

7. You should now see a screen asking if you want to migrate to Microsoft Azure or if you want to migrate to Hyper-V. Choose the Migrate to Hyper-V option.

8. Click Next.

9. Enter a name or an IP address for your Hyper-V server.

10. Enter a set of credentials for an account with Domain Admin privileges.

11. Click Next.

12. Enter the UNC name for the file share where you will initially be storing the virtual machines on your Hyper-V server (see Figure 6-11).

Figure 6-11. *Enter the UNC name for the file share that you created earlier*

13. Choose whether you want to create fixed-size virtual hard disks or dynamically expanding virtual hard disks on the Hyper-V server. Fixed-length virtual hard disks tend to perform better, but require more disk space up front.

14. Choose whether you want to create VHD- or VHDX-based virtual hard disks. You should always use VHDX unless you are planning to eventually migrate the virtual machines to an older version of Hyper-V (pre-Windows Server 2012) or to Microsoft Azure.

15. Click Next.

16. Enter an IP address, computer name, or fully qualified domain name for your vCenter server. As an alternative, you can connect directly to an ESX or ESXi server, but my instructions are based on connecting to a vCenter server.

17. Enter a set of credentials that can be used to connect to your VMware server.

18. Click Next.

19. Select a virtual machine to convert (see Figure 6-12). Unfortunately, you cannot select multiple virtual machines.

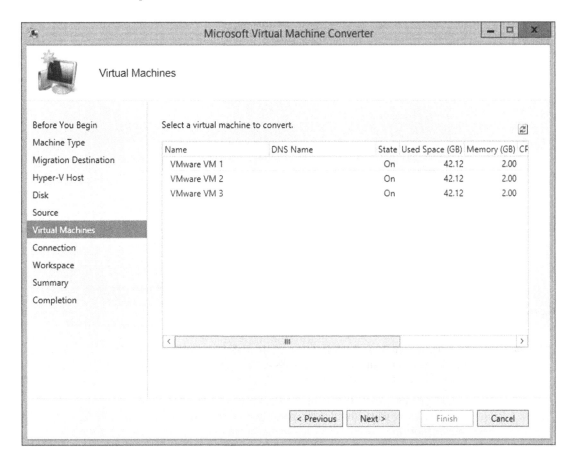

Figure 6-12. *Select a virtual machine to convert*

20.   Click Next.

21.   Enter a set of credentials for logging in to your virtual machine. You must use the same account for which you previously enabled remote WMI access.

22.   Select the final state of the source virtual machine (usually off).

23.   Select the final state of the destination virtual machine (usually on) (see Figure 6-13).

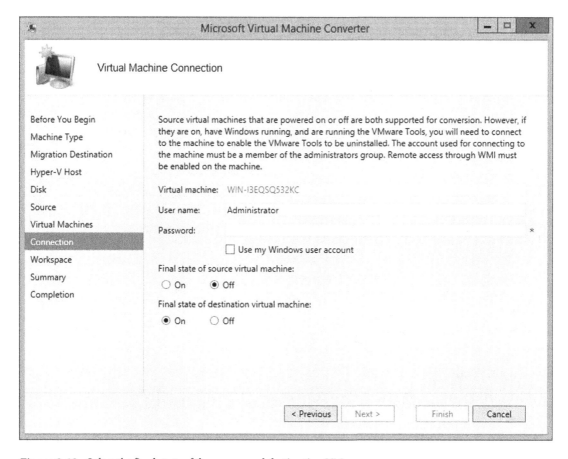

Figure 6-13. *Select the final state of the source and destination VMs*

24.   Click Next. The converter will validate your credentials. If you receive an error message, check to make sure that no firewalls are blocking the connection. Remember, VMware and Windows each have their own firewalls.

25.   Create a folder on the server that is running the Microsoft Virtual Machine Converter. This folder will be used to temporarily store converted virtual hard disks and therefore must reside on a volume that contains enough free space to accommodate all of the converted disks. You must also make sure to set the security settings so that you will have full control over the folder.

26. Enter the path to the folder that you have created into the wizard (see Figure 6-14).

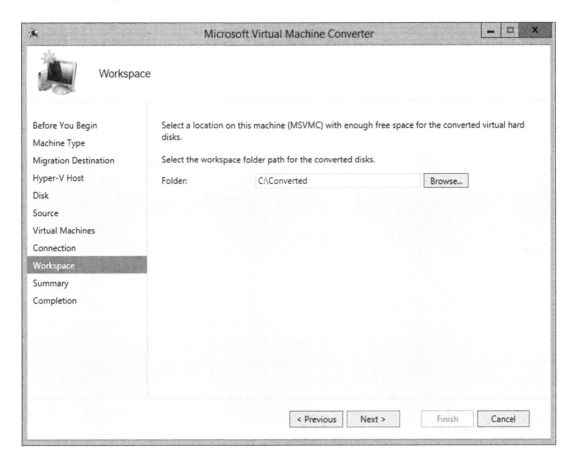

***Figure 6-14.** Enter the path to the folder that you created*

27. Click Next.

28. Verify the summary information for the virtual machines and address any warnings that might be displayed (see Figure 6-15).

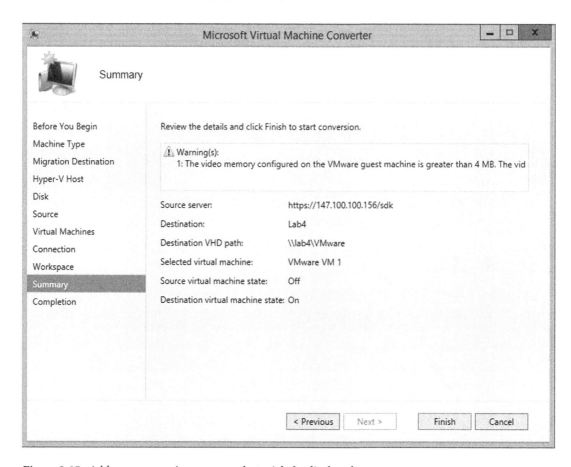

Figure 6-15. *Address any warning messages that might be displayed*

29. When all of the warnings have been addressed, click Finish. This will cause the conversion process to begin (see Figure 6-16).

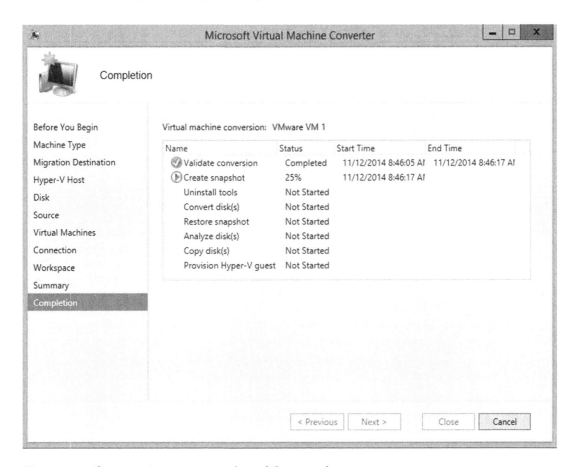

Figure 6-16. *The conversion process can take a while to complete*

30. When the conversion completes, click Close (see Figure 6-17). As you can see in the figure, the conversion of this one virtual machine took about 32 minutes to complete. This was a small lab machine, so it is very possible that a production VM could take much longer to convert.

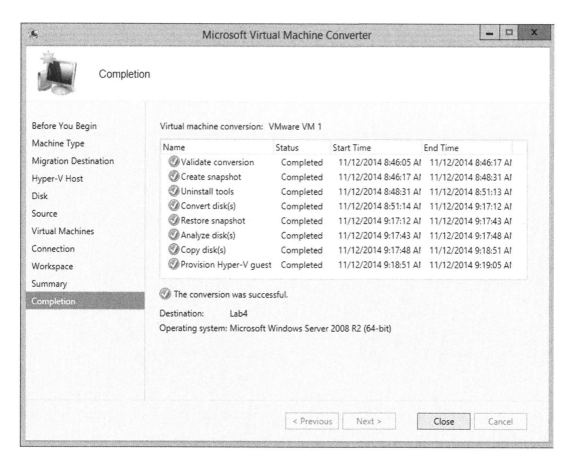

Figure 6-17. *The conversion process has completed successfully*

31. Verify that the virtual machine exists in Hyper-V Manager and that it is running and accessible (see Figure 6-18).

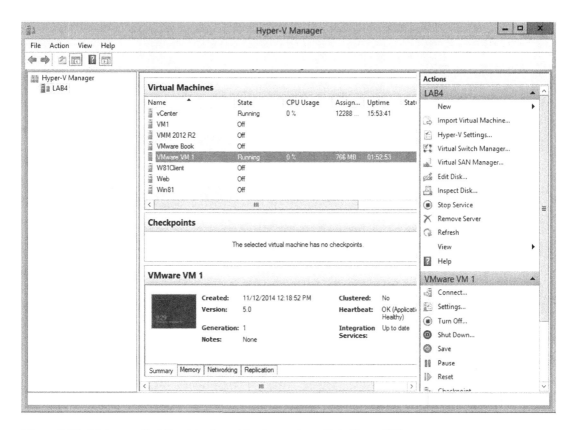

Figure 6-18. *Make sure that the virtual machine is running within Hyper-V Manager*

32.   Verify that the virtual machine still exists as a VMware virtual machine, but is not running (see Figure 6-19).

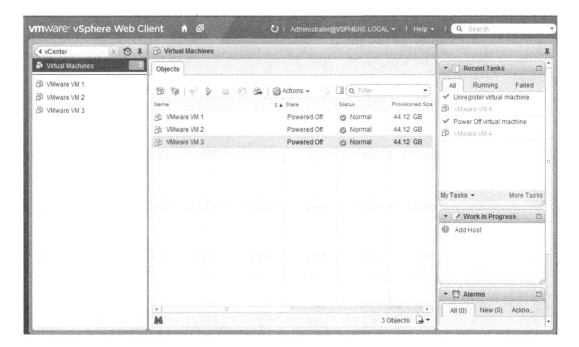

Figure 6-19. *The virtual machine should still exist in the VMware environment, but it should not be running*

33.   Install Hyper-V Integration Services if necessary.

34.   When you are satisfied that the virtual machine is working properly on Hyper-V, delete the VMware virtual machine.

35.   Repeat the process for any additional virtual machines that you want to migrate.

Third-Party Migration Tools

If, for whatever reason, neither of the Microsoft approaches to virtual machine migration meet your needs then there are a couple of third-party products that you can use. Please keep in mind that I am not endorsing these solutions. I am merely presenting them as alternative options. It is up to you to figure out which tool best meets your own migration needs.

Vision Solutions Double-Take Move

Vision Solutions Double-Take Move (`www.visionsolutions.com/Products/DT-Move.aspx`) supports Physical-to-Physical (P2P), Physical-to-Virtual (P2V), and Virtual-to-Physical (V2P) migrations. Migration sources can include Windows Server, VMware, and Amazon Web Services. Virtual machines can be migrated to Windows Server, Hyper-V, and Microsoft Azure.

Double-Take's primary strengths are its flexibility with regard to supported sources and destinations and the fact that migrations can usually be completed with minimal downtime. However, Double-Take requires an agent to be installed within the source and target operating systems, and there is a per-VM migration cost.

5nine V2V Easy Converter

Another third-party solution is 5nine V2V Easy Converter (`www.5nine.com/vmware-hyper-v-v2v-conversion-free.aspx`). This is a free, standalone migration tool that doesn't require any additional 5nine software licenses. This tool does not perform a true online conversion, but it is designed to minimize downtime during the conversion process. The tool is designed to work with Windows, Ubuntu, and CentOS VMs.

Moving On

In this chapter, I walked you through the process of using the Microsoft Virtual Machine Converter to migrate virtual machines from VMware to Hyper-V. Along the way, I also introduced a few third-party tools. If you would like to learn more about the Microsoft Virtual Machine Converter, then Microsoft has an excellent video available at

`http://channel9.msdn.com/Events/TechEd/NorthAmerica/2014/DCIM-B331#fbid=`

In the next chapter, I want to spend some time talking about ways of protecting your Hyper-V virtual machines against data loss. The last chapter of the book will talk about the day-to-day management and maintenance of Hyper-V virtual machines.

■ ■ ■

CHAPTER 7

Virtual Machine Protection

So far in this book, I have shown you some of the basics of working with Hyper-V as well as how you can migrate virtual machines from a VMware host to a Hyper-V server. There are still some things that I want to show you regarding the day–to-day management and maintenance of Hyper-V. Before I get to that, however, I want to take a time out and talk about protecting your Hyper-V virtual machines.

When your VMs existed in a VMware environment, you no doubt used backups and possibly some other protective mechanisms to protect your virtual machines. Now that you have migrated those VMs to Hyper-V, your existing protective mechanisms are no longer going to provide any protection (assuming that those protective mechanisms were VMware specific). That being the case, I think that it makes a lot of sense to spend some time talking about various ways of protecting your Hyper-V virtual machines.

A Crash Course in Hyper-V Backups

Backing up a Hyper-V environment is very similar to backing up a VMware environment. A lot of the same concepts apply to both environments. Even so, there are a few best practices for Hyper-V backups.

I don't want to spend too much time talking about backups, as there are a lot of other things that I want to get to. Besides, most of the best practices for Hyper-V backups are backup-application specific.

So, what are some of the things that you should look for in a Hyper-V backup solution? The biggest things to look for are Hyper-V awareness and application awareness. Let me explain.

When Hyper-V was first released, very few backup applications supported virtual machine backups. As such, backups had to be made at the guest level by installing a backup agent into each individual virtual machine. This method worked, but it was tedious and didn't provide any hypervisor-level protection. For example, virtual machine snapshots were not included in the backup because the backup agent was unaware that it was running on a virtual machine.

Pretty much all modern Hyper-V backup solutions run at the host level. Some of the earlier host-level backup solutions lacked granularity. For example, you might not be able to restore individual components within a virtual machine. You might only be able to restore at the virtual machine level. Thankfully, this has changed over time, and almost all of the current backup solutions offer true granularity for Hyper-V recovery. It's just important to make sure that the backup application that you choose is able to automatically detect the newly created or newly migrated virtual machines.

The other important thing to look for is application awareness. As with any other backup solution, the product that you choose to use for backing up Hyper-V needs to be able to back up and restore applications such as Exchange Server or SQL Server that are running inside of a virtual machine.

- A backup solution must be Hyper-V aware and must automatically discover and protect newly created or recently migrated virtual machines.

- Guest-level backups will work in a pinch, but host-level backups are almost always preferable.

Checkpoints

Another protective feature that I want to discuss is the virtual machine checkpoint. In versions of Hyper-V earlier than Windows Server 2012, checkpoints were referred to as snapshots. As the name implies, Hyper-V snapshots (or checkpoints) are very similar to VMware snapshots.

A checkpoint gives you the ability to roll a virtual machine back to the state in which it existed at an earlier point in time. The nice thing about checkpoints is that creating and using them is a very quick and easy process. You can usually create or use a checkpoint within a matter of a few seconds. Needless to say, this is much faster than creating or restoring a backup. As helpful as checkpoints are, however, there are three very important things that you need to know before using them.

Understanding Checkpoints

The first thing that you need to know about checkpoints is that they are not application aware, at least not yet. There is no rule that says that you cannot create a checkpoint on a production virtual machine. However, using the checkpoint to revert the virtual machine to an earlier point in time can have some unintended consequences, especially for application servers. Because the checkpoint process is not application aware, applying a checkpoint to an application server can cause data corruption within the application or it can cause the application to be placed into a dirty shutdown state. It is worth noting, however, that Microsoft is introducing application-aware checkpoints in the next release of Hyper-V.

Another important thing that you need to know about checkpoints is that they do not provide the same degree of protection as a backup. When you create a backup, you are creating a copy of the data that you are trying to protect. Checkpoints do not create copies of data. Instead, checkpoints are based on the use of differencing disks.

When you create a checkpoint, Hyper-V creates a differencing disk that has a parent/child relationship to the virtual machine's virtual hard disk. At that point, the virtual hard disk becomes read only, and all of the write operations are directed to the differencing disk. If the virtual machine needs to be rolled back to an earlier point in time, then the differencing disk is deleted and write operations are redirected to the original virtual hard disk. The original virtual hard disk is still in the same state that it existed in at the time that the checkpoint was created.

One last thing that I want to quickly mention about checkpoints is that if you accumulate a large number of checkpoints for a virtual machine, those checkpoints can degrade read performance. Windows is smart enough to know that the most recently created checkpoint (or rather its differencing disk) contains the most recently written data. When a read operation occurs, the reoperation is directed against the most recent differencing disk. If the requested data is not found within that differencing disk, then Hyper-V redirects the read requests to the next most recent differencing disk. Read operations progress further and further down the chain of differencing disks until either the data is found or the original virtual hard disk has been examined. The more checkpoints that exist for a virtual machine, the more differencing disks will also exist, and the longer that read requests will take.

Important Points:

- Checkpoints are a convenience feature, not a disaster-recovery feature. They do not create copies of your data.

- Checkpoints do not provide backup-grade protection. In fact, a checkpoint is likely to exist on the same volume as its associated virtual hard disk.

- Checkpoints are not application aware, although application awareness is going to be a part of the next version of Hyper-V. Using a checkpoint to roll back an application server can severely damage the application.

- Keeping an excessive number of checkpoints for a VM can degrade the VM's read performance.

Working with Checkpoints

Now that I have spent some time talking about checkpoints, I want to show you how to create and use checkpoints in Hyper-V. It is worth noting that although it is possible to create checkpoints using the Hyper-V Manager, this chapter will focus on using System Center Virtual Machine Manager (VMM).

Creating a Checkpoint

You can create a checkpoint for a virtual machine by completing these steps:

1. Open the VMM console.

2. Select the VMs and Services workspace.

3. Right click on the VM for which you want to create a checkpoint and then select the Create Checkpoint command from the shortcut menu (see Figure 7-1).

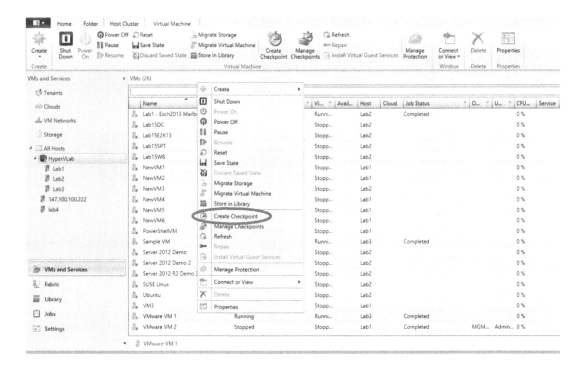

Figure 7-1. *Right click on the VM and select the Create Checkpoint command from the shortcut menu*

4. Enter a name for the checkpoint that you are creating. Although not a requirement, it is also a really good idea to enter a description of why the checkpoint was created (see Figure 7-2).

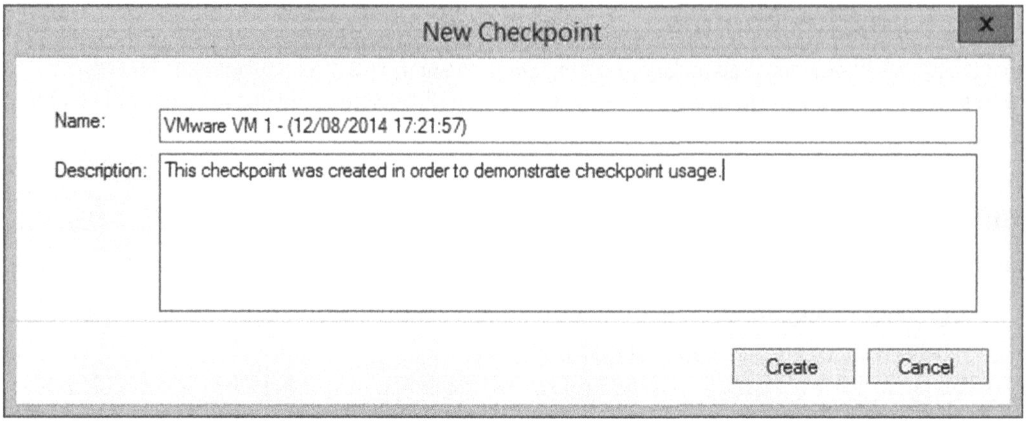

Figure 7-2. *Enter a name and a description for your checkpoint*

5.   Click the Create button.

6.   Look at the most recent job (in the Recent Job section) to confirm that the checkpoint was created successfully (see Figure 7-3).

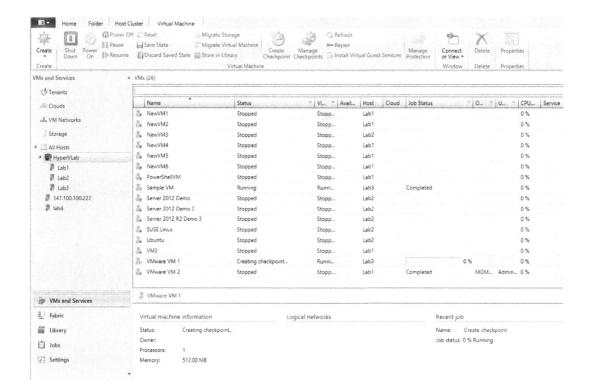

Figure 7-3. *Make sure that the checkpoint has been created successfully*

Restoring a Checkpoint

Now that I have shown you how to create a checkpoint for a virtual machine, let's take a look at how to revert a virtual machine to a previous state by restoring a checkpoint. You can restore a checkpoint by completing the following steps:

1. Open the VMM console.

2. Select the VMs and Services workspace.

3. Right click on the virtual machine for which you want to restore the checkpoint and choose the Manage Checkpoints command from the shortcut menu. This will cause Windows to display the virtual machine's Properties dialog box, with the Checkpoints tab selected (see Figure 7-4).

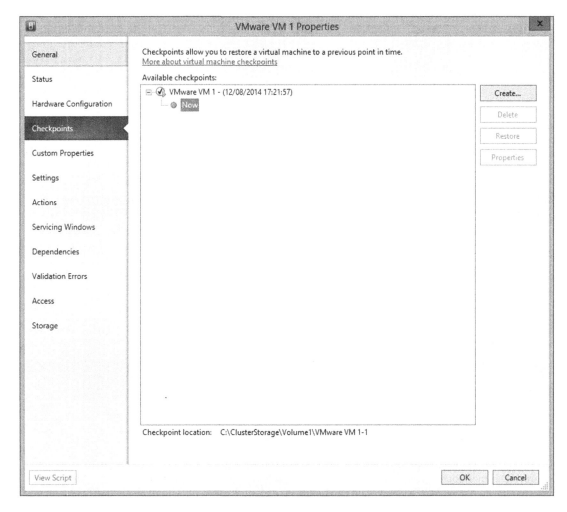

Figure 7-4. The Checkpoints tab allows you to manage checkpoints for the virtual machine

4. Select the checkpoint that you want to restore. Although only a single checkpoint is shown in Figure 7-4, it is possible for a VM to have multiple checkpoints.

5. Click on the Restore button.

6. When prompted, click Yes to confirm that you want to restore the checkpoint.

7. Click OK.

8. Check the Recent Job section to confirm that the restoration has been successful (see Figure 7-5). It is also a good idea to check the virtual machine's status. Windows virtual machines that have Integration Services installed will usually continue to display a status of Running, but other types of VMs may be put into a saved state, which means that you will have to manually start the VM.

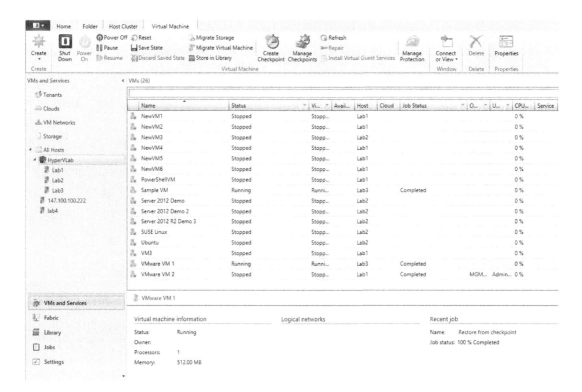

Figure 7-5. *Make sure that the Restore from Checkpoint job was successful*

Checkpoint Details

The procedure that I just demonstrated was really simple because there was only one checkpoint to restore. As previously mentioned, however, a virtual machine can have multiple checkpoints. Entering a meaningful description when you create a checkpoint can help you to identify each checkpoint and its purpose later on. However, if you look at Figure 7-4, you will notice that the checkpoint description is not shown. So, how can you go about accessing the checkpoint description?

If you look at Figure 7-6, you will see that I have created several checkpoints for my VM. If I needed to identify a particular checkpoint, I could select it and click the Properties button. This causes Virtual Machine Manager to display additional, detailed information about the checkpoint (see Figure 7-7).

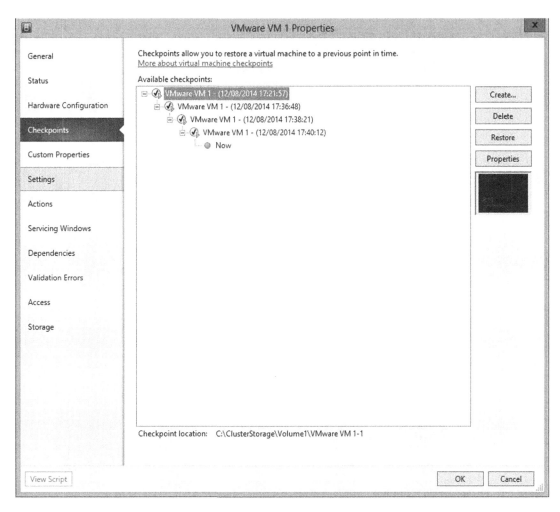

Figure 7-6. *Select the checkpoint for which you want to access the description*

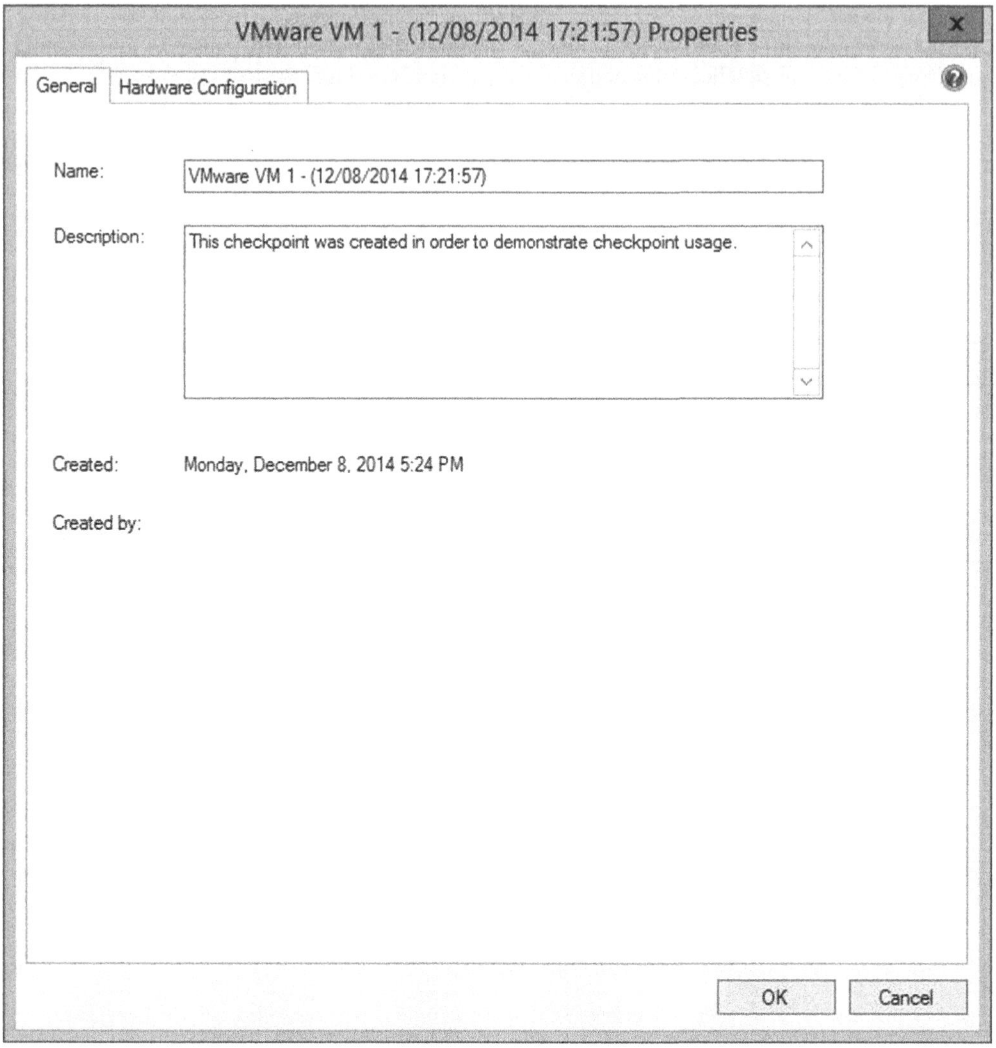

Figure 7-7. *Virtual Machine Manager displays detailed information about the checkpoint*

As you look at this figure, you will notice that the dialog box contains a Hardware Configuration tab. The reason for this is that it is entirely possible that an administrator could make a checkpoint, shut down the VM, make significant hardware allocation changes, and then power up the VM. The end result is that the checkpoint is associated with a completely different hardware configuration than currently exists. The Hardware Configuration tab (see Figure 7-8) allows you to see the hardware allocation as it existed at the time that the checkpoint was created.

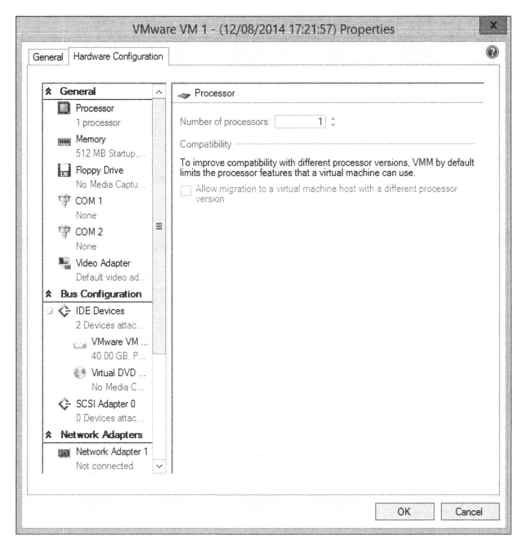

Figure 7-8. *The Hardware Configuration tab shows the virtual machine's hardware configuration at the time that the checkpoint was created*

Deleting a Checkpoint

As I explained earlier, checkpoints are based on the use of differencing disks, which have a parent–child relationship to one another. In spite of this relationship, VMM will allow you to delete checkpoints on an as-needed basis without impacting the other checkpoints in a checkpoint chain.

The procedure for deleting a checkpoint is almost identical to the procedure for restoring a checkpoint. You can delete a checkpoint by completing these steps:

1. Open the VMM console.

2. Select the VMs and Services workspace.

3. Right click on the virtual machine for which you want to delete a checkpoint and choose the Manage Checkpoints command from the shortcut menu. This will cause Windows to display the virtual machine's Properties dialog box, with the Checkpoints tab selected.

4. Select the checkpoint that you want to delete.

5. Click on the Delete button.

6. When prompted, click Yes to confirm that you want to delete the checkpoint.

7. Click OK.

8. Verify that the Remove Checkpoint job has completed successfully (see Figure 7-9).

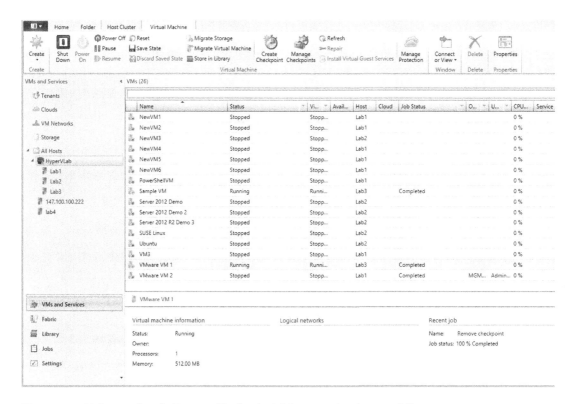

Figure 7-9. *Make sure that the Remove Checkpoint job has completed successfully*

Replication

One more protective mechanism that I want to talk about is replication. Hyper-V replication is similar to VMware's vSphere Replication. The replication feature allows you to create a standby copy of a virtual machine. You can fail over to the replica in the event of a disaster.

Before I show you how to use the replication feature, there are a few things that you need to know. First, replication is not a substitute for failover clustering. Failover clustering provides high availability for virtual machines. Replication does not. Replication provides you with a standby virtual machine copy that can be activated in the event that the primary virtual machine copy is badly damaged or destroyed.

Another thing that you need to know is that Hyper-V is extremely flexible with regard to its support for the replication feature. You can replicate a virtual machine in the following ways:

- From one cluster to another

- From a cluster to a standalone Hyper-V host

- From one standalone Hyper-V host to another

- From a standard Hyper-V host to a cluster

Hyper-V replication is not a substitute for a true backup. While it is true that a replica is a full copy of a virtual machine, and that you can create recovery points that allow you to revert a replica to the state in which it existed at an earlier point in time, Hyper-V replication simply is not as flexible and does not provide as comprehensive of protection as a true backup.

So, why use replication at all? Replication is a good continuity-of-business feature because it allows for a full copy of a virtual machine to be standing by on another host or another cluster. This replica is ready to go in the event that something happens to the primary virtual machine. You don't have to take the time to restore a backup.

Installing the Hyper-V Replica Broker

If you are going to use replication in conjunction with failover clustering, any clusters involved in the replication process will need to be provisioned with the Hyper-V Replica Broker. Replication normally occurs from one Hyper-V host to another. The Hyper-V Replica Broker allows replication to work at the cluster level rather than at the host level. Installing the Hyper-V Replica Broker is relatively easy. To do so, complete these steps:

1. Log on to one of your cluster nodes as an administrator.

2. Open Server Manager.

3. Select the Failover Cluster Manager command from the Tools menu.

4. When the Failover Cluster Manager opens, select the listing for your cluster.

5. Click on the Configure Role link, found in the Actions pane (see Figure 7-10). This will cause the High Availability Wizard to open.

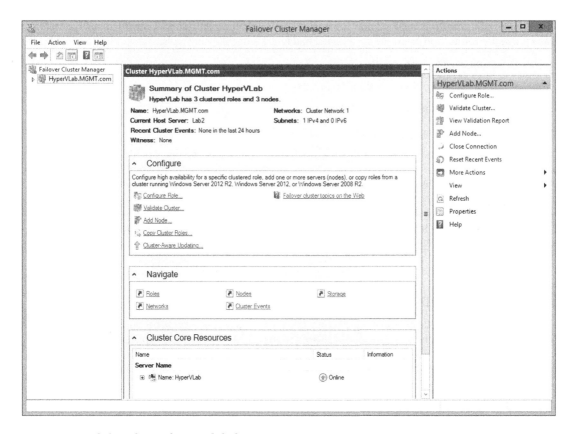

Figure 7-10. *Click on the Configure Role link*

6. Click Next to bypass the wizard's welcome page.

7. Select the Hyper-V Replica Broker from the list of roles (see Figure 7-11).

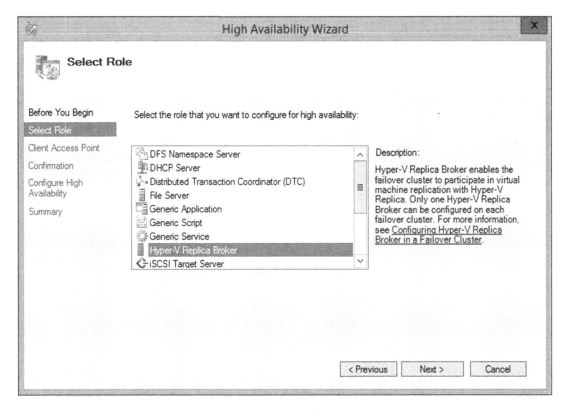

Figure 7-11. *Select the Hyper-V Replica Broker role from the list*

8. Click Next.

9. Enter a NetBIOS name and an IP address that can be used by the Replica Broker (see Figure 7-12). Microsoft refers to the NetBIOS name as the Client Access Point Name. You will need to make note of the name and IP address you choose for later use.

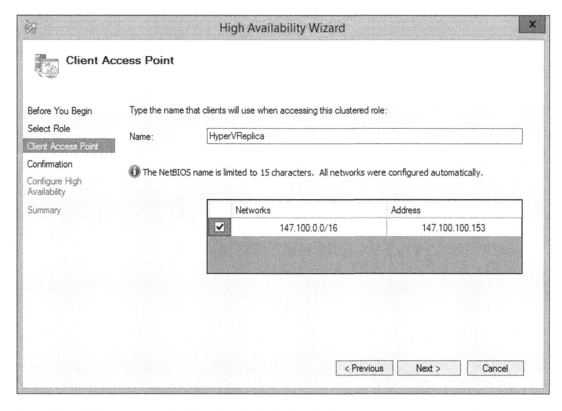

Figure 7-12. Enter a name and an IP address for the Replica Broker to use as a client access point

10. Click Next.

11. Take a moment to view the summary information.

12. Click Next.

13. When the process of deploying the Hyper-V Replica Broker completes, click Finish.

14. From within the Failover Cluster Manager, select the Hyper-V Replica Broker role that you just created (see Figure 7-13).

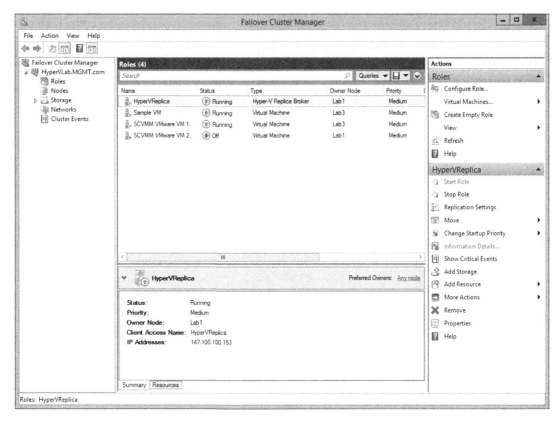

Figure 7-13. *Select the Hyper-V Replica Broker*

15. Click on the Replication Settings link, found in the Actions pane. This will cause Windows to open the Hyper-V Replica Broker Configuration dialog box.

16. Select the Enable This Cluster as a Replica Server check box (see Figure 7-14).

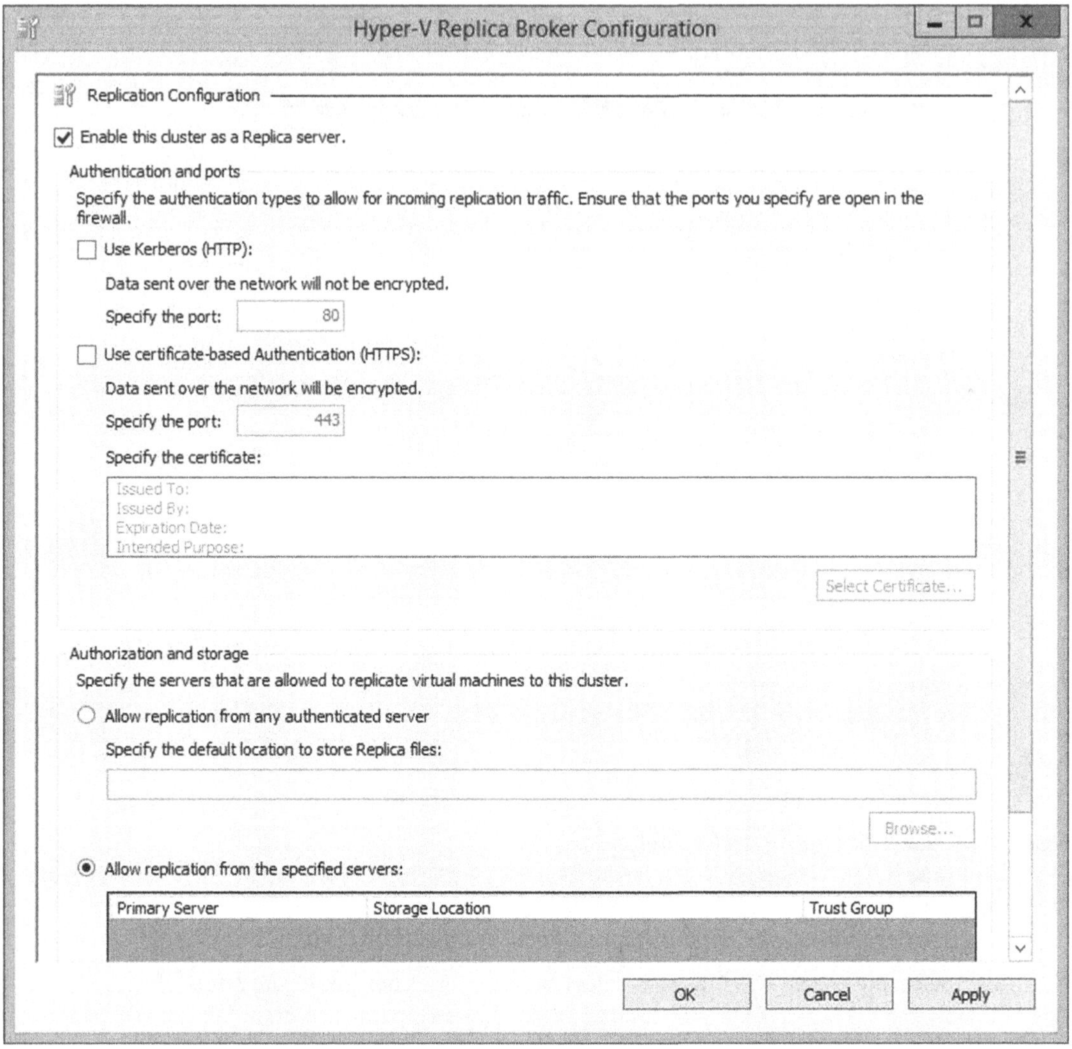

Figure 7-14. *Select the Enable This Cluster as a Replica Server check box*

17. You will need to choose an authentication type for the replication process to use. Assuming that all of the servers that will be participating in the replication process are members of a common management domain, you should use Kerberos authentication. Otherwise, you will need to choose the option to use certificate-based authentication (you will also have to provide a certificate). For the purposes of this book, I will be using Kerberos authentication.

18. Now, you must choose whether to allow replication from any authenticated server or to only allow replication from specific servers. In either case, you will have to specify a path in which replicas will be stored. In the case of a cluster, this should be your cluster-shared volume. In a real-world deployment it is a good idea to specify the servers that you want to use. Otherwise it may become possible for someone to replicate rogue VMs to your cluster. For the sake of this book, however, I am going to use the Allow Replication from Any Authenticated Server option, because doing so allows me to reduce the authentication and storage settings to a single screen capture (see Figure 7-15).

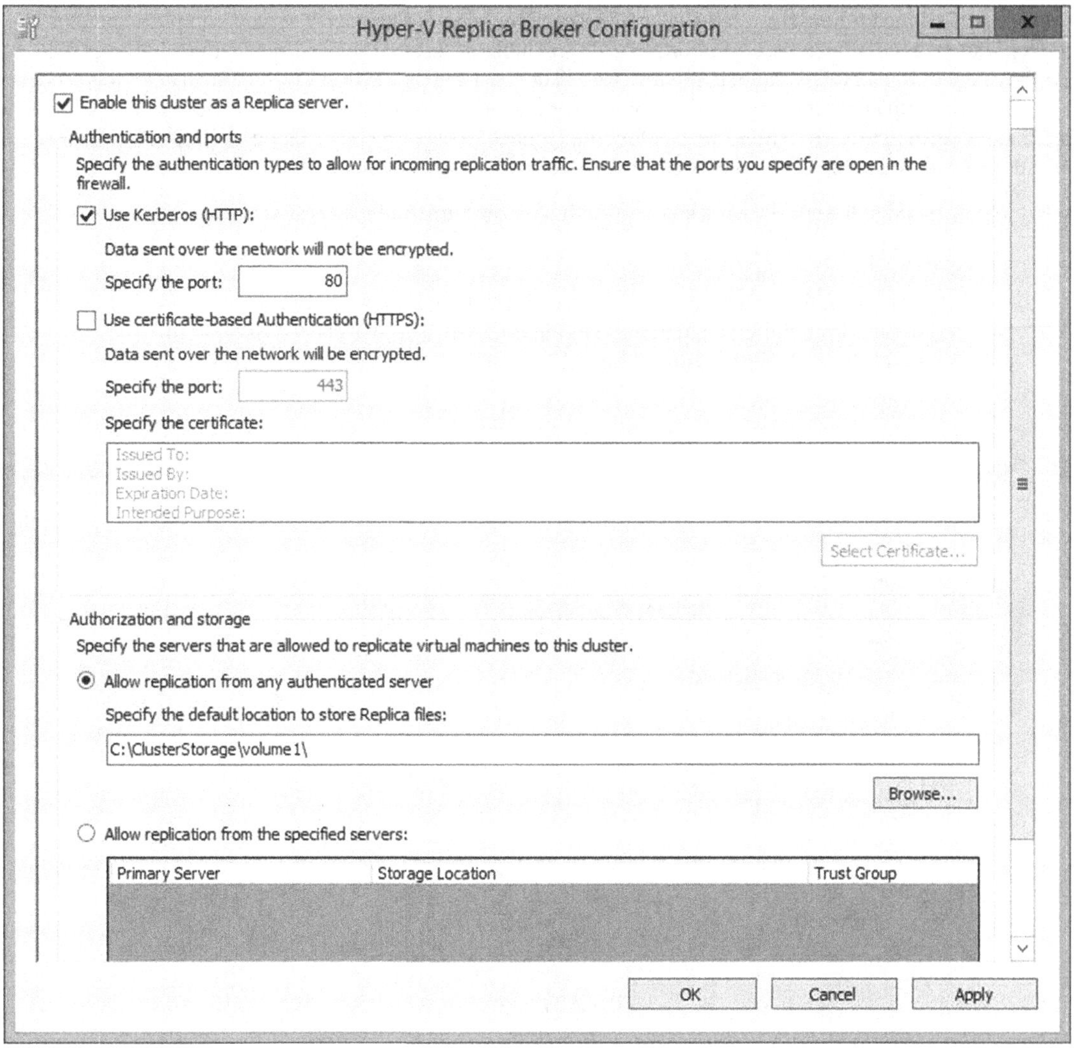

Figure 7-15. *Choose your authentication and storage options*

19. Click OK.

20. Click OK again to acknowledge the warning message indicating that you must configure the firewall on each cluster node to allow inbound traffic on TCP port 80 and that you must enable the Hyper-V HTTP Listener (TCP-in) rule on each cluster node. You will need to do this for any Hyper-V server that participates in the replication process, including individual cluster nodes.

Enabling Replication for Non-Clustered Hyper-V Servers

As you saw in the previous section, we had to enable our cluster to participate in Hyper-V replication. The same thing must be done for non-clustered Hyper-V servers. Non-clustered Hyper-V servers can participate in the replication process, but must be authorized to do so. Unlike a clustered Hyper-V deployment however, the Hyper-V Replica Broker is not required. As such, we will not be using the Failover Cluster Manager for this process.

This brings up an interesting point. For whatever reason, Microsoft chose not to expose Hyper-V replication through System Center Virtual Machine Manager. Thus, we will be using the Hyper-V Manager for this process. To enable a non-clustered Hyper-V server for replication, complete these steps:

1. Log on to the server using an account that has administrative permissions.

2. Open the Hyper-V Manager.

3. Right click on the listing for your server and select the Hyper-V Settings command from the shortcut menu (see Figure 7-16). This will cause Windows to open the Hyper-V Settings dialog box.

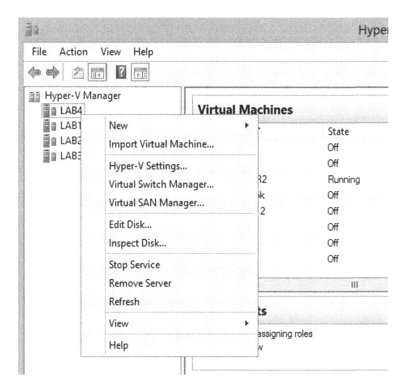

Figure 7-16. *Right click on your Hyper-V server and select the Hyper-V Settings command from the shortcut menu*

4. Select the Replication Configuration option.

5. Select the Enable This Computer as a Replica Server check box.

6. You will need to choose an authentication type for the replication process to use. Assuming that all of the servers that will be participating in the replication process are members of a common management domain, you should use Kerberos authentication. Otherwise, you will need to choose the option to use certificate-based authentication (you will also have to provide a certificate). For the purposes of this book, I will be using Kerberos authentication.

7. Now, you must choose whether to allow replication from any authenticated server or to only allow replication from specific servers. In either case, you will have to specify a path in which replicas will be stored. In a real-world deployment it is a good idea to specify the servers that you want to use. Otherwise it may become possible for someone to replicate rogue VMs to your server. For the sake of this book, however, I am going to use the Allow Replication from Any Authenticated Server option, because doing so allows me to reduce the authentication and storage settings to a single screen capture (see Figure 7-17).

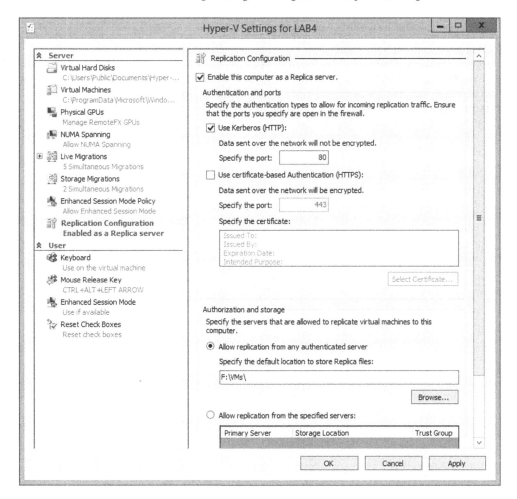

Figure 7-17. *Choose your preferred authentication settings and your authorization and storage settings*

8. Click OK.

Creating a Replica

Creating a replica of a Hyper-V virtual machine involves working through the Enable Replication Wizard. The wizard is launched in two different ways, depending on whether the virtual machine is acting as a clustered role. Regardless of which method you use, the process of working through the wizard is exactly the same. Here are the steps that you will need to use to enable replication for a VM:

1. Launc h the Enable Replication Wizard using one of the following options:

   - If you are creating a replica of a clustered VM, you can access this wizard from within the Failover Cluster Manager by right clicking on a virtual machine and then selecting the Replication ➤ Enable Replication commands from the shortcut menu.

   - You can enable replication for non-clustered virtual machines through the Hyper-V Manager by right clicking on the virtual machine and selecting the Enable Replication command from the shortcut menu.

2. Click Next to bypass the wizard's welcome page.

3. When prompted, enter the name of the replica target (see Figure 7-18). If the target is a non-clustered Hyper-V server, then you can enter the server name. If the replica will reside on a failover cluster, then you will have to enter the client access point name that you assigned to the Hyper-V Replica Broker. In either case, the source and the target will each need to be enabled for replication.

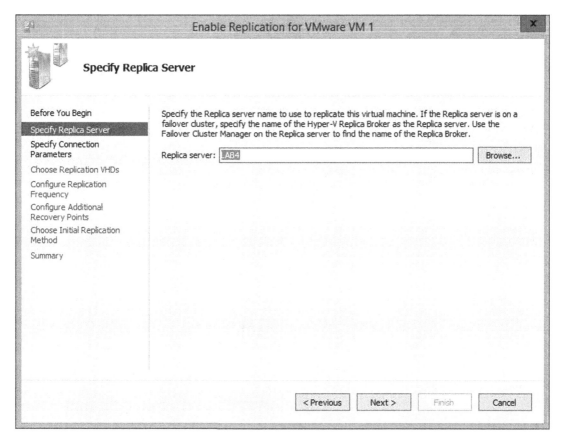

Figure 7-18. *Enter the name of the replication target*

4. Click Next.

5. Take a moment to verify that the replica server (the destination server), the replica server port, and the authentication type are all set correctly. It is also a good idea to select the Compress the Data That Is Transmitted over the Network checkbox (see Figure 7-19). Doing so minimizes the amount of network bandwidth consumed by the replication process.

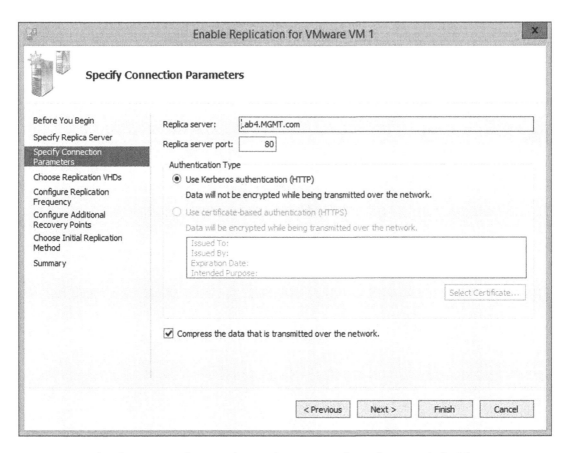

Figure 7-19. *Select the Compress the Data That Is to be Transmitted over the Network check box*

6. Click Next.

7. Hyper-V replication occurs on a per-virtual-hard-disk basis. Therefore, you will need to select the checkboxes corresponding to the virtual hard disks that you want to replicate. Under normal circumstances you should select all of the available checkboxes.

8. Click Next.

9. Select your desired replication frequency. You can replicate at 30-second, five-minute, or fifteen-minute intervals. I recommend using 30-second intervals on wired, on-premises networks, because doing so will provide the most up-to-date replicas. For networks that are connected by slow or unreliable links, it is better to use a long replication interval. Long intervals have the best chance of keeping a replica in sync in the event of intermittent link failures because of the way that the timeout/retry algorithm works.

10. Click Next.

11. Choose the number of recovery points that you want to maintain (see Figure 7-20). By default, Hyper-V replicas maintain only a single recovery point, which essentially means that the replica VM acts as an offline spare copy of the VM. Creating additional recovery points gives you the ability to roll back the replica to an earlier point in time.

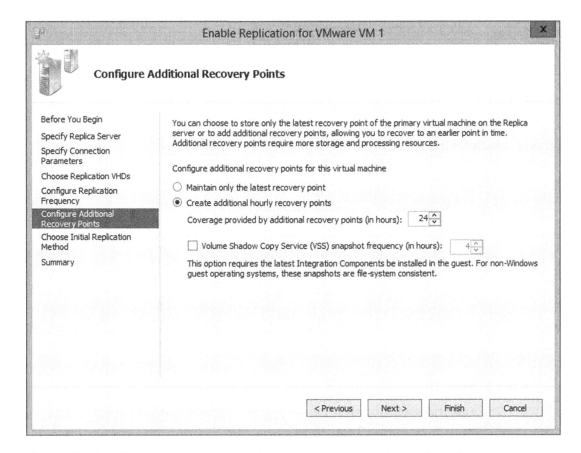

Figure 7-20. *Specify the number of recovery points that you want to maintain on the replica*

12. Click Next.

13. You must now choose how you want to initiate the replication process (see Figure 7-21). There are two things that you will have to consider. First, you have to decide when you want to begin the replication process. You can initiate the replication process immediately or later on at a scheduled time. The other thing that you will need to do is to choose a replication method. Hyper-V performs the initial copy process over the network by default, but doing so can be problematic for excessively large VMs or for slow network connections. Other options include seeding the replica through the use of external media or via a virtual machine that already exists on the replica server.

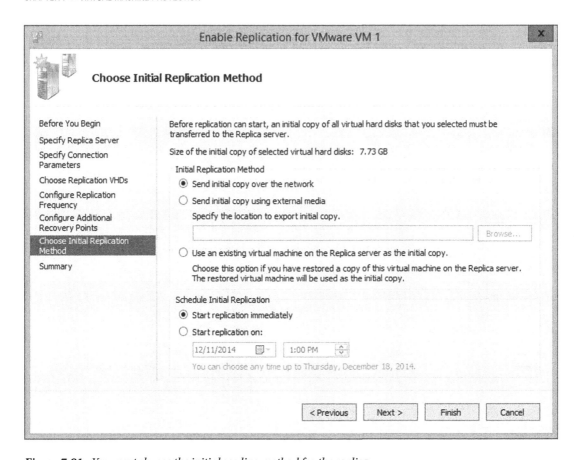

Figure 7-21. *You must choose the initial seeding method for the replica*

14. Click Next.

15. Take a moment to verify the replication summary information to be sure that it is correct.

16. Click Finish.

17. If you have chosen to seed the replica from an existing VM on the replica server or by using removable media, then you will need to follow the remaining prompts. Otherwise, check the virtual machine's status to make sure that the replication process is underway (see Figure 7-22).

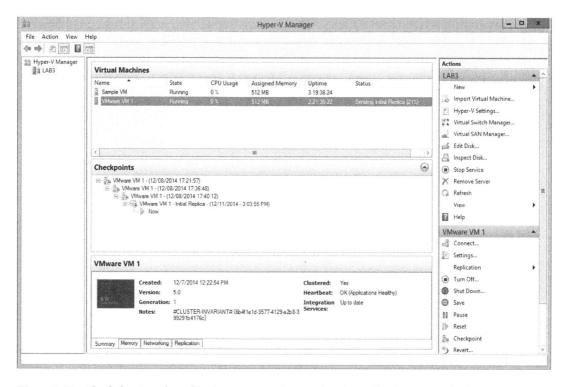

Figure 7-22. *Check the virtual machine's status to make sure that the replication process begins*

Verifying Replication Health

Being that replication is a mechanism for protecting your virtual machine infrastructure by creating standby copies of your virtual machines, it is a good idea to periodically verify the health of your replicas. Fortunately, this is quite easy to do.

Before I show you how to verify replica health, I need to point out that if a problem does occur with a replica, then the health status might not necessarily be accurate. I have encountered real-world situations in which the source server indicated that the replication process was healthy, while the replica server reported a problem. I have also seen the opposite situation in which the replica server reported a healthy replica, while the source server reported a problem. In any case, the lesson is that when you are verifying replica health, you need to check both the source and the replica servers.

You can check the replication health by completing these steps:

1. Open the Hyper-V Manager.

2. Click on the virtual machine for which you want to check the replication health.

3. Select the replication tab at the bottom of the screen (see Figure 7-23). This tab will provide you with some basic replication statistics.

233

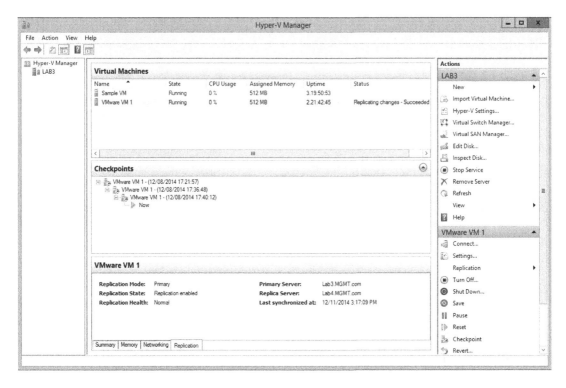

Figure 7-23. *The Replication tab provides a few basic replication statistics*

4. Right click on the virtual machine and select the Replication ➤ View Replication
    Health commands from the shortcut menus (see Figure 7-24).

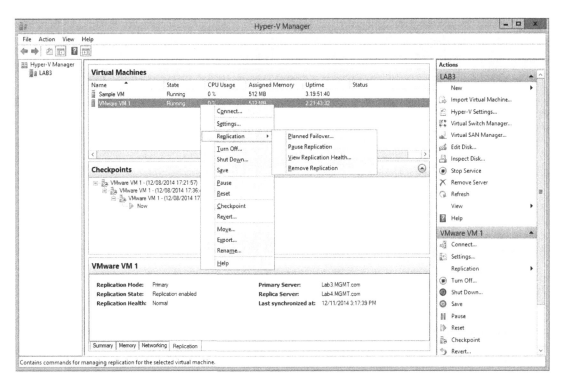

Figure 7-24. *Right click on the virtual machine and select the Replication ➤ View Replication Health commands from the shortcut menus*

When you follow the procedure described here, Windows will display the Replication Health dialog box (see Figure 7-25). You can view the replication health information on screen, or you can use the Save As button to save the replication health information for later viewing.

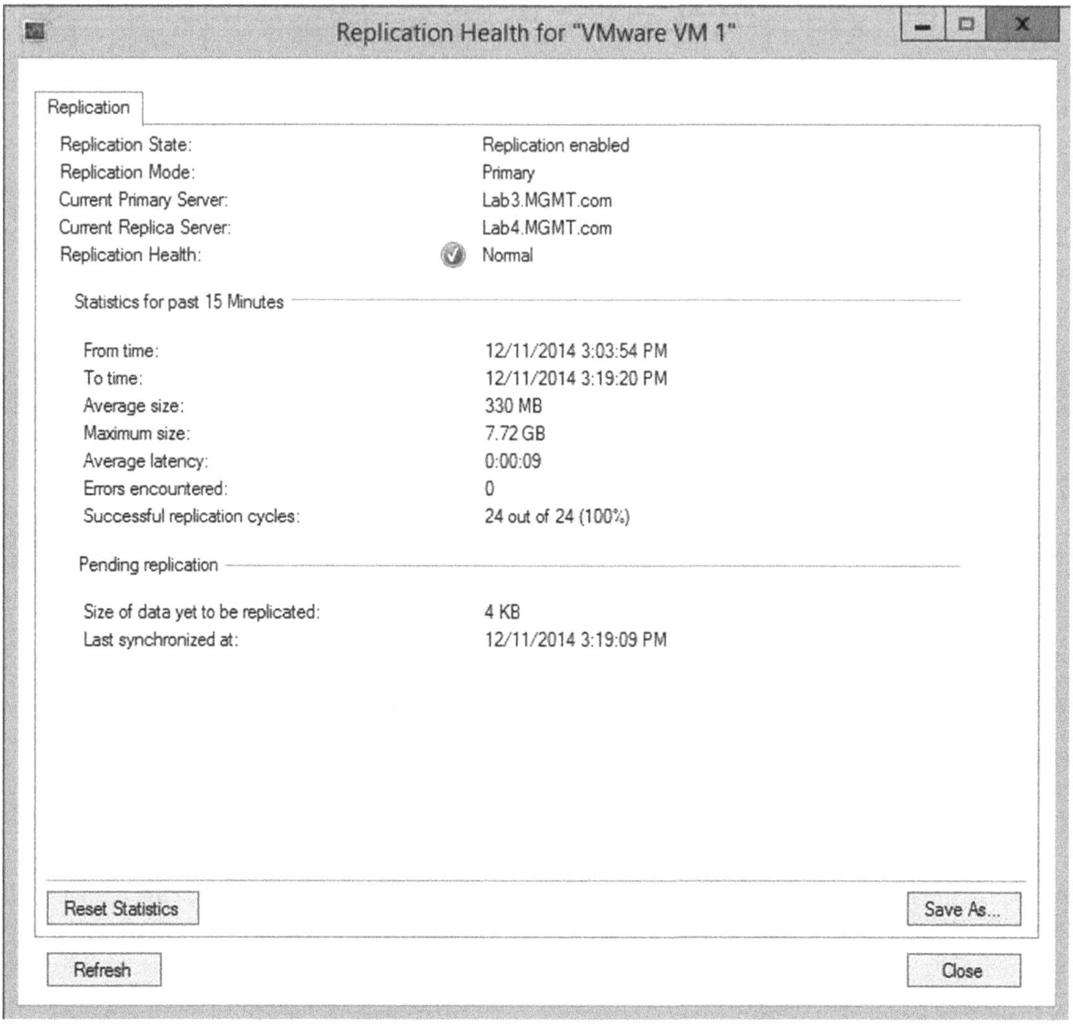

Figure 7-25. *This is what the Replication Health dialog box looks like*

The most important thing that you need to know about the Replication Health dialog box is that the status is not always accurate. If you look at Figure 7-25, you will notice that there is a section called Statistics for Past 15 Minutes. The information shown in the Replication Health dialog box represents what has happened over a period of time. As such, if there is a problem with a replica and you resolve the problem, the Replication Health dialog box may continue to show an error or a warning condition for a while, even after the problem has been fixed. The best way to make sure that you are viewing current information is to click the Reset Statistics button.

Creating an Extended Replica

One of the really great features that Microsoft introduced in Windows Server 2012 R2 was the ability to extend a replica. This feature allows you to create two replicas of a virtual machine. Typically, one replica is kept on-premises while another is kept in a secondary data center.

To create an extended replica, complete the following steps:

1. Open the Hyper-V server on your replica server (the procedure will not work if you use the source server; it has to be the replica server).

2. Right click on the VM and choose the Replication ➤ Extended Replication commands from the shortcut menu (see Figure 7-26). This will cause Windows to launch the Extend Replication wizard.

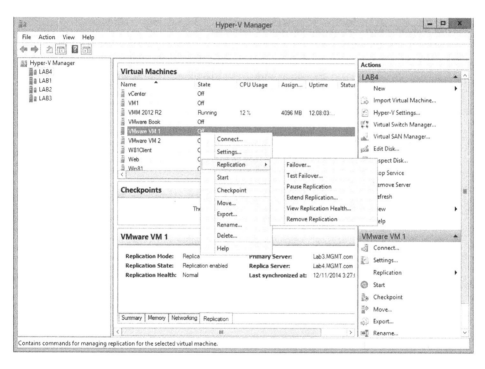

Figure 7-26. *Right click on the virtual machine and choose the Replication ➤ Extended Replication commands from the shortcut menus*

3. Click Next to bypass the wizard's Welcome page.

4. Enter the name of the server that will host the extended replica. Once again, if the extended replica will reside on a failover cluster then you will need to enter the client access point name that has been assigned to the Hyper-V Replica Broker.

5. Click Next.

6. Verify that the replica server name, the replica server port, and the authentication type are correct. You should also select the Compress the Data That Is Transmitted over the Network checkbox.

7. Click Next.

8. Select the desired replication frequency. Because this is an extended replica, your only options are 5 minutes and 15 minutes.

9. Click Next.

10. Choose the number of recovery points that you want to maintain for the extended replica.

11. Click Next.

12. Choose the initial replication method.

13. Click Next.

14. Take a moment to verify the options that you have chosen for the extended replica (see Figure 7-27).

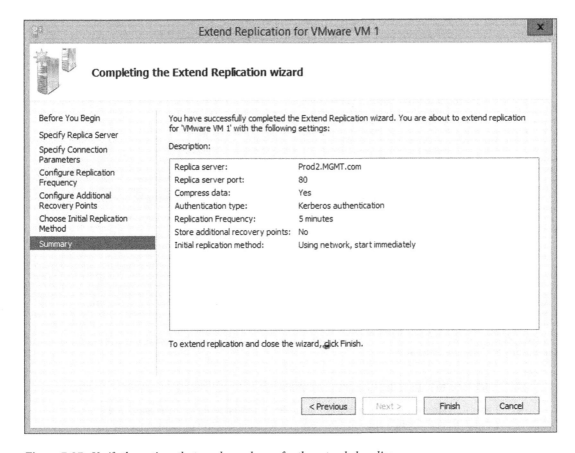

Figure 7-27. *Verify the options that you have chosen for the extended replica*

15. Click Finish.

Testing a Replica

One of the coolest things about Hyper-V replication is that you can actually boot up a replica VM to make sure that the replica works as expected. The best part is that the testing process is non-disruptive. The replication process continues to occur in the background, keeping the replica up to date. The replica is isolated from your production virtual machines, so there is no danger of a conflict occurring.

Testing a replica is simple. To do so, complete these steps:

1. Log in to your replica server as an administrator (this will not work on a source server).

2. Right click on the replica VM and choose the Replication ➤ Test Failover commands from the shortcut menu (see Figure 7-28).

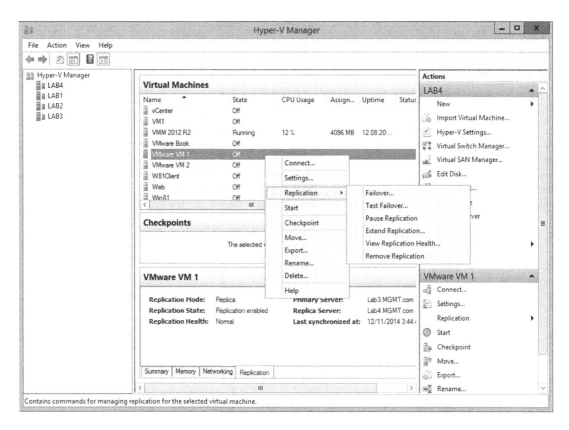

Figure 7-28. *Right click on the replica and choose the Replication ➤ Test Failover commands from the shortcut menus*

3.   Select the recovery point that you want to test (see Figure 7-29).

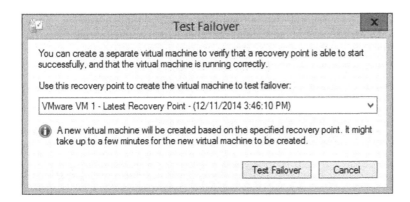

Figure 7-29. *Select the recovery point that you want to test*

4.   Click the Test Failover button.

The reason why it is possible to test a replica without causing problems with the replication process or causing conflicts on the production network has to do with the way that Hyper-V constructs the test environment. If you look at Figure 7-30, you will notice that Hyper-V has created a brand new virtual machine called VMware VM 1 - Test. This is our test virtual machine. It was created automatically. Our original replica virtual machine is named VMware VM 1. As you can see in the figure, that virtual machine still exists. It is also still receiving synchronization data from the source VM (which you can also see in the figure).

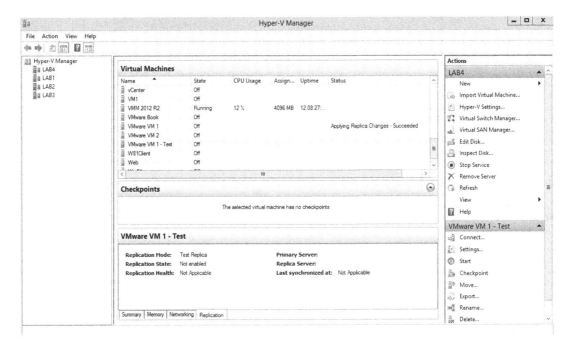

Figure 7-30. *Hyper-V automatically creates a test VM*

Now, let's take a look at the hardware settings for the test VM. As you can see in Figure 7-31, the test VM is not connected to the network. This is why it is possible to boot (and use) the test virtual machine without fear of network conflicts.

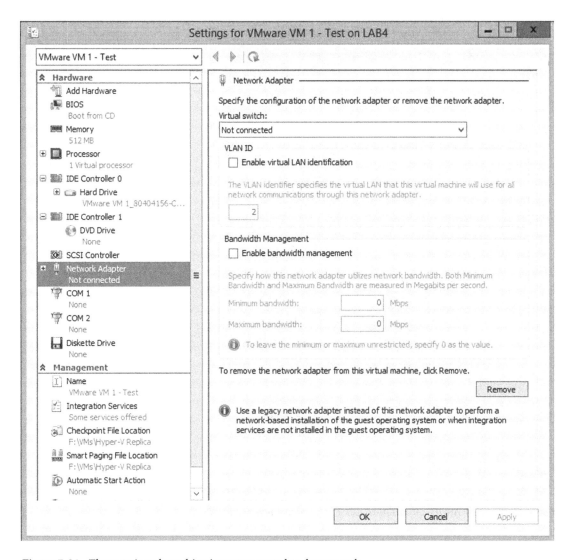

Figure 7-31. The test virtual machine is not connected to the network

Now check out Figure 7-32. Virtual machine replicas are stored in the Hyper-V Replica folder. If I peek inside of F:\VMs\Hyper-V Replica\Virtual Hard Disks, I can see the virtual hard disks that are in use by the replica and the test environment. Incidentally, I used F:\VMs as the path in which to write the replica, so that's where the F:\VMs portion of the path came from. This portion of the path will be something different in your environment, and will reflect the location where you have chosen to store the virtual machines.

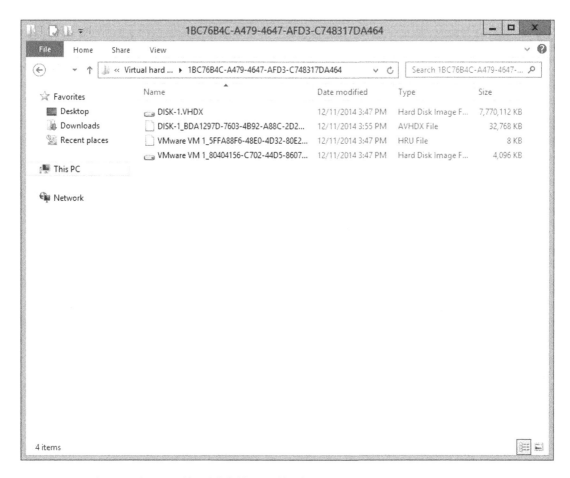

Figure 7-32. *These are the virtual hard disk files used by the replica VM*

As you can see in Figure 7-32, there are multiple VHDX and AVHDX files in use, even though the virtual machine only has a single virtual hard disk. The reason for this is that the replica is using a method that is very similar to creating a checkpoint. It's kind of like a double checkpoint.

Like a checkpoint, the virtual machine's virtual hard disk is placed into a read-only state, and all of the write operations are directed to a differencing disk that has a child relationship to the original (parent) virtual hard disk. The way that this differs from a normal checkpoint is that a second differencing disk is also created off of the parent virtual hard disk. This second differencing disk is used by the test virtual machine. At this point, both the replica VM and the test VM are using differencing disks that are linked to the original virtual hard disk file. This allows the replica VM to continue receiving updates and allows you to interact with the test VM without causing any problems with the replica VM or the replication process.

If you are curious as to which files are being used for which purpose, it is easy to find out. If you look at Figure 7-33, you will see that a checkpoint was created for the original VM. If I right click on the checkpoint and click Settings, I can see that, prior to the checkpoint being made, the VM was using DISK1.VHDX as its virtual hard disk (see Figure 7-34). The Disk1.VHDX file now serves as the parent to the differencing disks that are being used by the replica VM and the test VM. A quick look at the hardware settings for either the replica VM or the test VM shows us which differencing disks are being used (see Figure 7-35).

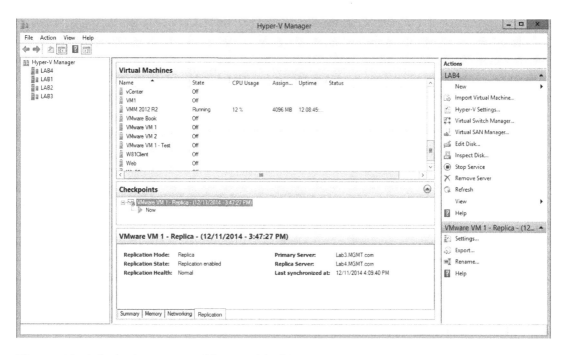

Figure 7-33. *A checkpoint was created for our original VM*

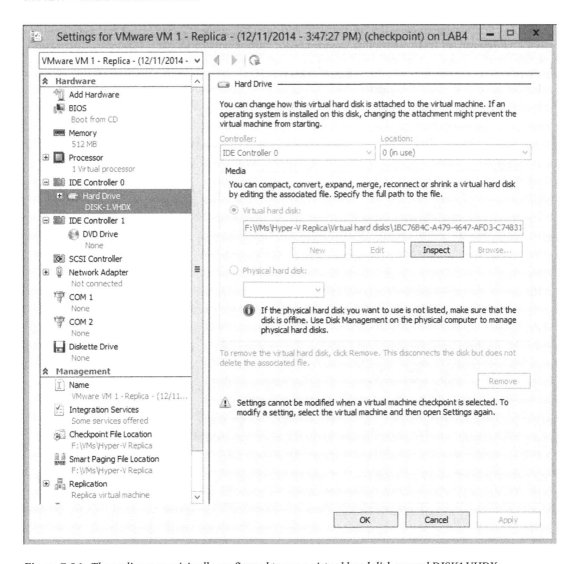

Figure 7-34. The replica was originally configured to use a virtual hard disk named DISK1.VHDX

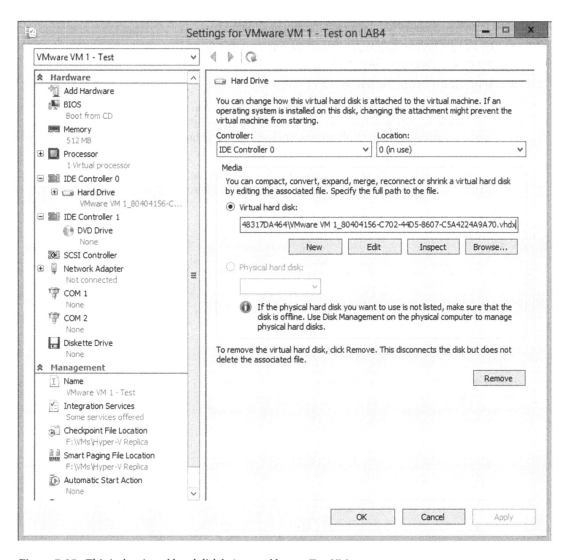

Figure 7-35. *This is the virtual hard disk being used by our Test VM*

When you are done testing the replica, you can put everything back to normal by right clicking on the replica VM and selecting the Replication ➤ Stop Test Failover commands from the shortcut menus. This will cause the test VM to be deleted. The replication data that has accumulated during the test will be merged back into the original virtual hard disk, and the checkpoint will be deleted. In other words, this process puts everything back to normal.

Performing a Planned Failover

There are two ways in which a replica VM can be used. One way is to do a planned failover. You might use a planned failover if you need to take the server that is hosting the active VM copy down for maintenance. Performing a planned failover requires the VM to be taken offline.

You can perform a planned failover by completing these steps:

1. Open the Hyper-V Manager on the server that is hosting the virtual machine (do not do this from the replica server).

2. Shut down the virtual machine.

3. Right click on the virtual machine and choose the Replication ➤ Planned Failover commands from the shortcut menus. Make absolutely sure that the menu option says Planned Failover, and not just Failover. Otherwise, data loss may occur.

4. When the Planned Failover dialog box appears, verify that the Start the Replica Virtual Machine after Failover checkbox is selected (see Figure 7-36).

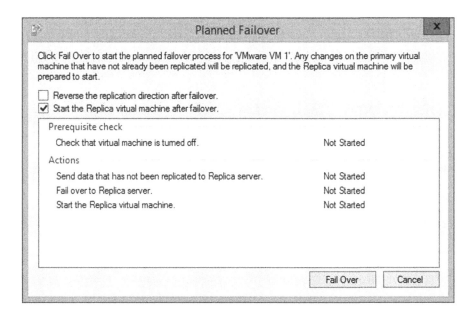

Figure 7-36. *Make sure that the Start the Replica Virtual Machine after Failover Checkbox is selected*

5. In most cases, you will probably also want to select the Reverse the Replication Direction after Failover checkbox. Doing so causes the primary virtual machine copy to become the replica and the replica virtual machine to become the primary. In other words, the primary and replica VMs trade roles if you select this checkbox. As a general rule, you should select this checkbox if you plan to continue using replication.

6. Click the Fail Over button.

Performing an Unplanned Failover

An unplanned failover is different from a planned failover in that an unplanned failover should only be performed in the event that the primary virtual machine is badly damaged or destroyed. If you perform an unplanned failover, any data that might have accumulated since the last successful synchronization will be lost.

You can perform a planned failover by completing these steps:

1. Shut down the virtual machine.

2. Open the Hyper-V Manager on the server that is hosting the replica virtual machine.

3. Right click on the replica virtual machine and choose the Replication ➤ Failover commands from the shortcut menus.

4. Choose the recovery point that you want to activate as a part of the failover (see Figure 7-37).

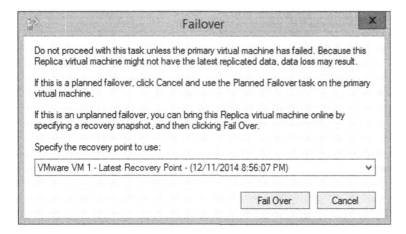

Figure 7-37. *Choose the recovery point that you want to activate*

5. Click the Fail Over button. It is worth noting that there is no "Are You Sure?" prompt. The failover occurs as soon as you click the button.

6. Verify that the virtual machine starts and that the Replication State indicates Failover Complete (see Figure 7-38).

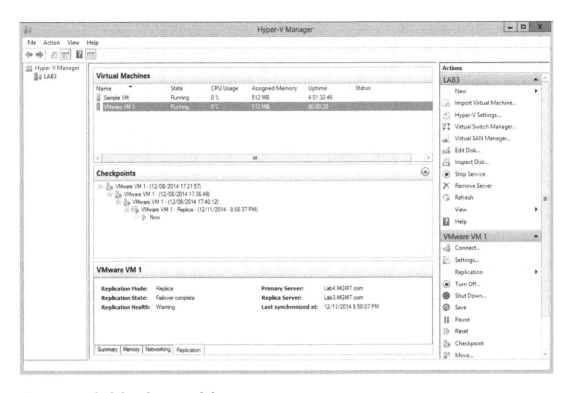

Figure 7-38. *The failover has succeeded*

Moving On

In this chapter, I talked about some various ways that you can protect Hyper-V. I started out by briefly talking about backups, but quickly moved on to a discussion on virtual machine checkpoints and replicas. My plan for the next chapter is to fill in some of the gaps that might still exist in your Hyper-V knowledge. In Chapter 8, I want to talk about some of the day-to-day management and maintenance tasks that you will likely have to perform as you migrate more virtual machines to Hyper-V.

CHAPTER 8

■ ■ ■

Keeping Hyper-V Healthy

So far in this book, I have shown you the basics of linking together your VMware and Hyper-V environments and then migrating virtual machines from VMware to Hyper-V. Although we have been working with management tools such as Hyper-V Manager, Failover Cluster Manager, and System Center Virtual Machine Manager (VMM) quite a bit up to this point, I have mostly limited the discussion to the mechanisms and features that are needed to complete the task at hand. In this chapter, I want to change that by showing you some other things that you can do with the various management tools.

As I said at the beginning of the book, this isn't intended to be a comprehensive discussion of every available management feature. Entire books have been written on such topics. Instead, I want to show you how to perform some day-to-day management tasks within the new environment. For instance, I plan to show you how to move virtual machine storage, how to make a VM highly available, and how to update your cluster nodes while the cluster remains online.

Storage Live Migration

The first thing that I want to show you is the storage live-migration feature. This probably isn't something that you are going to use every day, but it is important to know about. If you think back to the chapters on virtual machine migration, you will recall that there were instances in which I migrated a virtual machine from VMware to Hyper-V, but did not actually make the virtual machine a clustered resource within the Hyper-V environment. I did that on purpose so that I could show you how to use the storage live-migration feature later on.

Using Storage Live Migration

The storage live-migration feature allows you to move a virtual machine's storage from one physical location to another. This capability is especially useful when you want to cluster a non-clustered VM.

To show you how this works, I am going to be clustering a virtual machine named VMware VM 1. This virtual machine currently exists on a Hyper-V server called Lab3. Lab3 is a failover cluster node, but right now the virtual machine is not clustered.

One issue that needs to be resolved prior to clustering the VM is the VM's storage usage. If you look at Figure 8-1, you will see that the virtual machine's virtual hard disk currently resides at `c:\VMware\VMware VM 1`. Not only is it a bad idea to store virtual machines on a host's C: drive, but also the virtual machine isn't making use of our cluster-shared volume. As you may recall, earlier in the book we created an iSCSI-based cluster-shared volume. This cluster-shared volume is accessible through a logical mapping at `c:\ClusterStorage` (the cluster storage doesn't actually reside on the C: drive; the mapping just makes it look that way).

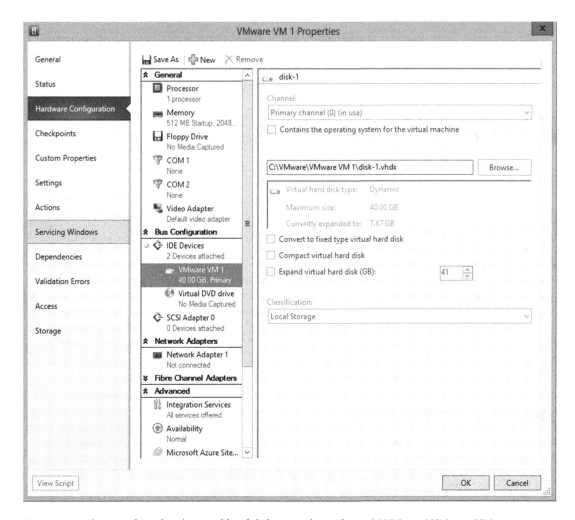

Figure 8-1. *The virtual machine's virtual hard disk currently resides at C:\VMware\VMware VM 1*

With that said, let's use the storage live-migration feature to move the virtual machine's virtual hard disk to our cluster-shared volume. To do so, complete the following steps:

1. Open the VMM console (storage live migrations can also be performed through the Hyper-V Manager, if necessary).

2. Select the VMs and Services workspace.

3. Select the host server on which the virtual machine currently resides.

4. Right click on the VM and select the Migrate Storage command from the shortcut menu (see Figure 8-2). This will cause Windows to launch the Migrate Storage Wizard.

Figure 8-2. *Right click on the VM and select the Migrate Storage command from the shortcut menu*

5. Click the Browse button found within the Storage Location for VM Configuration section (see Figure 8-3).

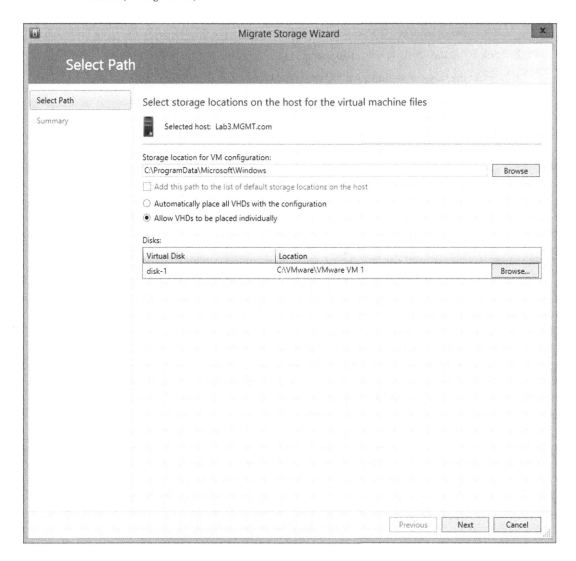

Figure 8-3. *Click the Browse button found within the Storage Location for VM Configuration section*

6. Select the location to which you want to move the VM configuration. For our purposes, I created a folder named VMware VM 1 at C:\ClusterStorage\Volume1 (see Figure 8-4). I will be using this folder for demonstration purposes.

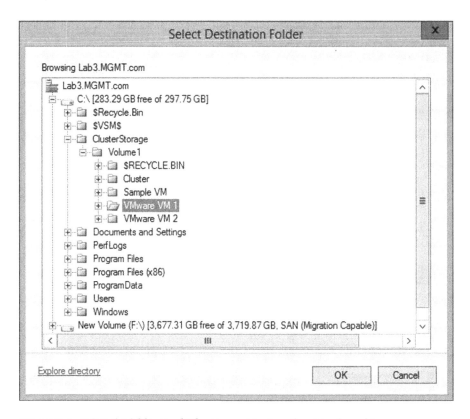

Figure 8-4. *Select the folder in which you want to store the virtual machine*

7. Click OK.

8. When you are returned to the main Migrate Storage Wizard page, click the Browse button that is located in the Disks section.

9. Select your desired storage location. I am going to use the same storage location I used previously.

10. Click OK.

11. When you have returned to the main Migrate Storage Wizard page, click Next.

12. Take a moment to verify the summary data to make sure that everything is correct.

13. Click the Move button.

14. When the move completes, take a look at the virtual machine's hardware settings and make sure that the virtual machine now exists in the correct location (see Figure 8-5).

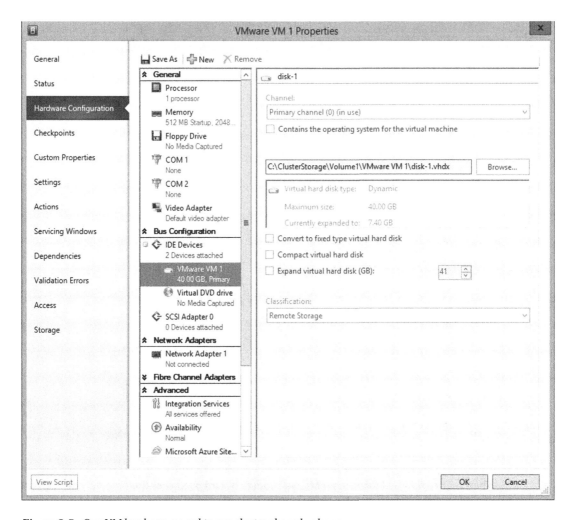

Figure 8-5. *Our VM has been moved to our cluster-shared volume*

What Went Wrong?

Normally, storage migration works without any problems. If the storage-migration process does fail, however, there are two things that you must check. First, open up the Hyper-V Manager and verify that the reported storage location matches the location that is being reported by VMM. Even though it doesn't happen very often, I have seen situations in which VMM misidentifies the virtual machine's physical location. If this happens, the storage migration will fail. The solution is to close the virtual machine's Properties dialog box, refresh the console, and then try it again. If that doesn't work then you can use Hyper-V Manager to perform the storage migration instead.

A permissions problem can sometimes cause a storage migration to fail as well. Make sure that VMM has permission to move the virtual machine to the new storage destination.

Making the VM Highly Available

Now that we have moved the VM to our cluster-shared volume, we can make it highly available. I previously showed you how to do this by using the Failover Cluster Manager, but I want to take a moment to show you how to use VMM to complete the task, because doing so is really tricky and non-intuitive.

To see what I mean, right click on the virtual machine that we just storage live migrated and select the Properties command from the shortcut menu. When the Properties dialog box opens, go to the Hardware Configuration tab, scroll down to the Advanced section, and select the Availability option. As you can see in Figure 8-6, the availability is set to Normal (the VM is not highly available). Furthermore, the check box labeled Make This Virtual Machine Highly Available is grayed out.

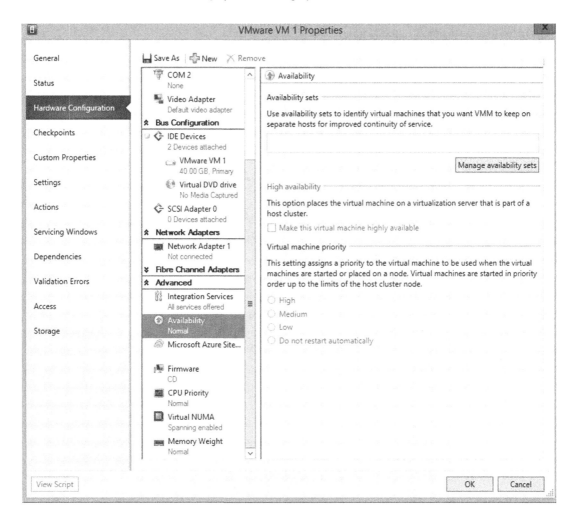

Figure 8-6. *The option to make the VM highly available is grayed out*

This screen is really deceptive. According to Microsoft (`http://blogs.technet.com/b/chrad/archive/2010/05/09/wait-a-minute-virtual-machine-isn-t-highly-available-though-it-is-on-a-clustered-host.aspx`), this check box is really more of a reporting mechanism than an on / off switch. You simply cannot use the check box to make the VM highly available.

The trick instead is to force high availability through a live migration. Live migrations are the Hyper-V equivalent of VMware's vMotion. Our virtual machine already exists on a cluster-shared volume, and the VM itself is hosted on a cluster node. The trick is to move the VM to another cluster node and force high availability in the process. Here is how it's done:

1. Open the VMM console and select the VMs and Services workspace.

2. Right click on the VM that you need to make highly available, and select the Migrate Virtual Machine command from the shortcut menu. This will cause VMM to open the Migrate VM Wizard.

3. Select the Make This VM Highly Available check box.

4. Select the current host as a migration target (see Figure 8-7). Do not attempt to migrate the VM to another host.

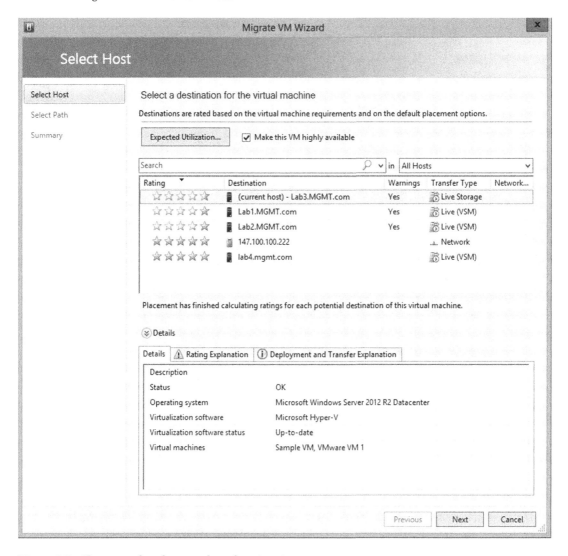

Figure 8-7. *Choose another cluster node as the migration target*

5. Click Next.

6. Make sure that the storage location remains the same.

7. Click Next.

8. Take a second to verify the summary information.

9. Click Move. VMM will now perform an in-place live migration (see Figure 8-8).

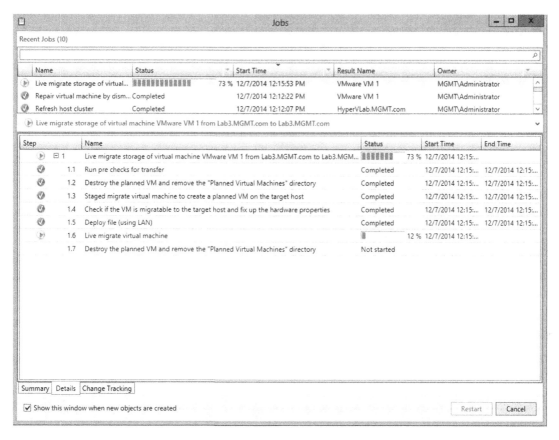

Figure 8-8. *VMM will go through the motions of a live migration, even though the VM isn't actually going anywhere*

10. When the process completes, verify that the virtual machine has been made highly available (see Figure 8-9).

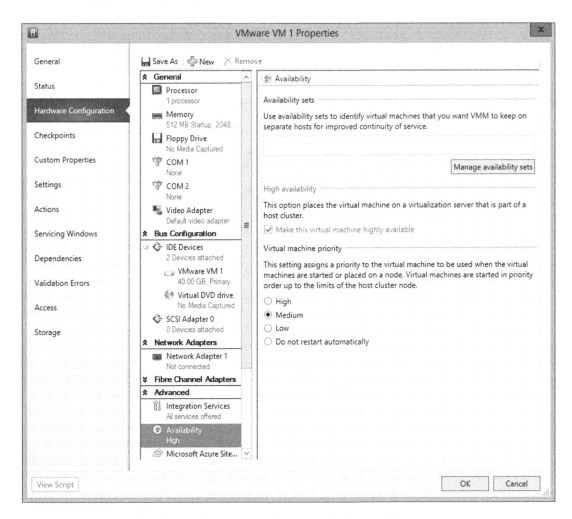

Figure 8-9. *Make sure that the virtual machine has been made highly available*

Cluster-Aware Updating

If you have worked with Windows servers in the past, then you know that Microsoft tends to release a lot of updates to the Windows Server operating system. Prior to the release of Windows Server 2012, updating the nodes that make up a Windows failover cluster was a tedious, manual process. Thankfully, Windows Server 2012 and 2012 R2 include a feature known as cluster-aware updating. Cluster-aware updating allows the failover cluster nodes to be updated without an administrator having to manually update each node. Best of all, the process allows VMs and other clustered roles to remain online throughout the update.

The process works by automatically live migrating VMs off of one cluster node and onto another. Once the cluster node has been drained of VMs it is placed into maintenance mode, updated, and then rebooted. The process is then repeated on the other cluster nodes. The exact steps that occur as a part of a cluster-aware update are:

1. Place a node into cluster maintenance mode.

2. Move the clustered roles off of the node.

3. Install all required updates.

4. Reboot the server (if required).

5. Take the cluster node out of maintenance mode.

6. Move the clustered roles back to the node.

7. Repeat the process on the next node.

Cluster-aware updating supports two different modes. One mode is known as self-aware updating. In this mode, the cluster-aware updating service is treated as a cluster role. The role fails over from one node to the next as the update process progresses.

The other option is to use remote-updating mode. This mode uses a server that is not a part of the cluster as an update coordinator.

For the purposes of this book, we will be using self-aware updating. The only real advantage to using remote-updating mode is that cluster resources are not consumed by running the cluster-aware updating role.

Configuring Cluster-Aware Updating

There are a number of components that must be installed in order to use cluster-aware updating. If you have been following the examples in this book then all of the necessary components should already be in place, and you can move forward with using cluster-aware updating. If you would like to read more about the required components then read this helpful article on TechNet at: `http://technet.microsoft.com/en-us/library/jj134234.aspx`.

To configure cluster-aware updating, complete the following steps:

1. Log in to one of your cluster nodes using an account with administrative privileges.

2. Open Server Manager.

3. Select the Cluster-Aware Updating option from Server Manager's Tools menu. You should now see the Cluster-Aware Updating interface (see Figure 8-10).

Figure 8-10. *This is the interface that you will use to perform cluster-aware updates*

4. Click on the Connect to a Failover Cluster drop-down list and select the name of your cluster.

5. Click the Connect button. The Cluster-Aware Updating tool should now list all of the cluster nodes and show a status of Not Available for Last Updating Run and Last Updating Status (see Figure 8-11).

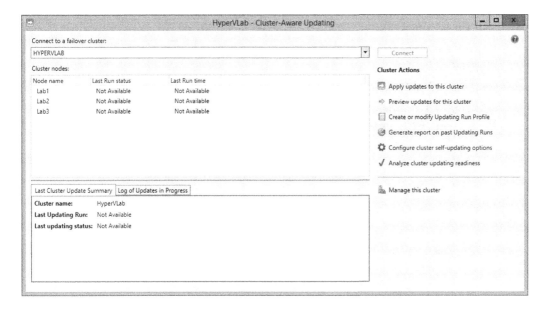

Figure 8-11. *The tool has established a connection to the cluster*

6. Click on the Configure Cluster Self-Updating Options link. This will cause Windows to launch the Configure Self-Updating Options Wizard.

7. Click Next to bypass the wizard's Getting Started page.

8. Select the Add the CAU Clustered Role, with Self-Updating Mode Enabled, to This Cluster check box (see Figure 8-12).

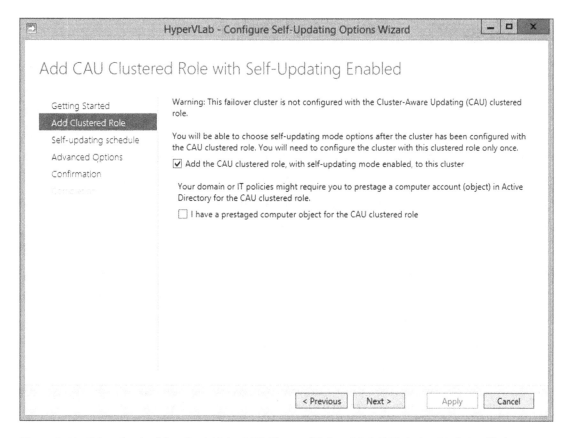

Figure 8-12. *Select the check box for Add the CAU Clustered Role, with Self-Updating Mode Enabled, to This Cluster*

9. Click Next.

10. Cluster-aware updating runs on a scheduled basis, so you will need to set a schedule that meets your organization's needs (see Figure 8-13). It is also possible to manually launch an update cycle on an as-needed basis. I will show you how to do so in the next section.

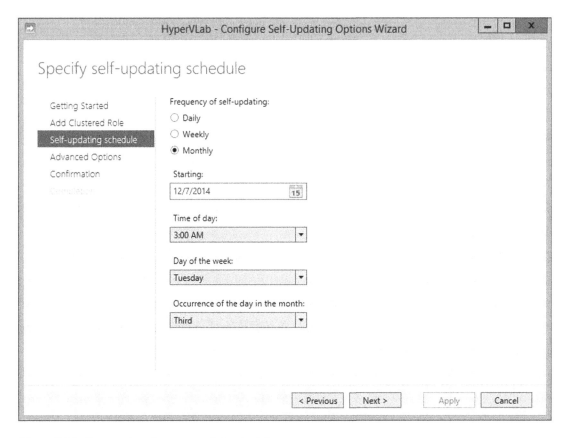

Figure 8-13. *You must configure an update schedule*

11. Click Next.

12. At this point you will see a screen that allows you to customize the update process. For instance, you can set the maximum number of retries or make it so that updates will only occur if all nodes are online. You don't have to enter any values into this screen, but if you do want to fine tune the update process, then this is where you do it (see Figure 8-14).

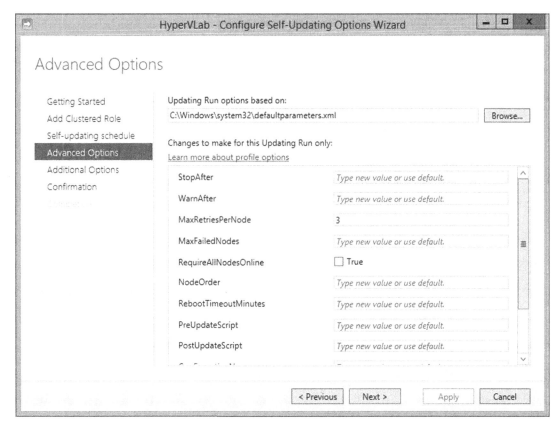

Figure 8-14. *Enter any necessary custom options*

13. Click Next.

14. Choose whether or not you want to receive recommended updates in the same way as you do important updates.

15. Click Next.

16. Take a moment to verify the information shown on the Confirmation screen.

17. Click Apply. The CAU clustered role will now be created and enabled.

18. When the process completes, click Close. You will now be returned to the main Cluster-Aware Updating interface.

19. At this point, we need to test our Cluster-Aware Updating configuration. To do so, click on the Analyze Cluster Updating Readiness link. Doing so will launch a series of automated tests to make sure that your cluster is properly configured.

20. Verify that the tests have completed successfully and then click Close (see Figure 8-15). It's OK if you receive warnings, but you shouldn't receive any errors.

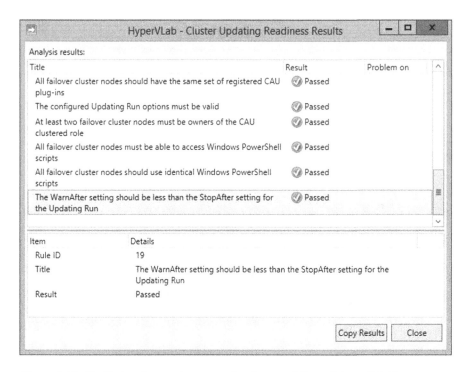

Figure 8-15. *Verify that the tests have completed successfully and then click Close*

Manually Updating the Cluster

I want to wrap up the section on cluster-aware updating by showing you how to manually launch the update process. Keep in mind that whether you manually initiate the updates or simply wait for the updates to occur on a scheduled basis, the updates apply only to the clustered Hyper-V hosts, not to the virtual machines. Virtual machines have to be updated separately using Windows Update, WSUS, or something similar.

With that said, you can manually initiate an update by completing these steps:

1. Log in to a cluster node using an account that has administrative permissions.

2. Open the Server Manager.

3. Select the Cluster-Aware Updating option from the Tools menu. This will cause Windows to launch the Cluster-Aware Updating tool.

4. Connect to your cluster, if necessary.

5. Click on the Apply Updates to this Cluster link (see Figure 8-16). This will cause Windows to launch the Cluster-Aware Updating Wizard.

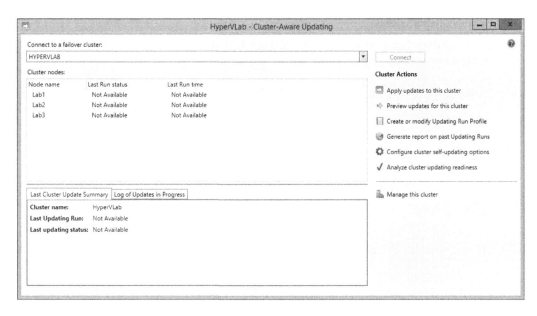

Figure 8-16. *Click on the Apply Updates to this Cluster link*

6. Click Next to bypass the wizard's Getting Started screen.

7. Confirm that the correct cluster is selected for updating (see Figure 8-17).

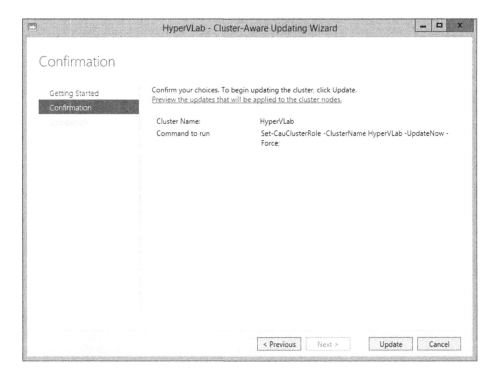

Figure 8-17. *Make sure that the correct cluster name is listed*

8. Click the Update button.

9. Verify that the Schedule Immediate Updating in Self-Updating Mode task is configured successfully (see Figure 8-18).

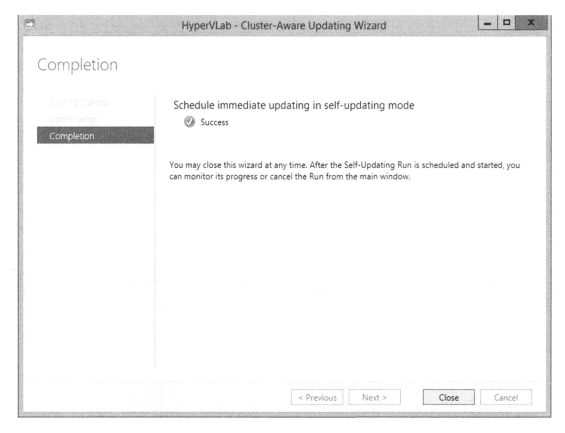

Figure 8-18. *Make sure that the server has successfully acknowledged your request for an immediate update*

10. Click Close.

11. You can watch the update in progress through the Cluster-Aware Updating tool until it is time for the current server to be rebooted (see Figure 8-19).

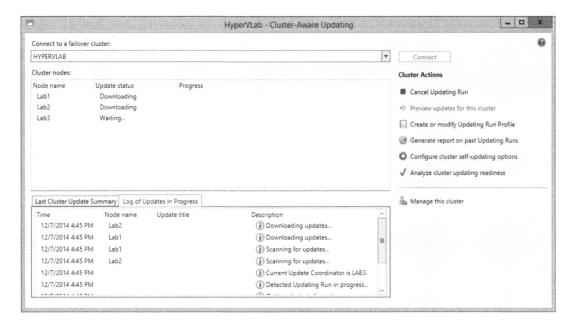

Figure 8-19. *The update process has begun*

Live Migration

VMware includes a feature called vMotion that allows a running virtual machine to be moved from one host server to another without interruption. Hyper-V includes a similar feature called Live Migration. Throughout this book, I have danced all around the topic of live migration, but I haven't directly addressed it. That being the case, I want to take the opportunity to show you how live migration works in a Hyper-V environment.

As is the case in a VMware environment, live migration is really simple to do. You can live migrate a virtual machine by completing these steps:

1. Open the VMM console.

2. Select the VMs and Services workspace.

3. Right click on the virtual machine that you want to live migrate and select the Migrate Virtual Machine command from the shortcut menu. This will cause the Migrate VM Wizard to be launched.

4. Select the destination host (see Figure 8-20).

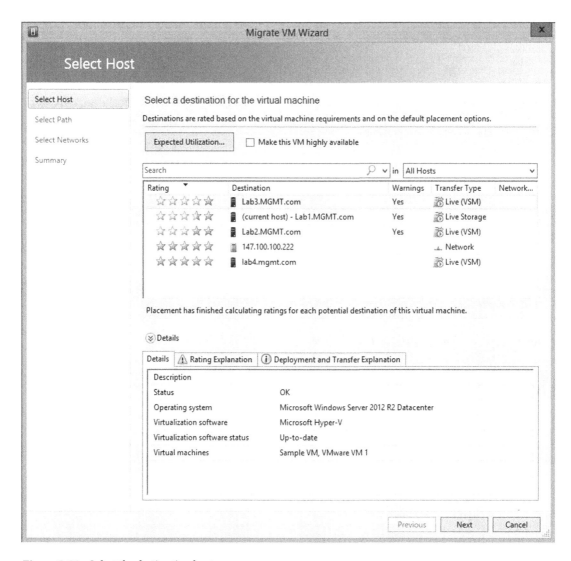

Figure 8-20. *Select the destination host*

5. Click Next.

6. Choose the storage location for the VM configuration.

7. Click Next.

8. Select the virtual network that you want the virtual machine to connect to on the destination host.

9. Click Next.

10. Take a moment to review the summary information to make sure that your migration options are correct.

11. Click the Move button.

It is worth noting that live migrations are a native Hyper-V feature and do not require a VMM license. If you do not have VMM, you can perform live migrations from the Hyper-V Manager instead.

Virtual Machine Placement (Star Rating)

It you followed the instructions in the previous section and performed a live migration, then you saw a screen on which host servers were assigned a star rating (see Figure 8-20). In fact, you have probably seen similar screens throughout this book. This screen provides some useful information, and yet I have not had much of a chance to talk about it. That being the case, I want to take this opportunity to talk about virtual machine placement.

As you have probably guessed, the star rating is an indication of which destination host is the most suitable for running the virtual machine. The destination hosts are arranged from most suitable (at the top of the list) to least suitable. Suitability is based on the resource usage on the destination host along with a number of other factors.

If you are preparing to place a VM that is running a production workload, then it is obviously important to pick a destination host that is going to do a good job of running that workload. VMM tries to use star ratings to help you predict which destination host is going to be the most suitable. However, VMM cannot predict how heavily the VM is going to be used. In some cases, you may need to give VMM a little bit of help. You can do this by clicking on the Expected Utilization button. Upon doing so, you will be given the chance to enter some data about the virtual machine's expected CPU, storage, and network utilization (see Figure 8-21). Entering accurate data here can help VMM make good recommendations about VM placement.

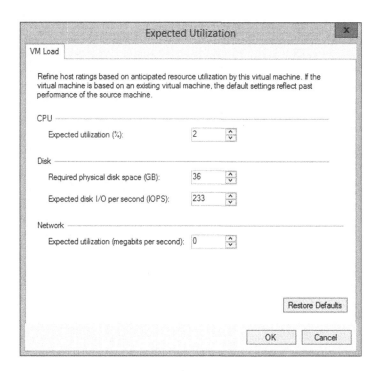

Figure 8-21. *Entering data about the virtual machine's resource usage can help VMM make better recommendations*

Before you commit to using a particular destination host (even if it is recommended with a high star rating), it is a good idea to click on the Rating Explanation tab. If the destination host has received anything less than a five-star rating, then there is some reason why VMM does not consider the host to be an ideal destination for the virtual machine. The Rating Explanation tab tells you what this reason is. If you look at Figure 8-22, for example, you can see that the host cluster is overcommitted.

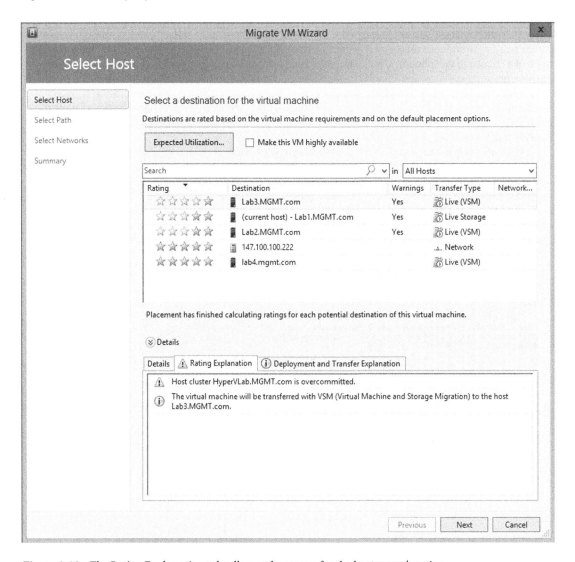

Figure 8-22. *The Rating Explanation tab tells you the reason for the host server's rating*

As you look at Figure 8-22, you will notice that the Rating Explanation tab also indicates that the virtual machine will be transferred via VSM (Virtual Machine and Storage Migration) to the host called Lab3.MGMT.com. If you want to find out what this means, then click on the Deployment and Transfer Explanation tab (see Figure 8-23).

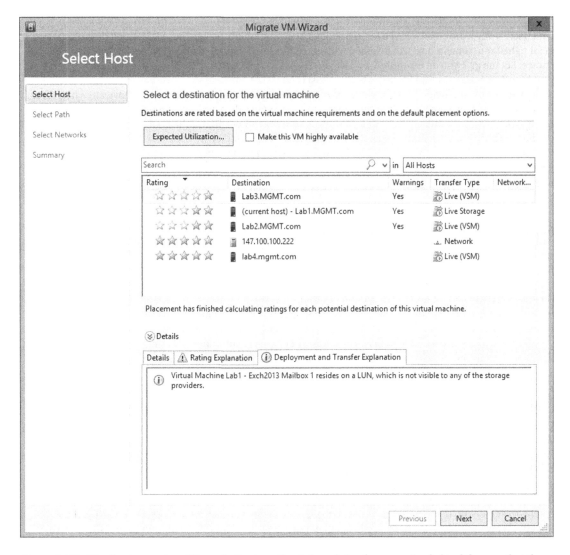

Figure 8-23. *The Deployment and Transfer Explanation tab explains the reasoning behind the way that the virtual machine is being migrated*

In this particular case, we see a message stating that the virtual machine resides on a LUN that is not visible to any of the storage providers. This message is displayed (at least in this case) because, although the virtual machine currently resides on a cluster node, it is not highly available and is not stored on a cluster-shared volume. The destination host does not have access to the virtual machine's current storage location. As such, all of the virtual machine's components (such as virtual hard disks) will have to be transferred over the network to the destination host. This isn't a problem (which is why no warning or error is displayed). It's just that the live migration will take longer than it would if the virtual machine's storage did not have to be moved. Incidentally, if we wanted to make this virtual machine highly available, the Select Host page includes a Make This VM Highly Available check box.

Occasionally, you may encounter a situation in which there are no hosts with favorable star ratings. This isn't necessarily a problem. VMM tries to predict a host's suitability for hosting a VM, but it doesn't always get it right. Sometimes a host will be listed with zero stars even though the host is a perfectly reasonable choice. Let me give you an example.

In my own organization I have a Hyper-V host (Lab4) that contains the VMs that I use when I write about various technologies. There are dozens of VMs on the server. The server doesn't have anywhere near the resources to run all of the VMs at the same time. Consequently, VMM always gives the host a zero-star rating. When I need to create a new VM, I simply ignore the rating and use the host anyway. It's fine for me to do that, because I rarely have an excessive number of VMs powered on at once.

Sometimes, however, VMM will block you from using a host with a zero star rating. For example, a host will receive zero stars if it is powered off, and VMM will not let you move forward with a VM deployment to the host.

Automated Live Migrations

Although it is helpful to be able to live migrate a virtual machine from one host server to another, there are times when the live-migration process is best handled by an automated procedure. Automated migrations can be used for a wide variety of purposes. The most common use is probably load balancing, but there are other reasons for using it, such as reduction of VM power consumption or automated host patching. You have already seen one example of automated live migrations in this chapter. Cluster-aware updating moves running virtual machines off of a cluster node automatically so that the node can be updated.

Hyper-V and VMM are able to perform some other types of automated live migrations. For instance, the dynamic optimization feature moved virtual machines in an effort to keep a cluster's workload balanced.

Dynamic Optimization

Earlier I talked about how VMM helps with virtual machine placement by using a star rating system to show you which host is best equipped to run the virtual machine that you are creating or migrating. Although this star rating is helpful, workloads can change over time, and today's optimal virtual machine placement might not be optimal tomorrow.

The dynamic optimization feature is designed to prevent any host within a clustered Hyper-V deployment from having to host an excessive workload. The feature evaluates the available resources on each host server and then compares the available resources to a predetermined threshold value. If the thresholds are exceeded, one or more virtual machines are live migrated to a different host. This process occurs on a scheduled basis (every ten minutes by default, once enabled).

Dynamic optimization is actually really easy to set up. Although dynamic optimization is technically a cluster-level function, it is configured at the host-group level. You can enable dynamic optimization by completing these steps:

1. Open the VMM console.

2. Go to the Fabric workspace.

3. Navigate through the console tree to Servers ➤ *<your host group>* ➤ *<your host cluster>*.

4. Click on the Host Cluster tab at the top of the window (see Figure 8-24).

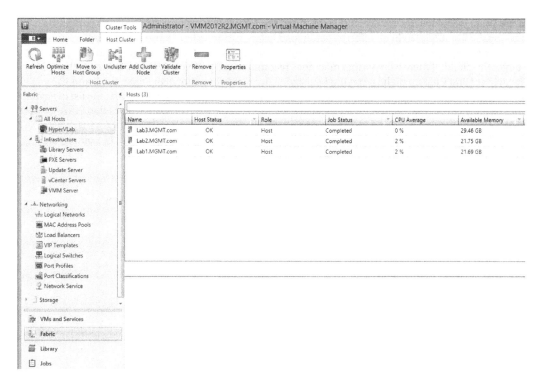

Figure 8-24. *Click on the Host Cluster tab*

5. Click on the Optimize Hosts button, found on the ribbon. This will cause Windows to open the Optimize Host Cluster dialog box (see Figure 8-25).

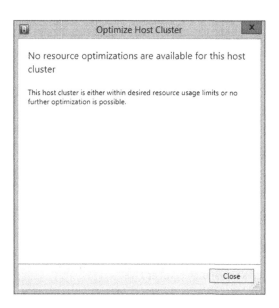

Figure 8-25. *VMM displays any resource optimizations that are available for the host cluster*

273

At this point, VMM will review the host servers and their available resources to see if any virtual machines can be live migrated in an effort to better load balance the cluster. As you can see in the figure above, VMM doesn't provide any recommendations if all of the hosts in the cluster fall within the resource-usage target threshold. If there were virtual machines recommended for live migration, however, those virtual machines and their target hosts would be listed in the dialog box shown in Figure 8-25, and you would be able to click a Migrate button to perform the live migration. It is worth noting that the list of virtual machines excludes those that are not highly available and also excludes any Hyper-V hosts that are in maintenance mode.

If you want to configure dynamic optimization to occur automatically, you can do so by completing these steps:

1. From within the VMM console, select the Fabric tab.

2. Click on the host group containing your cluster (do not click on the cluster itself).

3. Click on the Folder tab at the top of the screen (see Figure 8-26).

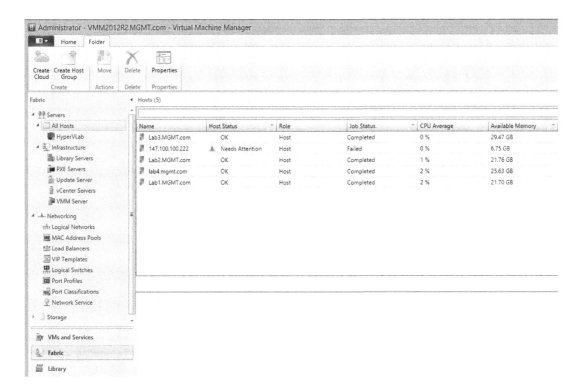

Figure 8-26. *Click on the Folder tab at the top of the screen*

4. Click on the Properties button, found on the ribbon. This will cause Windows to display the All Host Properties dialog box.

5. Click on Dynamic Optimization.

6. Select the Automatically Migrate Virtual Machines to Balance Load at This Frequency (Minutes) check box (see Figure 8-27).

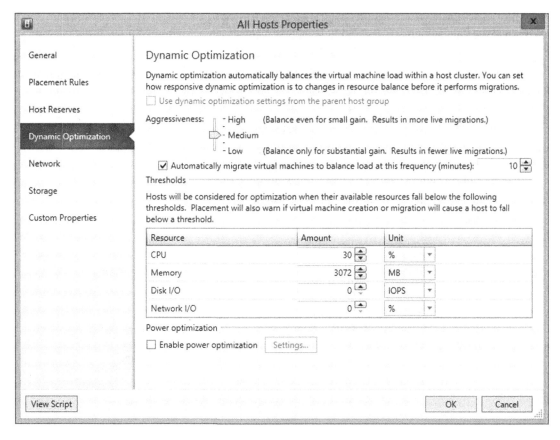

Figure 8-27. *Select the Automatically Migrate Virtual Machines to Balance Load at this Frequency (Minutes) check box*

7. Set the level of aggressiveness that you want to use.

8. Set the load-balancing frequency.

9. Adjust any necessary threshold values.

10. Click OK.

Workload Consolidation and Power Optimization

The dynamic optimization feature that I just discussed works really well for distributing virtual machines across all of the available hosts. However, doing so might not always be the most efficient action.

Consider an organization that runs a normal nine-to-five operation, but also has a much smaller night-shift operation. In such an environment, the virtual machines are probably going to be under a heavier load during the day than they will be at night. That being the case, the organization might be able to save some power by consolidating the virtual machines onto fewer host servers at night and then shutting down some of the now empty cluster nodes.

There are naturally a few things to consider before implementing power optimization. First, your servers must be BMC equipped so that out-of-band management can be performed. Your cluster must also be of sufficient size to allow some nodes to be shut down without the cluster losing quorum or sacrificing the ability to perform a failover.

The actual number of nodes that can be safely powered down depends on whether the cluster was created using VMM or the Failover Cluster Manager. The reason for this is that when VMM creates a cluster, it also creates a quorum disk that acts as part of the quorum model. The minimum number of nodes required in order to use power optimization is 4 if the cluster was created using VMM or 5 if the cluster was created outside of VMM. Of course you must still consider whether the cluster's workload allows for a node to be safely shut down. Microsoft provides the full guidelines for using power optimization at: `http://technet.microsoft.com/en-us/library/gg675109.aspx`.

You can configure power optimization by completing these steps:

1. From within the VMM console, select the Fabric tab.

2. Click on the host group containing your cluster (do not click on the cluster itself).

3. Click on the Folder tab at the top of the screen.

4. Click on the Properties button, found on the ribbon. This will cause Windows to display the All Hosts Properties dialog box.

5. Click on Dynamic Optimization.

6. Select the Automatically Migrate Virtual Machines to Balance Load at This Frequency (Minutes) check box. Although this check box is related to dynamic optimization, it must be selected if you want to enable power optimization.

7. Select the Enable Power Optimization checkbox (see Figure 8-28).

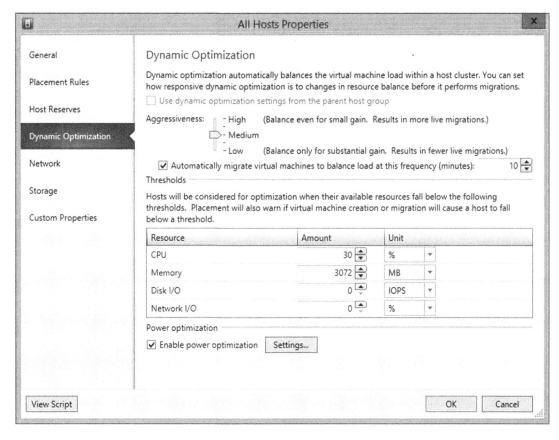

Figure 8-28. *Select the Enable Power Optimization check box*

8. Click the Settings button.

9. Configure the resource-usage thresholds for your cluster.

10. Configure the power optimization schedule (see Figure 8-29).

11. Click OK.

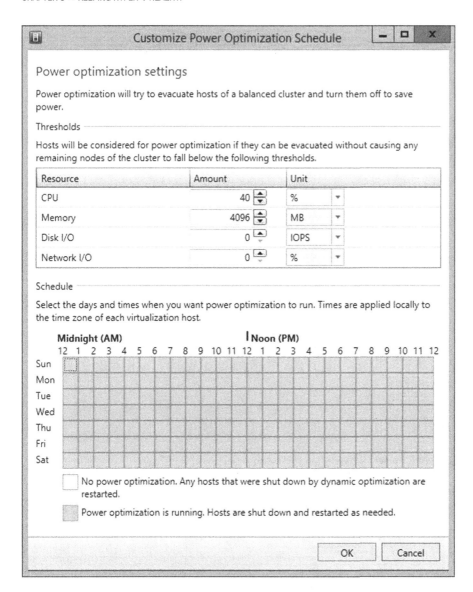

Figure 8-29. *Configure the cluster's power optimization schedule*

Virtual Machine Prioritization and Host Preferences

Back in one of the earlier chapters, I showed you how to build and operate a cluster, but I didn't really go into much depth regarding cluster options for protecting Hyper-V. At that point in the book, my goal was to get the cluster up and running as quickly as possible so that I could move on to talking about VMware. That being the case, I want to revisit the subject of clustering as it relates to your virtual machines. Specifically, I want to talk about ways in which you can protect your highly available virtual machines.

VMM offers two main mechanisms for protecting highly available virtual machines. One of these mechanisms is the virtual machine priority. The other is something called an availability set, which prevents set members from being hosted on a common server whenever possible.

Availability Sets

As I'm sure you recall, earlier in this book I walked you through the process of building a cluster for your Hyper-V virtual machines. Although I built the cluster on physical hardware, it is possible for a Windows Failover Cluster to exist purely on virtual hardware (although you can't nest Hyper-V). It is actually very common for virtual machines to act as cluster nodes. Oftentimes an organization might perform a P2V migration on a series of clustered nodes, for example, which results in the cluster nodes running on virtual hardware. A cluster whose nodes exist on virtual machines is referred to as a *guest cluster*.

With that in mind, think about the purpose of a physical cluster. A physical cluster exists as a way of making some application highly available. If a cluster node were to fail, then the application can fail over to another cluster node.

This behavior hasn't always translated well for guest clusters. Imagine for a moment that all of the nodes that make up a guest cluster are running on a common Hyper-V host. What happens if the host server fails? Unless all of the guest cluster nodes have been made highly available at the virtual machine level, then all of the nodes that make up the guest cluster will fail, thereby resulting in the failure of the highly available application.

The solution to this problem is to make all of the guest cluster nodes highly available (at the virtual machine level) and to use availability sets to prevent the guest cluster nodes from residing on a common host. An availability set will make a best-effort attempt to keep the set member VMs from residing on a common host server. I will show you how to create one in the following section.

Creating an Availability Set

You can create an availability set by completing the following steps:

1. Open the VMM console.

2. Click on the VMs and Services workspace.

3. Right click on the virtual machine that you want to work with and choose the Properties command from the shortcut menu. This will cause the virtual machine's Properties dialog box to be displayed.

4. Click on the Hardware Configuration tab.

5. Scroll down to the Advanced section.

6. Click on Availability (see Figure 8-30).

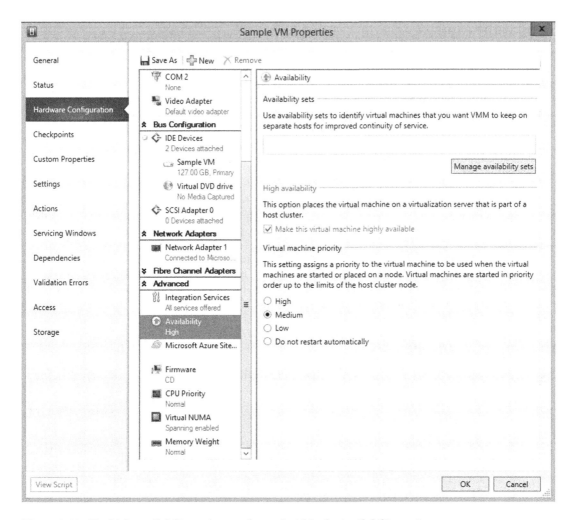

Figure 8-30. *The high-availability options are located within the Availability section*

7. Click the Manage Availability Sets button.

8. Click the Create button.

9. Enter a name for the availability set that you want to create. The availability set name typically reflects the name of the highly available application or the name of the guest cluster.

10. Click OK.

11. Click OK again. The virtual machine will be assigned to the newly created availability set (see Figure 8-31).

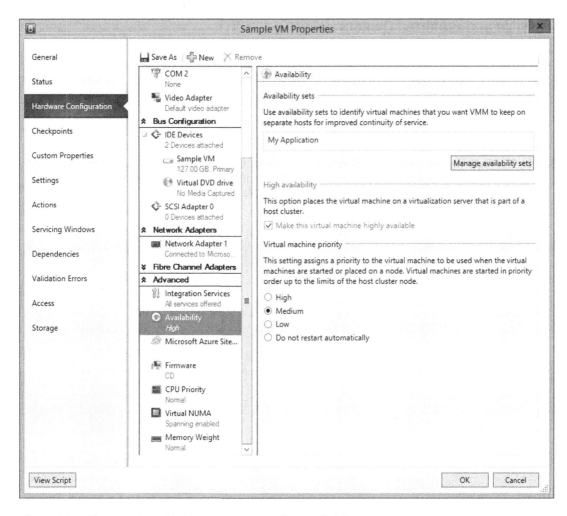

Figure 8-31. *The virtual machine is now a member of an availability set*

Other virtual machines can be added to the availability set by clicking on the virtual machine's Manage Availability Sets button, selecting the availability set that you want to use, and then clicking the Add button, followed by OK.

Possible and Preferred Owners

Availability sets are not the only mechanism that you can use to control which cluster nodes are able to host which virtual machines. Another option is to configure possible and preferred owners. This can only be done for highly available virtual machines. To configure a virtual machine's possible and preferred owners, complete these steps:

1. Open the VMM console.

2. Go to the VMs and Services workspace.

3. Right click on the highly available virtual machine that you want to configure and select the Properties command from the shortcut menu. This will cause the virtual machine's Properties dialog box to be displayed.

4. Click on the Settings tab (see Figure 8-32).

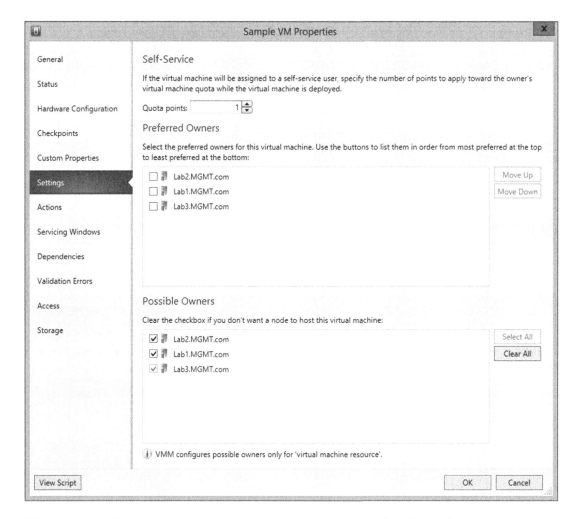

Figure 8-32. *The Preferred Owners and Possible Owners settings exist on the Settings tab*

The Preferred Owners and Possible Owners settings exist on the Settings tab. However, these settings will only be displayed if the virtual machine is highly available. Otherwise, only the Quota Points option will be displayed.

The Preferred Owners setting allows you to specify which host you would prefer to host the VM. However, Hyper-V does not guarantee that the virtual machine will reside on a preferred host.

The Possible Owners section lets you pick which cluster nodes are able to host the virtual machine. Your virtual machine will never reside on a host server that has not been designated as a possible owner.

If your goal is to keep virtual machines from ever coexisting on a common server, then your best option is to use availability sets. The preferred and possible owners settings are best used only in situations in which you need manual control over virtual machine placement.

Virtual Machine Priority

One of the problems that you can run into with highly available virtual machines is that a failover can cause a cluster node to become over committed. In other words, the destination cluster node might not have sufficient hardware resources to continue running its own workload, plus absorb highly available virtual machines that were running on the failed node.

Because it is somewhat common for cluster nodes to run out of hardware resources during a failover, it is a good idea to prioritize your virtual machines. Virtual machines are started or placed onto a node in order of priority until the host limits are reached. In other words, high-priority virtual machines fail over before low-priority VMs. You can configure a virtual machine's priority by completing these steps:

1. Open the VMM console.

2. Click on the VMs and Services workspace.

3. Right click on the virtual machine that you want to work with and choose the Properties command from the shortcut menu. This will cause the virtual machine's Properties dialog box to be displayed.

4. Click on the Hardware Configuration tab.

5. Scroll down to the Advanced section.

6. Click on Availability (see Figure 8-33).

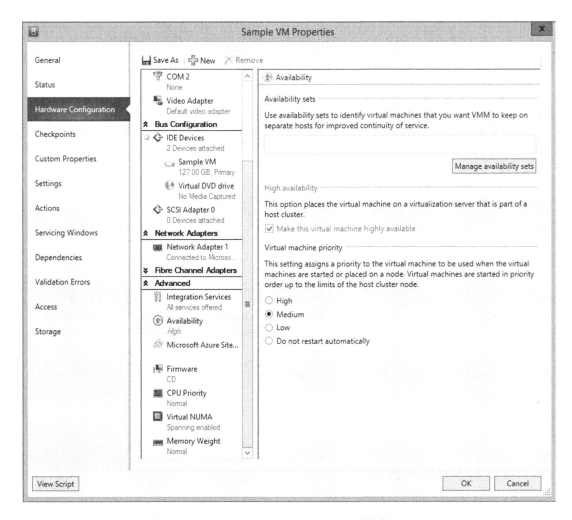

Figure 8-33. *The high-availability options are located within the Availability section*

7. Select a priority level for the virtual machine.

8. Click OK.

Moving On

In this chapter, I have discussed several VMM features that you can use to keep your virtual machines healthy and to gain a higher degree of control over the virtual machine management process. In the next chapter, I am going to conclude the book by discussing the use of library objects such as library shares, profiles, and templates for virtual machine creation.

■ ■ ■

CHAPTER 9

Virtual Machine Libraries and Templates

In this chapter, I want to wrap up the book by showing you some ways that you can make use of libraries and templates within System Center Virtual Machine Manager (VMM). Libraries and templates can go a long way toward simplifying (and in some cases even automating) the virtual machine creation process.

You got a brief look at templates back in Chapter 4, but there we were using templates solely as a mechanism for creating VMware virtual machines using VMM. Chapter 4 didn't go into templates deeply enough to illustrate their real benefits, and I didn't discuss library shares at all. With that said, my plan here is to show you how to create various library items and then use those items to build virtual machines.

Virtual Machine Libraries

In VMM, a library is basically just a collection of resources that can be used when building or configuring virtual machines. A library can contain virtual machine templates, DVD images (ISO files), and more.

In my own day-to-day interaction with VMM, I have found it to be extremely beneficial to have a library that contains all of my ISO files. As a technology writer, I am constantly downloading ISO files from MSDN. I used to burn these ISO files to DVD, but have discovered that it is a lot easier to keep track of the resources that I download if I place them into a library instead. Of course, placing an ISO file in a library share does not eliminate the opportunity to burn the ISO file to a DVD. It simply gives you the ability to use the ISO file, in place, without the need for a physical DVD.

Before I show you how to build a library share, I need to point out that library shares are useful for more than just storing ISO files. Remember what I said several chapters back about the inability of Generation 2 virtual machines to use a physical DVD drive? Well, the good news is that you can create a virtual DVD drive within a Generation 2 virtual machine, but the virtual DVD drive has to be linked to an ISO file rather than to a physical device.

Creating a Library Share

There are about a million different uses for library shares. I want to show you how to create a library share that you can use to store your ISO files. For all practical purposes, a library share is really just a file share that is exposed through VMM. The fact that VMM exposes the library share makes it possible to build virtual machines from the ISO files contained within the library share. You can create a library share by completing these steps:

1. Open File Explorer and create a folder that you can use to store ISO files. This storage should be local to the server, and the chosen location must have enough free space to accommodate the ISO files that you plan to share. For the purposes of this book, I will be calling the folder ISO.

2. From within File Explorer, right click on the folder that you just created and then choose the Share With ➤ Specific People commands from the resulting shortcut menus.

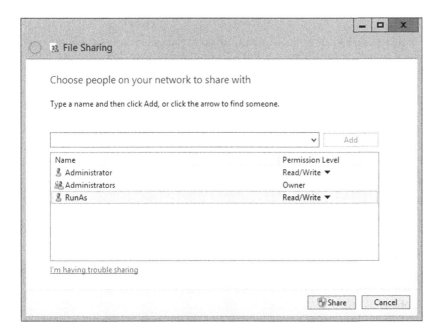

Figure 9-1. *Assign the necessary permissions to the file share*

3. When the File Sharing dialog box appears, set the necessary permissions for the file share. The permissions required will vary depending on how your organization is configured and on how you use VMM. Typically, you will need to assign Read / Write permissions to the Administrator account and to the RunAs account (see Figure 9-1).

4. Click Share.

5. Click Done.

6. Open the Windows Control Panel.

7. Click on Programs.

8. Click on Programs and Features.

9. When the list of installed programs appears, select the Microsoft System Center 2012 R2 Virtual Machine Manager option.

10. Click on the Uninstall / Change option. This will launch the Microsoft System Center 2012 R2 Virtual Machine Manager Setup Wizard (see Figure 9-2).

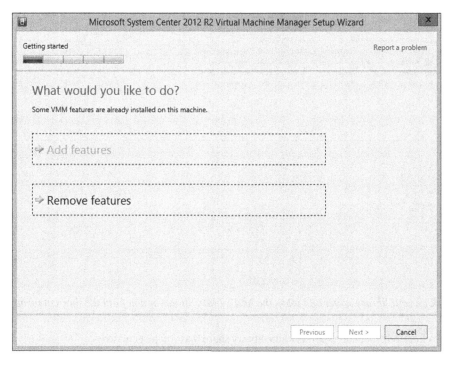

Figure 9-2. *The Microsoft System Center 2012 R2 Virtual Machine Manager Setup Wizard can be used to install or remove VMM components*

11. Check to see whether the Add Features button is grayed out (it is grayed out in Figure 9-2). If the Add Features option is grayed out then all of the available features are installed and you can click Cancel and move on to the next step. If the Add Features option is not grayed out then you will need to click on the Add Features link and then install the Virtual Machine Manager Library Server component. Library shares cannot be used unless the Virtual Machine Manager Library Server is installed.

12. Open the VMM console.

13. Select the Library workspace.

14. Navigate through the console tree to Library Servers ➤ *<your library server>*.

15. Right click on your library server and select the Add Library Shares command from the shortcut menu (see Figure 9-3). This will cause the Add Library Shares dialog box to be displayed.

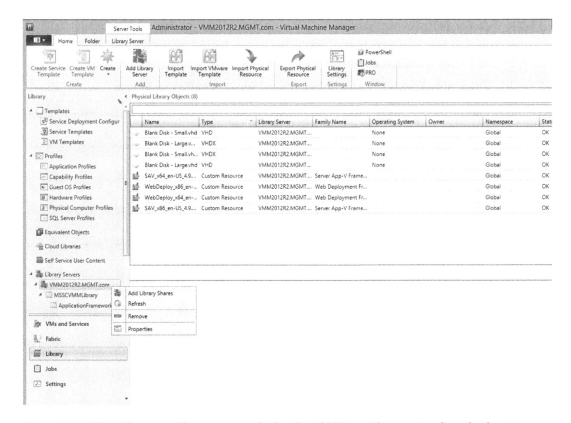

Figure 9-3. *Right click on your library server and select the Add Library Shares option from the shortcut menu*

16. Select the check box that corresponds to the library share that you just created (see Figure 9-4).

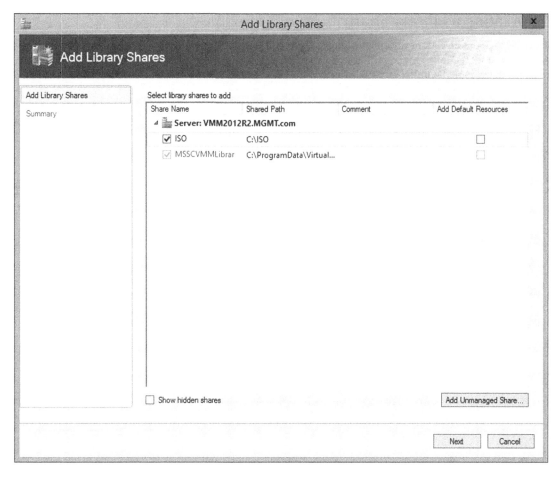

Figure 9-4. Select the check box that corresponds to the library share that you just created

17. Click Next.

18. Take a moment to verify that the share is going to be added.

19. Click the Add Library Shares button.

It is worth noting that you can create multiple library shares. Doing so gives you an easy way of organizing your ISO files. In the previous exercise, I created a generic library share named ISO, but I could have just as easily created a series of library shares with names like Server OS, Desktop OS, Server Applications, and Desktop Applications.

Populating a Library Share

It is easy to populate your newly created library share. All you have to do is use File Explorer to copy your ISO files into the shared folder. As you will recall, I shared a folder called ISO. If you look at Figure 9-5, you can see that I have copied Windows 8.1 and Windows Server 2012 R2 ISO files into this folder.

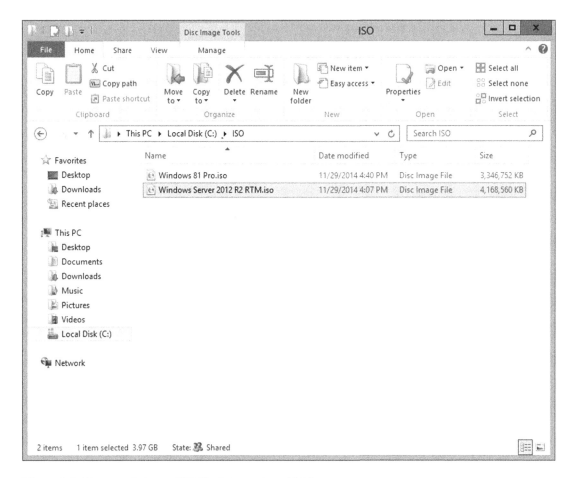

Figure 9-5. *I have copied some ISO files into my shared folder*

If you go back into the VMM console, the shared folder should appear in the console tree beneath the listing for your library server. There is a good chance that the file share will initially appear empty. If that happens, right click on the folder and choose the Refresh option from the shortcut menu (see Figure 9-6). Upon doing so, you should see your ISO files listed within the library share (see Figure 9-7).

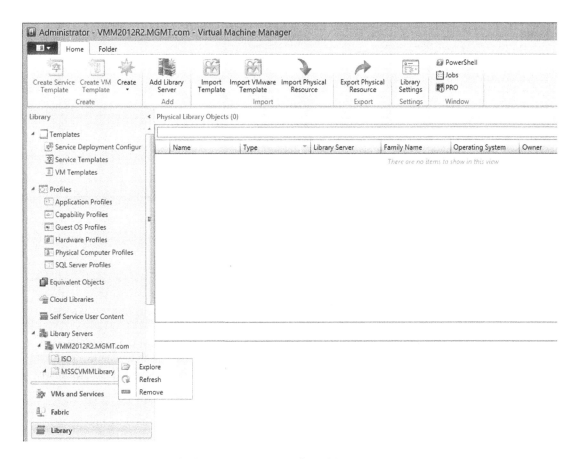

Figure 9-6. *You may need to refresh your library share after adding new content*

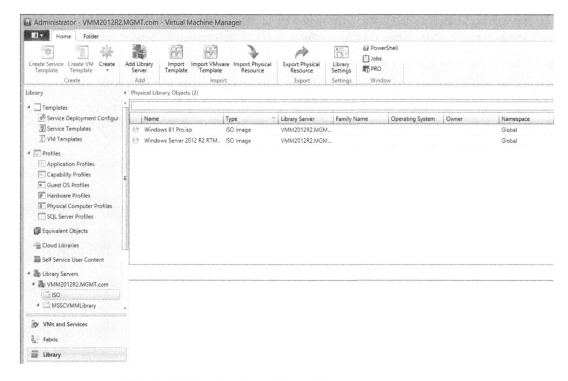

Figure 9-7. *Your ISO files should be listed within the library share*

Later in this chapter, I am going to show you how to build templates that can be used to automate virtual machine creation. When we get to that point, I will show you how to use the library share for virtual machine creation. For right now, though, there are some other pieces that I need to put in place before we start building virtual machines.

Virtual Machine Templates

Throughout this book, I have been using VMM primarily as a tool for creating and managing virtual machines. One thing that you have to understand about VMM, however, is that it offers functionality far beyond what is being covered in this book. For instance, VMM can be used as a tool for building your own private cloud. One of the features that makes this possible is the virtual machine template.

In a private cloud environment, authorized users typically have the ability to create their own virtual machines. In such environments, templates are used to automate the virtual machine creation process. Even if you aren't going to be building a private cloud, however, templates can provide a shortcut for creating new virtual machines, while also allowing virtual machines to be created in a consistent manner. In this section, I will show you how to create virtual machine templates, and how to build new virtual machines that are based on templates.

Templates and Profiles

In the previous section, I mentioned how virtual machine templates can be used to simplify the virtual machine deployment process. What I haven't mentioned up to now is that templates are not the only mechanism that can make your life easier. The VMM library allows for the creation of several different types of profiles that can aid in the creation of virtual machines. Since this book isn't intended to be a deep dive, I am not going to be covering all of the profile types in depth, but it is good to know what types of profiles exist and what they are used for. Figure 9-8 shows the available types of profiles.

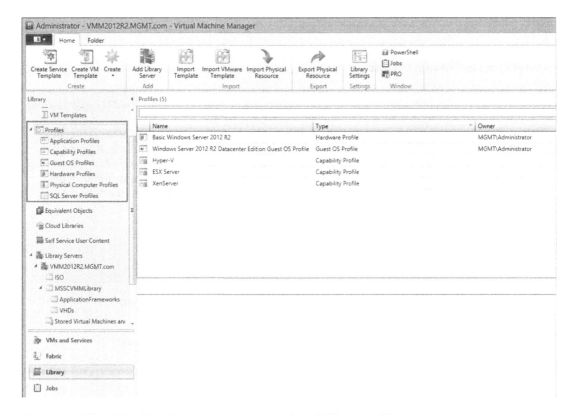

Figure 9-8. *Virtual Machine Manager supports a number of different profile types*

Here is a summary of the profile types supported by VMM:

- Application Profiles – Application profiles are used to automate the installation of applications. These can be App-V applications, Microsoft Web Deploy applications, scripts, and so forth.

- Capability Profiles – A few chapters back, you saw that VMM works with Hyper-V, VMware, and XenServer. Capability profiles define the limits of each hypervisor. For example, a capability profile can specify the maximum number of virtual processors that can be used by a particular hypervisor.

- Guest OS Profiles – A guest OS profile contains a list of values that are needed in order to complete an automated Windows Server deployment. For instance, a guest OS profile might contain a product key, computer name, and so on.

293

- Hardware Profiles – A hardware profile specifies the physical hardware that should be allocated to new virtual machines.

- Physical Computer Profiles – Physical computer profiles replace host profiles and are used as mechanisms for provisioning new Hyper-V hosts.

- SQL Server Profiles – SQL Server profiles allow for the automated deployment of SQL Server applications.

In the following sections, I will be showing you how to create guest OS profiles and hardware profiles. I have chosen these two profile types because they complement virtual machine templates, and we are going to be building virtual machine templates later on.

Creating a Hardware Profile

So far in this book, you have created a number of different virtual machines. As you know by now, when you create a Hyper-V virtual machine, you have to provision hardware to the virtual machine. This might include things like virtual CPUs, physical memory, or perhaps network adapters.

There is nothing wrong with manually provisioning hardware, but if you have a lot of VMs to set up, you may wish that there were a way to provision hardware in a consistent manner. Similarly, if your goal is to automate virtual machine provisioning then you will need a way to specify the hardware to allocate to the new virtual machine. Hardware profiles can help with both of these situations. A hardware profile is really nothing more than a list of hardware allocations. This list can later be used in the virtual machine creation process. To create a hardware profile, complete the following steps:

1. Open the VMM console.

2. Select the Library workspace.

3. Expand the Profiles container (if necessary) and then right click on the Hardware Profiles container; select the Create Hardware Profile command from the shortcut menu. This will cause Windows to display the New Hardware Profile dialog box.

4. Enter a name for the hardware profile that you are creating. The name should reflect what the hardware profile will eventually be used for.

5. Enter a description for the hardware profile. The description should ideally reflect the hardware allocations that are being made.

6. Select the generation of virtual machines that will be created using the hardware profile (see Figure 9-9). Remember that Generation 1 and Generation 2 VMs use different hardware.

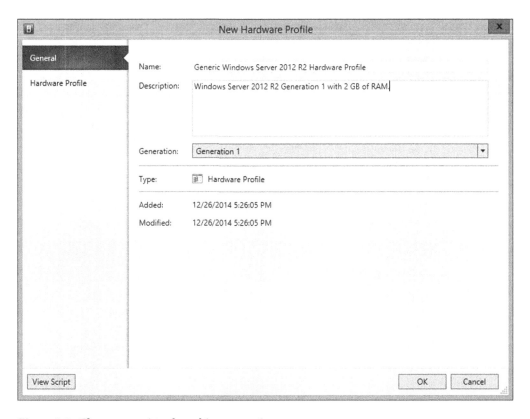

Figure 9-9. *Choose your virtual machine generation*

7. Click on the Hardware Profile tab.

8. Select the hardware profile's cloud compatibility (Hyper-V, VMware, Citrix) by selecting the check box corresponding to the hypervisor (see Figure 9-10).

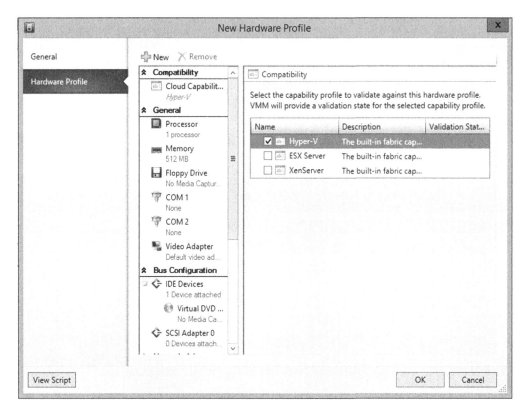

Figure 9-10. *Select the profile's cloud compatibility*

9. Configure the hardware allocations that you want to define within the profile (see Figure 9-11).

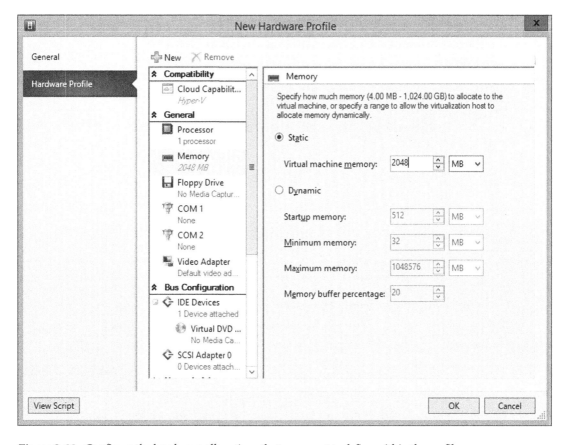

Figure 9-11. *Configure the hardware allocations that you want to define within the profile*

10. Click OK.

11. Verify that the new hardware profile is listed within the Hardware Profiles container (see Figure 9-12).

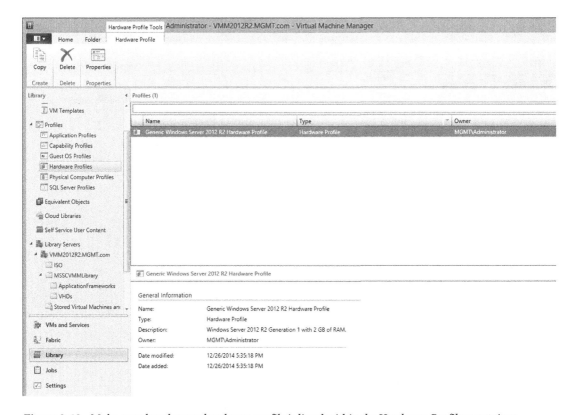

Figure 9-12. *Make sure that the new hardware profile is listed within the Hardware Profiles container*

I want to quickly mention that in a production environment you will likely use multiple hardware profiles. Each type of server in your organization (file server, exchange server, domain controller, and so on) will commonly require its own unique hardware profile.

Creating a Guest OS Profile

A guest OS profile is designed to automate the operating system installation on a virtual machine. Think back to the last time that you manually installed Windows Server. There were a lot of questions that you had to answer. You had to tell Windows what time zone you were in and what your product key was. After the installation completed, you might have specified a computer name, joined a domain, or installed some roles or features. A guest OS profile provides Windows Setup with the answers to the various Setup questions (and performs some post-installation tasks) so that you don't have to do it manually.

If you are familiar with the SYSPREP utility, then you have probably used a SYSPREP answer file. A guest OS profile is essentially the same thing. If you aren't familiar with SYSPREP then don't worry—I will show you how everything works in the next section.

Most production environments require multiple guest OS profiles because servers need to be configured differently based on what they are designed to do. For instance, a file server is going to be configured differently than a Web server. For the sake of demonstration, I will show you how to create a general-purpose guest OS profile.

To create a guest OS profile, complete the following steps:

1. Open the VMM console.

2. Select the Library workspace.

3. Expand the Profiles container (if necessary) and right click on the Guest OS Profile container; select the Create Guest OS Profile command from the shortcut menu (see Figure 9-13). This will cause Windows to display the New Guest OS Profile dialog box.

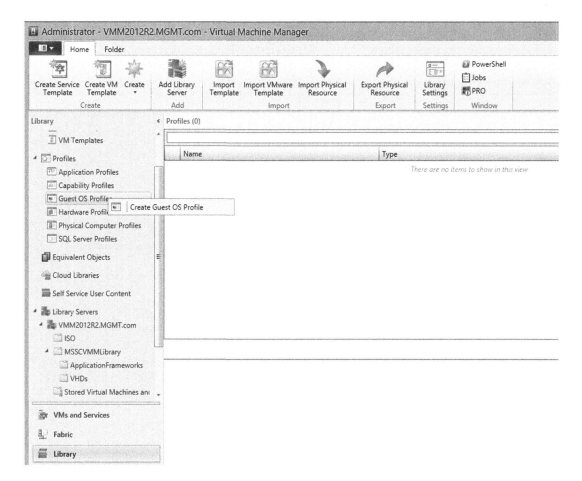

Figure 9-13. *Right click on the Guest OS Profile container and choose the Create Guest OS Profile command from the shortcut menu*

4. Enter a name for the new guest OS profile. The name should be something descriptive.

5. Enter a meaningful description of the guest OS profile.

6. Choose either the Windows option or the Linux option from the Compatibility drop-down menu (see Figure 9-14).

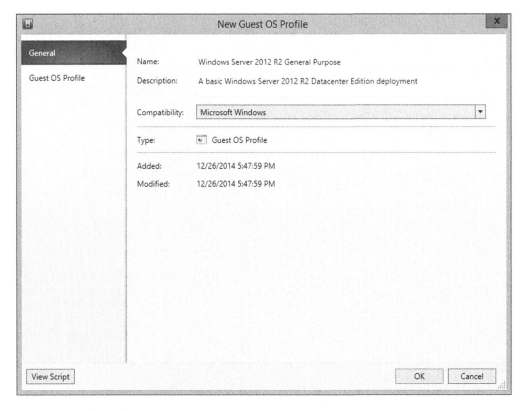

Figure 9-14. Choose the guest operating system type

7. Click on the Guest OS Profile tab.

8. Select the version of Windows (or Linux) that you want to use with the guest OS
    profile (see Figure 9-15).

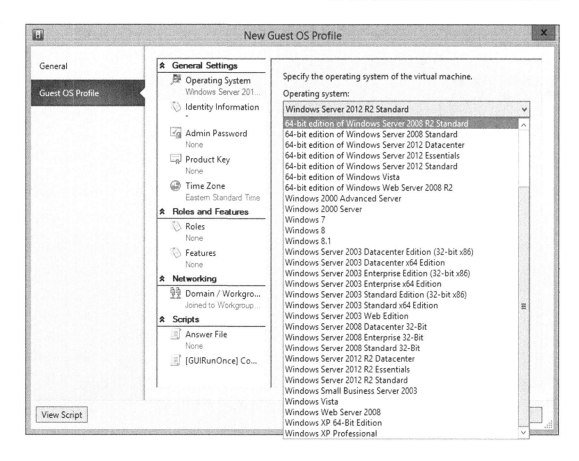

Figure 9-15. *You must select your operating system version*

9. Provide any remaining configuration details. In addition to basic installation data, you can also specify which roles and features you want to install and which domain you want to join (see Figure 9-16).

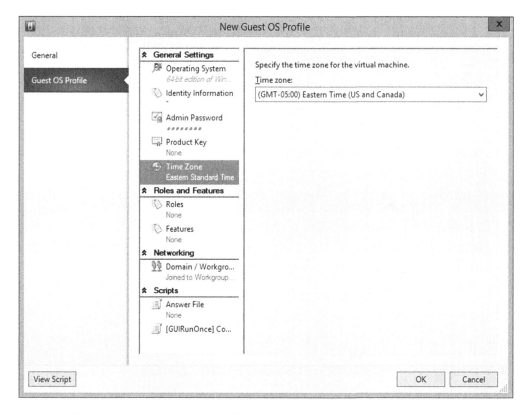

Figure 9-16. *Enter any remaining configuration details*

10. Click OK.

11. Make sure that the new guest OS profile is listed in the Guest OS Profile container (see Figure 9-17).

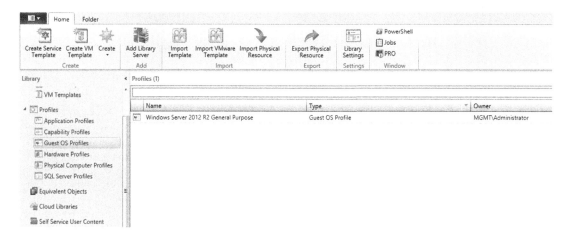

Figure 9-17. *Make sure that the new guest OS profile is listed in the Guest OS Profile container*

Creating a Virtual Machine Template

Now that we have created a library filled with ISO files, a guest OS profile, and a hardware profile, it is time to create a virtual machine template. Technically, you can create a virtual machine template without using a hardware profile, but going ahead and creating hardware profiles usually saves work (and time) in the long run. As you may recall, we created a template back in Chapter 4 and used it as a mechanism for creating VMware virtual machines from Hyper-V. Now I want to show you how to use templates for Hyper-V virtual machine creation.

When you create a virtual machine template, VMM gives you a choice of creating the template either from a virtual hard disk or from an existing virtual machine. We are going to create a virtual machine specifically for the purpose of building a template. You should always base templates off of brand new virtual machines, because the process of creating a template destroys the source VM.

Creating a Source VM

I have discussed the process of creating a new VM several different times. However, I want to walk you through the process one last time, because I want to show you how to use the pieces that we have put into place. When we are done creating this VM, we will use it to create a virtual machine template. To create a virtual machine, complete the following steps:

1. Open the VMM console.

2. Select the VMs and Services workspace.

3. Right click on a host server and select the Create Virtual Machine command from the shortcut menu. This will cause Windows to launch the Create Virtual Machine Wizard.

4. Select the Create the New Virtual Machine with a Blank Virtual Hard Disk option.

5. Click Next.

6. Enter the name of the virtual machine that you want to create.

7. Enter a description for the virtual machine.

8. Select the virtual machine's generation (see Figure 9-18).

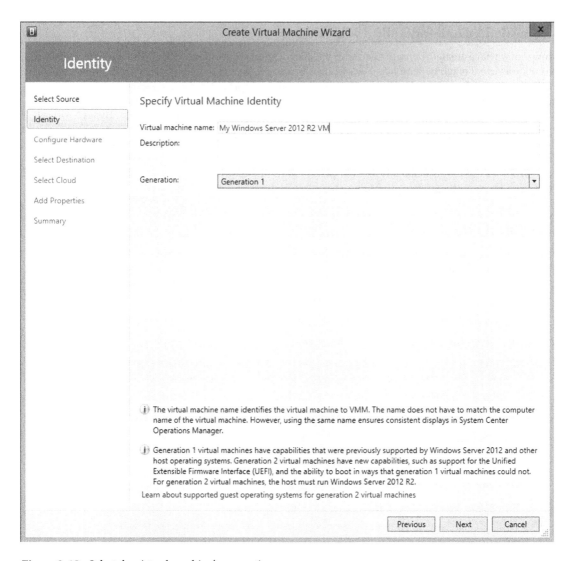

Figure 9-18. *Select the virtual machine's generation*

9. Click Next.

10. You should now be looking at the Configure Hardware page. Rather than manually provisioning hardware, use the Hardware Profile box at the top of the window to select the hardware profile that you created earlier (see Figure 9-19). The new virtual machine will use the hardware configuration specified within the hardware profile.

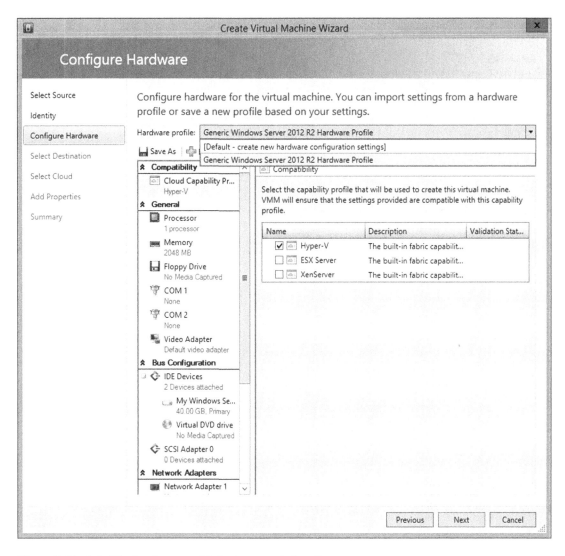

Figure 9-19. *Select the hardware profile that you created earlier*

11. Select the Virtual DVD drive.

12. Choose the Existing ISO Image option.

13. Click the Browse button.

14. Select the ISO file that corresponds to the desired operating system from your library (see Figure 9-20).

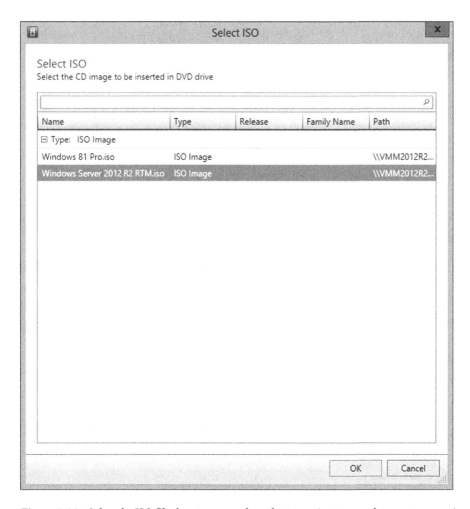

Figure 9-20. *Select the ISO file that corresponds to the operating system that you want to install*

15. Click OK.

16. Make sure that the Existing ISO Image field lists the correct ISO file (see Figure 9-21).

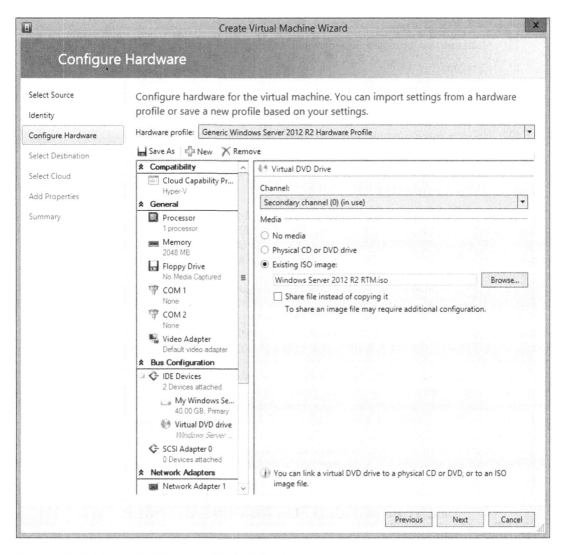

Figure 9-21. *Make sure that the correct ISO file is listed*

17. Click Next.

18. Choose the destination host group.

19. Click Next.

20. Select the host server on which you want to create the virtual machine.

21. Click Next.

22. Verify the virtual machine path.

23. Click Next.

24. Select the virtual machine network and virtual switch.

25. Click Next.

26. Make sure that the most appropriate automatic actions are selected.

27. Click Next.

28. Verify the virtual machine's summary information.

29. Click Create.

30. Once the virtual machine has been created, power the virtual machine on and then complete the operating system installation.

Preparing the Source VM

Creating a source virtual machine was only the first step in building a template virtual machine. The next part of the template-creation process involves running SYSPREP on the virtual machine that we just created. We don't have to manually run SYSPREP, however. VMM will run SYSPREP on the virtual machine for us. In case you aren't familiar with SYSPREP, it is a utility that prepares the operating system to be cloned. As you no doubt know, a Windows installation contains a lot of system-specific information. Things like the computer name, the IP address, and the SIDs and GUIDs that are in use are unique to that system. We can't include system-specific information in a template, so SYSPREP is used to get rid of anything system specific.

The most important thing to know about SYSPREP is that you must never use it on a production virtual machine. SYSPREP resets the virtual machine to a state that Microsoft refers to as the Out of the Box experience (OOBE). The Out of the Box experience is perfect for cloning a VM, but it will break a production VM.

In case you are wondering about the Out of the Box experience, it is very similar to what you see when you power up a brand new PC for the first time. If you have ever bought a PC from an electronics store or an online retailer, then you probably didn't have to use a Windows DVD to install the OS. Instead, you most likely booted the PC, answered a few quick questions, and then the PC completed the setup process on its own. This is exactly how the Out of the Box experience works.

You need to be careful about what you do to the virtual machine prior to running SYSPREP. The virtual machine should not be domain joined. Similarly, some applications can survive the SYSPREP process, but others cannot.

BEST PRACTICES FOR RUNNING SYSPREP

SYSPREP is a destructive process, and there are a number of considerations and best practices that you should review before moving forward. Here is a list of some important things to note:

- Never SYSPREP a production virtual machine, because doing so will destroy the VM.

- Make sure that the VM that you are about to SYSPREP is not joined to a domain.

- Try to avoid installing applications prior to running SYSPREP if possible. SYSPREP causes problems for some applications.

- Remove any antivirus software prior to running SYSPREP.

- Apply any available patches to the source VM prior to running SYSPREP.

You can create a template from a virtual machine by completing the following steps:

1. Select the VMs and Services workspace.

2. Start the virtual machine and open the virtual machine's console.

3. Shut down the virtual machine from which you are creating the template.

4. Go to the Library workspace.

5. Expand the Templates container (if necessary) and right click on the VM Templates container. Select the Create VM Template command from the shortcut menu. This will cause Windows to launch the Create VM Template Wizard.

6. Select the option to create a VM template from an existing virtual machine that is deployed on the host.

7. Click the Browse button.

8. Select the VM from which you want to create the template.

9. Click OK.

10. Verify that the correct virtual machine is listed (see Figure 9-22).

Figure 9-22. *Make sure that the correct virtual machine is listed*

11. Click Next.

12. Read the warning message indicating that creating a template will destroy the source virtual machine. If you are ready to move forward, click Yes (see Figure 9-23).

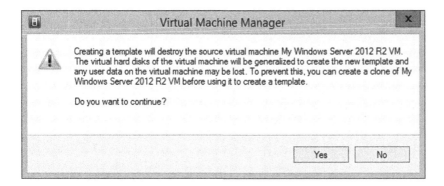

Figure 9-23. *Creating a template destroys the source virtual machine*

13. Enter a name for the template that you are creating.

14. Enter a description for the template (see Figure 9-24).

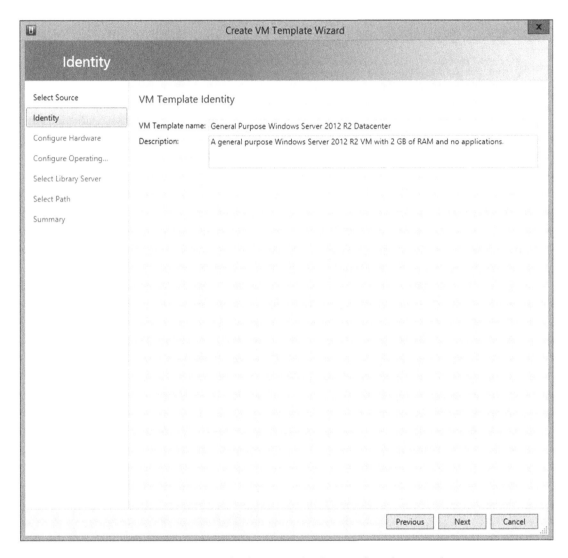

Figure 9-24. *Enter a meaningful name and a description for the virtual machine template*

15. Click Next.

16. You will now see the wizard's Create Hardware page. Notice in Figure 9-25 that all of the hardware configuration options are grayed out. The reason for this is that we are creating a template from an existing virtual machine. You will also notice, however, that the configuration from our previously used hardware profile has been retained.

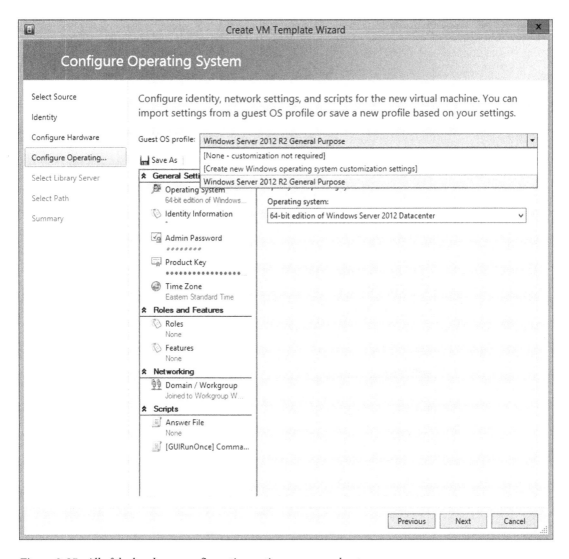

Figure 9-25. *All of the hardware configuration options are grayed out*

17. Click Next.

18. You will now be taken to the Configure Operating System page. Although you can manually configure the operating system deployment settings, it is easier to select the guest OS profile that we created earlier (see Figure 9-26).

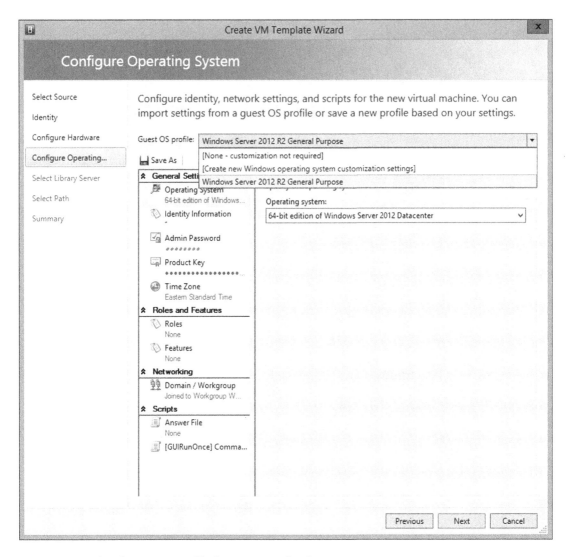

Figure 9-26. *Select the guest OS profile that you created earlier*

19. Click Next.

20. You will now be taken to the Select Library Server page. Virtual machine templates are stored in a library, so you will need to select a library server.

21. Click Next.

22. The next page that you will see is the Select Path page. You can use this page to choose the location within the library where the new virtual machine template will be stored. Be sure to make note of the location that you have chosen.

23. Click Next.

24. Click Create.

25. When the creation process completes, you should see your new virtual machine template listed within the library at your chosen location (see Figure 9-27).

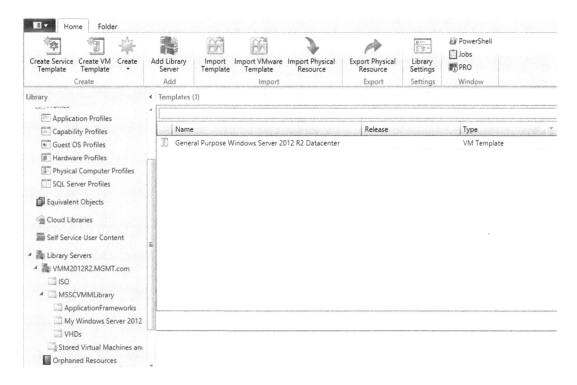

Figure 9-27. *The new template has been created*

Creating a Virtual Machine from a Template

Now that we have created a hardware profile, an operating system profile, and a virtual machine template, I want to wrap things up by showing you how to create virtual machines from a template. You will find that the process of creating a new virtual machine is quite a bit different from what we have done so far. You can create a new virtual machine from the template by completing these steps:

1. Open the VMM console and select the Library workspace.

2. Right click on your newly created VM template and select the Create Virtual Machine command from the shortcut menu (see Figure 9-28). This will cause Windows to launch the Create Virtual Machine Wizard.

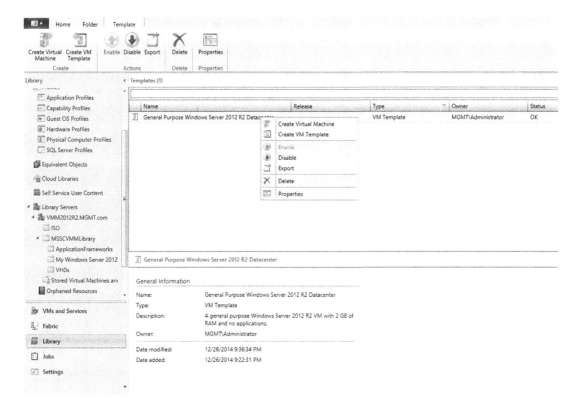

Figure 9-28. *Right click on your VM template and select the Create Virtual Machine command from the shortcut menu*

3. Enter a name for the virtual machine that you want to create.

4. Click Next.

5. The wizard will now display the Configure Hardware page. Although you can make changes to the hardware configuration, you shouldn't have to, because the template was based on your hardware profile.

6. Click Next.

7. You will now be taken to the Configure Operating System page. Once again, you can make changes to the operating system configuration, but you shouldn't need to, because your guest OS profile has already been applied.

8. Click Next.

9. Select your virtual machine destination.

10. Click Next.

11. Select the host server on which you want to create the VM.

12. Click Next.

13. You can make changes to the operating system configuration, but you shouldn't need to, because your guest OS profile has already been applied.

14. Click Next.

15. Click Create.

16. When VMM finishes creating the new virtual machine, go to the VMs and Services workspace, turn on the virtual machine, and open the console.

If you have done everything correctly, the new virtual machine should be ready to use and should not require any additional setup (see Figure 9-29).

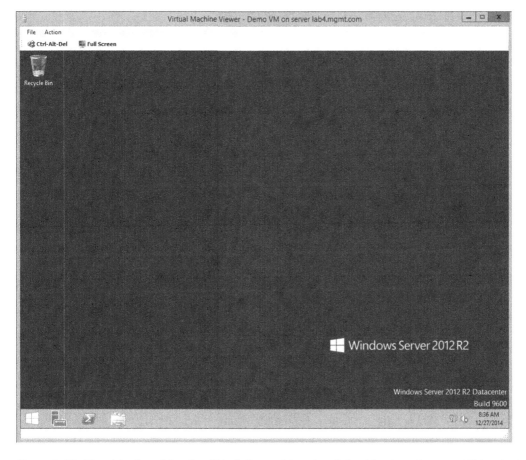

Figure 9-29. *The virtual machine should be fully provisioned and should not require any additional setup*

I will be the first to admit that we went through a lot of work in this chapter just to deploy a VM. Now that you have the various templates and profiles at your disposal, however, it should be quick and easy to create new virtual machines in the future.

Moving On

I hope that you have enjoyed reading this book as much as I have enjoyed writing it, and that you have found the lab exercises to be helpful. If you want to learn more about Hyper-V or VMM, then I recommend visiting Microsoft TechNet (http://technet.microsoft.com). The TechNet site contains the full documentation for Windows Server, Hyper-V, VMM, and many other Microsoft server products. Another great reference that may be worth checking out if you want to learn more is the Microsoft Virtual Academy (www.microsoftvirtualacademy.com).

Index

■ W, X, Y, Z

Get the eBook for only $5!

Why limit yourself?

Now you can take the weightless companion with you wherever you go and access your content on your PC, phone, tablet, or reader.

Since you've purchased this print book, we're happy to offer you the eBook in all 3 formats for just $5.

Convenient and fully searchable, the PDF version enables you to easily find and copy code—or perform examples by quickly toggling between instructions and applications. The MOBI format is ideal for your Kindle, while the ePUB can be utilized on a variety of mobile devices.

To learn more, go to www.apress.com/companion or contact support@apress.com.

Get the eBook for only $5!

Why limit yourself?

Now you can take the weightless companion with you wherever you go and access your content on your PC, phone, tablet, or reader.

Since you've purchased this print book, we're happy to offer you the eBook in all 3 formats for just $5.

Convenient and fully searchable, the PDF version enables you to easily find and copy code—or perform examples by quickly toggling between instructions and applications. The MOBI format is ideal for your Kindle, while the ePUB can be utilized on a variety of mobile devices.

To learn more, go to www.apress.com/companion or contact support@apress.com.

Printed in the United States
By Bookmasters